THE VANISHING AMERICAN
LAWYER

THE VANISHING AMERICAN LAWYER

THOMAS D. MORGAN

OXFORD
UNIVERSITY PRESS

OXFORD
UNIVERSITY PRESS

Oxford University Press, Inc., publishes works that further Oxford University's objective of excellence in research, scholarship, and education.

Oxford   New York
Auckland   Cape Town   Dar es Salaam   Hong Kong   Karachi   Kuala Lumpur   Madrid
Melbourne   Mexico City   Nairobi   New Delhi   Shanghai   Taipei   Toronto

With offices in
Argentina   Austria   Brazil   Chile   Czech Republic   France   Greece   Guatemala   Hungary
Italy   Japan   Poland   Portugal   Singapore   South Korea   Switzerland   Thailand
Turkey   Ukraine   Vietnam

Library of Congress Cataloging-in-Publication Data
Morgan, Thomas D.
    The vanishing American lawyer / Thomas D. Morgan.
       p. cm.
    Includes bibliographical references and index.
    ISBN 978-0-19-973773-4 ((hardback) : alk. paper)
    1. Lawyers—United States. 2. Practice of law—United States.
    3. Law—Study and teaching—United States. I. Title.
    KF300.M67 2010
    340.023'73–dc22   2009036764

2 3 4 5 6 7 8 9
Printed in the United States of America on acid-free paper

Note to Readers
This publication is designed to provide accurate and authoritative information in regard to the subject matter covered. It is based upon sources believed to be accurate and reliable and is intended to be current as of the time it was written. It is sold with the understanding that the publisher is not engaged in rendering legal, accounting, or other professional services. If legal advice or other expert assistance is required, the services of a competent professional person should be sought. Also, to confirm that the information has not been affected or changed by recent developments, traditional legal research techniques should be used, including checking primary sources where appropriate.

(Based on the Declaration of Principles jointly adopted by a Committee of the American Bar Association and a Committee of Publishers and Associations.)

You may order this or any other Oxford University Press publication by
visiting the Oxford University Press website at www.oup.com

CONTENTS

PREFACE

In the legal world's game of musical chairs, 2009 was the year the music stopped. Lawyers who had been chasing more and more work at an ever faster pace found themselves looking for a secure place—almost any place—to survive the disorienting fall in demand for their services. Lawyers hope the music will begin again, and of course it will. But if the predictions of this book are correct, the melody lawyers hear will be quite different.

This book is divided into six chapters. The first three analyze where lawyers are and how they got there. The last three examine the implications of the new reality for law firms, law schools and the public that often looks to lawyers for civic leadership.

My work on this book has extended for more than a decade. Today, some of the ideas found here may seem self-evident. For much of the time in which lawyers were riding high, however, it was hard to get lawyers or those who study them to take seriously the changes that have now overtaken the legal profession.

Any book such as this is the product of what the author has learned from too many people to mention individually. Special thanks, however, go to Jim Jones, the late Lew Rudnick, and Richard Susskind who understood these issues in the early days of the project, and to Steve Chitwood, Robert Creamer, Anthony Davis, Jennifer DelMonico, Steven Karl, Fred Lawrence, Kathryn Morgan, Jim Pyle, Mitt Regan, Richard Salomon and Robert Tuttle who have read and commented on earlier drafts of this book.

1. THE UNSETTLED WORLD OF AMERICAN LAWYERS

A. PERVASIVE LAWYER ANXIETY

American lawyers are worried. Attracted by the prospect of an honorable—possibly influential—career with above-average financial rewards, many of them have spent up to a quarter-million dollars for the education required to obtain a law license. Many have gone deeply into debt for that education, and others have spent unrecoverable years trying to build the practice to which they had aspired.

Even before the current recession, reports had been heard that many lawyers were "pathologically unhappy" and "hate themselves [for] what they have become, what the [legal] profession has made of them."[1] The profession itself was said to be "dead or dying" and "rotting away."[2] Lawyers were described as feeling "betrayed"[3] and dominated by "rascals" engaged in "widespread greed, hype, and self-dealing."[4] Studies show that almost twice as many lawyers as other adults abused drugs and alcohol.[5] Books such as *Running from*

1. Douglas Litowitz, The Destruction of Young Lawyers: Beyond One L 9, 16 (2006); Patrick J. Schlitz, *On Being a Happy, Healthy, and Ethical Member of an Unhappy, Unhealthy, and Unethical Profession*, 52 Vand. L. Rev. 871, 891 (1999).

2. Carl T. Bogus, *The Death of an Honorable Profession*, 71 Ind. L. Rev. 911 (1996).

3. Sol M. Linowitz with Martin Mayer, The Betrayed Profession: Lawyering at the End of the Twentieth Century (1994).

4. Peter Megargee Brown, Rascals: The Selling of the Legal Profession 5 (1989).

5. *See, e.g.*, Connie J.A. Beck, Bruce D. Sales & G. Andrew H. Benjamin, *Lawyers' Distress: Alcohol-Related Problems and Other Psychological Concerns Among a Sample of Practicing Lawyers*, 10 J.L. & Health 1, 5–6 (1995); Andrew H. Benjamin et al., *The Prevalence of Depression, Alcohol Abuse, and Cocaine Abuse Among United States Lawyers*, 13 Int'l J.L. & Psychiatry 233 (1990); Association of American Law Schools, *Report of the AALS Special Comm. on Problems of Substance Abuse in the Law Schools*, 44 J. Legal Educ. 35 (1994).

the Law[6] and inside jokes about being a "recovering lawyer" were a familiar part of the dialogue among law students, lawyers, and former lawyers.[7] Indeed, one distinguished observer had concluded that the legal profession "stands in danger of losing its soul."[8]

On top of that, many lawyers now have doubts about their economic future. The current global economic crisis has led many clients to abandon deals that were the backbone of law firm practice.[9] The American Bar Association urges new law school graduates to have "backup plans."[10] Over 4,000 lawyers—some of them experienced partners—have lost their positions at major American firms

---

6. DEBORAH L. AARON, RUNNING FROM THE LAW: WHY GOOD LAWYERS ARE GETTING OUT OF THE LEGAL PROFESSION (1989). Lest the title seem the only provocative part, the book contains chapter titles such as *Prison Unrest* and *The Scene of the Crime. See also* WALT BACHMAN, LAW V. LIFE: WHAT LAWYERS ARE AFRAID TO SAY ABOUT THE LEGAL PROFESSION (1995); STACY M. DeBROFF, ET AL., THE GREAT FIRM ESCAPE: HARVARD LAW SCHOOL'S GUIDE TO BREAKING OUT OF PRIVATE PRACTICE AND INTO PUBLIC SERVICE (2000).

7. Among the stories of former lawyers are Tresa Baldas, *The Show Biz Bar*, NAT'L L.J., Sept. 25, 2005, at 1 (former litigator who has turned to writing television shows); Vivia Chen, *A Thing for Ming*, AMERICAN LAWYER, Apr. 2003, at 39 (former Skadden Arps associate who has opened a Chinese design gallery); Bryan Gottlieb, STUDENT LAWYER, Dec. 1999, at 15 (lawyer who runs a law office out of "Legal Grind," his coffee house business). *See also* GARY A. MUNNEKE, ET AL., NONLEGAL CAREERS FOR LAWYERS (5th ed. 2006).

8. ANTHONY T. KRONMAN, THE LOST LAWYER: FAILING IDEALS OF THE LEGAL PROFESSION (1993) (the author is a professor at Yale Law School and was Dean at Yale when he wrote the book). Dean Kronman's book calls attention to society's seeming loss of respect for lawyers' "practical wisdom" and the corresponding loss of lawyer-"statesmen" in the tradition of Robert Jackson, Dean Acheson, Cyrus Vance, and Carla Hills.

9. *See, e.g.,* Anthony Lin, *Corporate Law Firms See Dark Days Ahead*, N.Y. LAWYER, Sept. 16, 2008, at http://www.nylawyer.com/display.php/file=/news/08/09/091608a; Jacqueline Bell, *Wall Street Woes Spell Trouble for Law Firms*, LAW 360, Sept. 16, 2008, at http://competition.law360.com/print_article/69369.

10. Molly McDonough, *New Law Grads Urged to Have Backup Plans*, A.B.A. J., Oct. 20, 2008, at http://www.abajournal.com/news/new_law_grads_urged_to_ have_backup_plans. The A.B.A. was saying much the same thing the year before. Debra Cassens Weiss, *Law School Secret: Bad Job Market*, A.B.A. J., Sept. 29, 2007, at http://www.abajournal.com/news/law_school_secret_bad_job_market.

in 2009.[11] Job offers to many 2009 law graduates have been "deferred" to a later, often-unspecified date.[12] Law firm partners have tried to keep their own earnings steady, but "as the chair of one firm put it, 'We can't beat the donkeys any harder.'"[13] In short, says another writer wryly, "a law degree isn't necessarily a license to print money these days."[14]

Observers of the current state of the American legal profession do not always agree what the central problems are, but this book suggests that lawyers are right to be concerned. Those who practice law face a world in which the demand for lawyers is determined by what clients need lawyers to do. The premise of this book is that lawyers are facing fundamental changes in both what they will be asked to do and whether the work they once did will continue to be done by lawyers at all. The world that many lawyers decry and others fear, in short, may in fact be the world in which they and other lawyers are destined to live.[15]

---

11. Debra Cassens Weiss, *Legal Sector Lost 2000 Jobs Last Month, 58 Jobs Last Week*, A.B.A. J., Oct. 5, 2009, at http://www.abajournal.com/news/ legal_sector_lost_2000_jobs_last_month_58_jobs_last_week/. In the last half of 2008, the Heller Ehrmann and Thatcher Proffitt firms collapsed, the venerable firm of Cadwalader, Wickersham & Taft laid off ninety-six lawyers, and Sonnenschein Nath & Rosenthal laid off twenty-four lawyers to add to the thirty-seven it had laid off six months earlier.

12. Some firms are paying deferred associates a portion of what they would have earned if they work at a public service agency. *See, e.g.*, Mark Fass, *Fellows Program Seen to Benefit Deferred Associates, D.A. and Firms*, N.Y.L.J., Sept. 22, 2009, at http://www.law.com/jsp/nylj/PubArticleNY.jsp? id=1202433960500.

13. David Bario, *Fog Advisory: Managing Partners are Nervous About What 2008 Will Bring*, AM. LAWYER, December 2007, at 114. *See also* Brian Katkin, *BigLaw Associates' Pay Unlikely to Rise, But Their Hours. . .*, NEW YORK LAWYER, Sept. 29, 2008, at http://nylj.com/nylawyer/news/08/09/0929081. html. Anthony Lin, *Corporate Law Firms See Dark Days Ahead*, NEW YORK LAWYER, Sept. 16, 2008, at http://nylj.com/nylawyer/news/08/09/091608a. html.

14. Amir Efrati, *Hard Case: Job Market Wanes for U.S. Lawyers*, WALL ST. J., Sept. 24, 2007, at 1.

15. Some authors believe personality traits such as a need to be able to control all variables disproportionately appear in people who decide to be lawyers. If so, lawyers are perhaps inherently more sensitive to change than the

B. WHAT IS A LAWYER?

The legal definition of an American lawyer is someone who has been issued a license to "practice law." The license is typically granted by the supreme court of one of the fifty states or the District of Columbia.[16] The practice of law, in turn, is best described as the application of general legal principles to concrete client problems.[17] While individuals may represent themselves or work on their own legal problems, only a lawyer may perform that service for others.

To receive a license to practice law, a person ordinarily must complete four years of college, plus three years of graduate training in a law school accredited by the American Bar Association.[18] After finishing law school, the candidate for a license must then pass a bar examination. That examination is administered by the state in which the lawyer is applying for a license, but most states use the "multistate" examination prepared by the National Conference of Bar Examiners. Much of that examination consists of multiple choice questions about legal issues arising anywhere in the country. Only some of the questions asked to applicants will focus on the law of the state whose license the applicant seeks.

When most non-lawyers think of a lawyer, they probably imagine someone who knows the law, tells others what it requires, and goes to court to defend charges that their clients have violated the law's provisions. Lawyers, however, know that such a description is incomplete

---

general public. *See, e.g.,* Martin E.P. Seligman, Paul R. Verkuil & Terry H. Kang, *Why Lawyers Are Unhappy,* 23 Cardozo L. Rev. 33 (2001); Susan Daicoff, *Lawyer, Know Thyself: A Review of Empirical Research on Attorney Attributes Bearing on Professionalism,* 46 Am. U. L. Rev. 1337 (1997). *See also* Walt Bachman, Law v. Life 15–21 (1995) (describing experiments showing unusual levels of stress experienced by persons who have responsibility for the welfare of others but who lack the ability to control all relevant variables).

16. *See generally* Restatement (Third) of The Law Governing Lawyers § 1 (2001).

17. Model Code of Prof'l Responsibility EC 3–5 (1969). *See also* Restatement (Third) of The Law Governing Lawyers § 4, cmt. c (2001).

18. California is one notable exception to this rule, allowing graduates of state-accredited law schools to take its bar examination even if the schools are not A.B.A.-accredited.

and inaccurate. The law's provisions are so numerous and i many aspects of life that no lawyer can possibly know m small fraction of its requirements. A typical lawyer under there are many kinds of legal regulation, knows one or i of legal analysis, and can determine ways to get additional informa-tion. Beyond those general similarities, however, lawyers' substantive knowledge and personal skills differ radically. Realistically, all law-yers limit their practice if they hope to deliver services efficiently and effectively.[19]

Furthermore, few people ask a lawyer for legal information. Occasionally they want a formal legal opinion about the legality of a course of action, but what most clients want is help accomplishing a particular objective—starting a new business, for example, resolving a dispute, or getting a divorce. An understanding of legal require-ments may be implicit in achieving the objective, but for most clients, knowledge of the law and even a commitment to follow its dictates are not ends in themselves.[20]

While all lawyers have the same basic license earned the same way, what each actually does with the license is more different than alike. The reality of the differences among lawyers is only increasing

---

19. In other fields of employment, such limitations on practice might be called "specialization," but lawyers have long resisted applying that label to most such limitations of practice. MODEL RULES PROF'L CONDUCT R. 7.4 (2004).

20. People who know lawyers primarily from popular media may see law-yers as unattractive and the practice of law as suspect. There is now an exten-sive literature examining popular culture images of lawyers, *e.g.*, PAUL BERGMAN & MICHAEL ASIMOV, REEL JUSTICE: THE COURTROOM GOES TO THE MOVIES (1996); ROBERT M. JARVIS & PAUL JOSEPH, EDS., PRIME TIME LAW: FICTIONAL TELEVISION AS LEGAL NARRATIVE (1998); Michael Asimow, *Embodiment of Evil: Law Firms in the Movies*, 48 UCLA L. REV. 1339 (2001); Marc Galanter, *The Faces of Mistrust: The Image of Lawyers is Public Opinion, Jokes & Political Discourse*, 66 U. CINN. L. REV. 805 (1998); Carrie Menkel-Meadow, *Can They Do That? Legal Ethics in Popular Culture: Of Characters and Acts*, 48 UCLA L. REV. 1305 (2001); Robert C. Post, *On the Popular Image of the Lawyer: Reflections in a Dark Glass*, 75 CAL. L. REV. 379 (1987). *See also* Richard Brust, *The 25 Greatest Legal Movies: Tales of Lawyers We've Loved and Loathed*, A.B.A. J., Aug. 2008, at 38.

today, and as a result, the idea of an identity that lawyers have in common can be said to be vanishing rapidly.

C. WHY LAWYERS' ANXIETY MAY BE INTENSIFYING

For a number of years, the greatest single complaint heard from lawyers was that they were required to work too hard.[21] In part, the burden was self-imposed by lawyers who liked the income that working long hours produces, but there was no denying that demands on lawyers to devote extensive time to their careers was intense. Annual law firm billable-hour requirements of 1,300 hours in the 1950s became 1,600 hours in the 1970s, 2,000 hours in the 1990s, and 2,200 or more hours of billable work per year in the current decade. Adding several hundred hours of non-billable time in the office to a 2,200 billable-hour requirement—and adding a commute to and from the office and time off the clock for lunch each day—could easily result in a young lawyer investing seventy hours per week or more in his or her career.[22]

But billable-time requirements cannot be the whole story of lawyer dissatisfaction. Many people work hard, and issues of work-life balance are far from unique to lawyers. Furthermore, if hard work were the problem, one would expect that today's business slowdown

---

21. The literature on this subject was extensive. *See, e.g.,* Susan Saab Fortney, *The Billable Hours Derby: Empirical Data on the Problems and Pressure Points,* 33 FORDHAM URBAN L.J. 171 (2005); Susan Saab Fortney, *Soul for Sale: An Empirical Study of Associate Satisfaction, Law Firm Culture, and the Effects of Billable Hour Requirements,* 69 UMKC L. REV. 239 (2000); Alex M. Johnson, Jr., *Think Like a Lawyer, Work Like a Machine: The Dissonance Between Law School and Law Practice,* 64 S. CAL. L. REV. 1231 (1991). If demand for lawyer services decreases, of course, lawyers may yearn for the bad days of too much to do.

22. AM. B. FOUND. & N.A.L.P. FOUND. FOR LAW CAREER RES. & EDUC., AFTER THE JD: FIRST RESULTS OF A NATIONAL STUDY OF LEGAL CAREERS 33 (2004), reports that fifty was the median number of hours worked by the respondents and that the image of most new lawyers as "worked to the point of exhaustion" is "greatly exaggerated." About 20 percent of the lawyers—most of them in large firms—reported, however, that they work sixty hours or more each week. *Id.*

would be seen as exciting rather than as a cause for alarm. Other factors must be part of lawyer discontent.

A second source of lawyers' disquiet seems to be the fact that many lawyers are under pressure to attract more clients and bring more work into their firm. Until the late 1970s, it was considered unseemly for lawyers to market their services to potential clients, and it was unusual for a client to move its work from one law firm to another. That meant that if there was more work to do than a lawyer would prefer, it was most likely because existing clients needed more help at the moment. Later, things would revert to normal. Today, no matter how large and lucrative last year's base of business, firms do not see it as enough, and economic issues faced by clients only compound the problem. Yesterday's work may be attracted away by others, and overwork has sometimes seemed the only alternative to having no work at all.

A third reality facing lawyers is the fact that most of the time, they find their work involves solving problems defined by their clients. This is not new, of course. Lawyers have rarely been in control of their own activity except in the sense that they may turn down a client's matter altogether.[23] How lawyers respond to the reality that others define what they do may indeed be what affects some lawyers' attitudes about their work. For many lawyers, one of the things that makes work interesting and satisfying is the chance to work with other bright people on complex matters involving the constantly changing activities of multiple clients. For other lawyers, having their day always defined by what is important to other people represents a fundamental loss of their own personhood.

Fourth, lawyers express in various forms a loss of the sense of being part of a public profession that helps keep the country's legal standards focused on a commitment to justice.[24] Thoughtful lawyers

---

23. Professor Geoffrey Hazard suggests that a tension remains between the profession's view of itself as independent and its ethical standards as a form of "self-government" and the view that "the profession takes its shape in response to pressures and demands from outside forces." Geoffrey C. Hazard, Jr., *The Future of Legal Ethics*, 100 YALE L.J. 1239, 1241 (1991). This book argues that the latter view is the more realistic one today.

24. *See, e.g.,* DAVID LUBAN, LAWYERS AND JUSTICE: AN ETHICAL STUDY (1988); DEBORAH L. RHODE, IN THE INTERESTS OF JUSTICE: REFORMING THE

have long had a schizophrenic sense of their professional identity. They have been trained by their parents and teachers to think about maximizing the ways in which their lives affect the public good, but realistically, while some lawyers help clients achieve just results at least some of the time, many lawyers find that private clients have little interest in what an objectively just result would be.

Indeed, at least some clients affirmatively want to avoid doing what the law requires. The ultimate limitation on lawyer conduct is that lawyers may not themselves commit a crime or fraud, nor may they help their clients do so.[25] Thus, what lawyers do mostly is (1) help their clients avoid illegal behavior, (2) assist their clients in arguing that the law does not apply to them, or (3) argue that their client's conduct will not or did not violate the law. Only the first of those functions is largely congruent with a sense of the lawyer as advancing the public good, so a thoughtful lawyer's schizophrenia about his or her choice of career is almost inevitable.

Fifth, some lawyers have a financial incentive to keep people fighting rather than solving their problems. In practice, much of the business of the courts is a form of intimidation by one person or corporation seeking to impose financial burdens on a supplier, customer, or competitor. Litigation can even be a form of bullying, as the pretense of a dispute lets a lawyer force a client's adversary into an expensive discovery process that can force that adversary to lay bare important secrets or pay the aggressor to go away.[26] Adversaries can

LEGAL PROFESSION (2000); WILLIAM H. SIMON, THE PRACTICE OF JUSTICE: A THEORY OF LAWYERS' ETHICS (1998). *See also* SOL M. LINOWITZ WITH MARTIN MAYER, THE BETRAYED PROFESSION: LAWYERING AT THE END OF THE TWENTIETH CENTURY 1–2 (1994); ANTHONY T. KRONMAN, THE LOST LAWYER: FAILING IDEALS OF THE LEGAL PROFESSION (1993); PETER MEGARGEE BROWN, RASCALS: THE SELLING OF THE LEGAL PROFESSION 46–47, 68, 90–92 (1989).

25. MODEL RULES OF PROF'L CONDUCT R. 1.2(d).

26. For a vigorous assertion of this idea, *see, e.g.*, PHILIP K. HOWARD, THE COLLAPSE OF THE COMMON GOOD: HOW AMERICA'S LAWSUIT CULTURE UNDERMINES OUR FREEDOM (2002); WALTER K. OLSON, THE RULE OF LAWYERS: HOW THE NEW LITIGATION ELITE THREATENS AMERICA'S RULE OF LAW (2003); WALTER K. OLSON, THE LITIGATION EXPLOSION: WHAT HAPPENED WHEN AMERICA UNLEASHED THE LAWSUIT (1991). To get some perspective on today's litigation and the alleged litigation explosion, *see, e.g.*, HERBERT M. KRITZER, THE JUSTICE BROKER: LAWYERS AND ORDINARY LITIGATION (1990);

try to seek mediation or some other less intrusive processes, but even asking may be seen as a sign of weakness, and thus the cycle of mutual destruction can continue.

If, on the other hand, a genuine victim seeks redress, an aggressive opposing lawyer can often make the process of recovery so costly that it is not worth the effort. Law seen this way—especially from the inside—can become the height of lawlessness, and responsible lawyers can correctly see themselves as victimizers. Professor William Simon wisely explains that lawyers sometimes conclude that they must practice immorally in the short run but try to persuade themselves that in the long run such a system produces just results. Lawyers, as well as the public, become uncertain, however, whether the long run will ever come.[27] Thus, again, today's lawyers have legitimate reasons to be troubled by the role they have chosen to assume.

D. PUTTING SOME OF THE CONCERNS INTO PERSPECTIVE

Serious concerns such as these deserve to be taken seriously, although Professor Deborah Rhode observes that "[l]awyers belong to a profession permanently in decline."[28] Indeed, viewed another way, the legal profession has never seemed more attractive and alive. Over 140,000 students take the Law School Admission Test each year, and over

---

Marc S. Galanter, *Reading the Landscape of Disputes: What We Know and Don't Know (and Think We Know) About Our Allegedly Contentious and Litigious Society,* 31 UCLA L. REV. 4 (1983).

27. WILLIAM H. SIMON, THE PRACTICE OF JUSTICE: A THEORY OF LAWYERS' ETHICS 2 (1968). *See also* Norman W. Spaulding, *Reinterpreting Professional Identity,* 74 U. COLO. L. REV. 1 (2003).

28. DEBORAH L. RHODE, IN THE INTERESTS OF JUSTICE: REFORMING THE LEGAL PROFESSION 1 (2000). Many examples support Professor Rhode's observation, e.g., early in the last century, one prominent law school dean complained that "in the dominant attitude, the Law is no more than a trade, an occupation, a business." John H. Wigmore, *Introduction, in* ORRIN N. CARTER, ETHICS OF THE LEGAL PROFESSION xxi (1915). More recently, Marc Galanter observed that nostalgia "has been a constant accompaniment of elite law practice at least since the formation of the large firm a hundred years ago." Marc Galanter, *Lawyers in the Mist: The Golden Age of Legal Nostalgia,* 100 DICK. L. REV. 549, 552 (1996).

80,000 of those apply to law schools in order to enter the allegedly troubled profession.[29] Just under 50,000 of those applicants annually enroll in A.B.A.-accredited law schools, and a high proportion of that number graduate and become lawyers.[30]

Americans pay over $236 billion each year for legal services.[31] Interest in entering law school has undoubtedly been stimulated in part by starting salaries in some law firms of up to $165,000 per year, plus bonuses.[32] Partners at the nation's most successful law firms report earning more than $1 million per year.[33] Most lawyers are not paid those sums, of course, but the median American lawyer's annual income exceeds $100,000, and practicing law surely looks to many like a way to make a relatively good living.[34]

---

29. Law School Admission Council, Tests Administered and Volume Summary Data 1998–2008, at http://members.lsac.org/Public/MainPage.aspx. Test volume rose from 107,200 in 1999–2000 to 151,400 in 2008–2009. The number of law school applicants was 74,600 in 1999–2000 and 83,400 in 2007–2008, although the largest number of applicants was 100,600 in 2004–2005. First year enrollment in accredited U.S. law schools has steadily risen from 43,500 in 1999–2000 to 49,414 in 2007–2008. *Id.*

30. A.B.A. Section Legal Educ. & Admission to the Bar, SYLLABUS 8 (Spring 2007). The 2006 data show 48,937 first-year students in accredited U.S. law schools, and total law school enrollment of 148,698.

31. U.S. CENSUS BUREAU, 2008 STATISTICAL ABSTRACT OF THE UNITED STATES, NAICS Code 5411, Table 6.1. The data is current through 2006.

32. PETER MEGARGEE BROWN, RASCALS: THE SELLING OF THE LEGAL PROFESSION 78–79 (1989), points out that this was not always the case. New lawyer Franklin D. Roosevelt began his career in 1907 for no salary at all in the first year and only a small salary in the second year. The accepted principle at that time was that young lawyers needed training, got it at the law firm, and paid for it in the form of their uncompensated services. *See also* MICHAEL H. TROTTER, PROFIT AND THE PRACTICE OF LAW: WHAT'S HAPPENED TO THE LEGAL PROFESSION 9–10 (1997), reporting that the annual pay of a starting associate at a top Atlanta firm in 1960 was about $3,600 per year.

33. Judge Learned Hand noted in 1921: "I feel sorry for lawyers; they seem to me to be so earnest and to work so hard, and when all is said and done to get very little out of life, except, perhaps, money." Letter from Learned Hand to Felix Frankfurter, *quoted in* Wayne K. Hobson, *Symbol of the New Profession: Emergence of the Large Law Firm, 1870–1951, in* THE NEW HIGH PRIESTS: LAWYERS IN POST–CIVIL WAR AMERICA 9 (Gerard W. Gawalt ed., 1984).

34. *See* AM. B. FOUND. & N.A.L.P. FOUND. FOR LAW CAREER RESEARCH & EDUCATION, AFTER THE JD: FIRST RESULTS OF A NATIONAL STUDY OF LEGAL

Further, when lawyers have been asked about their career satisfaction, the responses of a large majority have been positive. While some reported dissatisfaction, an American Bar Association study of lawyers in the year 2000 reported that 80 percent surveyed were "very satisfied" or "satisfied" with their current job.[35] That same level of satisfaction was also reported by the American Bar Foundation and National Association of Law Placement after the comprehensive, national "After the JD" study completed in 2004.[36] On the other hand, lawyers know that they only get paid when clients use their services. The current economic slowdown has only increased lawyer anxiety about the long-term prospects for sustaining lawyer incomes.[37]

CAREERS 43 (2004) (reported 2002 income of 25th percentile of solo practitioners entering practice in 2000 was $45,000, the median salary of such lawyers in firms of over 20 lawyers was $97,000, and the 75th percentile salary of such lawyers in firms over 250 lawyers was $158,000).

35. *See* A.B.A. YOUNG LAWYERS DIVISION, SURVEY: CAREER SATISFACTION (2000). AMERICAN BAR ASS'N YOUNG LAWYERS DIVISION, THE STATE OF THE LEGAL PROFESSION 1990, at 52 (1991) (76 percent were very satisfied or satisfied). In response, Deborah Rhode suggests that when lawyers are interviewed orally or asked a direct question about happiness, they tend to be more positive than when they can respond more confidentially or when indirect questions are used. DEBORAH L. RHODE, IN THE INTERESTS OF JUSTICE: REFORMING THE LEGAL PROFESSION 25 (2000).

36. AM. B. FOUND. & N.A.L.P. FOUND. FOR LAW CAREER RESEARCH, AFTER THE JD: FIRST RESULTS OF A NATIONAL STUDY OF LEGAL CAREERS (2004). Preliminary results of the second phase of the study, reported in February 2009, find 76 percent satisfaction even in the midst of an uncertain economy. Important current research focuses on *which* lawyers are happy and which are unhappy. *See, e.g.,* Ronit Dinowitzer & Bryant G. Garth, *Lawyer Satisfaction in the Process of Structuring Legal Careers,* 41 LAW & SOC'Y REV. 1 (2007) (lawyers in large firms are least satisfied, in spite of their higher incomes); Kenneth G. Dau-Schmidt & Kaushik Mukhopadhaya, *The Fruits of Our Labors: An Empirical Study of the Distribution of Income and Job Satisfaction Across the Legal Profession,* 49 J. LEGAL EDUC. 342 (1999) (minority and female lawyers are less satisfied than white male lawyers).

37. Professor Regan suggests that many lawyers may have personalities that are particularly unsettled by change; "many lawyers may be propelled by a 'never satisfied drive for success' that places a premium on controlling one's environment." MILTON C. REGAN, JR., EAT WHAT YOU KILL: THE FALL OF A WALL STREET LAWYER 298 (2006). What makes many lawyers successful is the ability "quickly to grasp the rules of the game." *Id.* at 303. When events

E. WHY SHOULD LAWYERS' ANXIETY INTEREST US?

The premise of this book is that we should not be surprised by the twin problems of significant lawyer anxiety amid the high level of reported lawyer satisfaction, and today's financial concern in the face of historic financial success. Indeed, the contrasts tell us less about the experience of lawyers than it does about the turbulent world in which all of us—not just lawyers—live. This book's premise is that the "lawyer" role known by generations of Americans and others is vanishing. In spite of the job satisfaction experienced by a majority of today's lawyers, most perceptive lawyers sense that the occupational life they have known is dissolving around them.

The world many lawyers imagine is the world of the 1950s and 1960s, a period now sometimes called the "golden age" of the American bar.[38] One can, of course, question that positive characterization. The bar was far from diverse during that era.[39] There was widespread discrimination against Jewish and Catholic lawyers, and the discrimination was even worse against women and minority lawyers.[40]

---

control a lawyer's world, one might expect that these lawyers will feel especially unsettled.

38. MARC GALANTER & THOMAS PALAY, TOURNAMENT OF LAWYERS: THE TRANSFORMATION OF THE BIG LAW FIRM 20–36 (1991). The characterization is affirmed in MARY ANN GLENDON, A NATION UNDER LAWYERS: HOW THE CRISIS IN THE LEGAL PROFESSION IS TRANSFORMING AMERICAN SOCIETY 20–24 (1994).

39. Erwin Smigel reports that New York firms in 1964 primarily wanted "lawyers who are Nordic, have pleasing personalities and 'clean-cut' appearances, are graduates of the 'right' schools, have the 'right' social background and experience in the affairs of the world, and are endowed with tremendous stamina." ERWIN O. SMIGEL, THE WALL STREET LAWYER: PROFESSIONAL ORGANIZATION MAN? 37 (1964). Smigel quotes a law school dean as saying: "If a man has any one of these things, he could get a job. If he has two of them, he can have a choice of jobs; if he has three, he could go anywhere." Id.

40. Id. at 44–47. See also Eli Wald, The Rise and Fall of the WASP and Jewish Law Firms, 60 STAN. L. REV. 1803 (2008). From 1950 to 1970, the proportion of women lawyers ranged between 2.5 percent and 2.8 percent. BARBARA A. CURRAN, ET AL., THE LAWYER STATISTICAL REPORT: A STATISTICAL PROFILE OF THE U.S. LEGAL PROFESSION IN THE 1980s 10 (1985). It appears that the number of minority lawyers was not even recorded before about 1970. See, e.g., RICHARD L. ABEL, AMERICAN LAWYERS 288 (1989). Even critics

Further, bar admission in the "golden age" was denied on political grounds,[41] accessible programs of group legal services were largely outlawed,[42] and lawyers in many states were required to charge at least specified minimum fees.[43] The sense of a once "golden age" remains, however, because the lives of lawyers' during those decades were relatively stable. An associate who worked hard could expect to have senior lawyers who would act as mentors. The young associate would likely become a partner and would likely retire from the firm in which he began his practice. Along the way, he would have earned an above-average income, worked on a variety of cases, and been a leader in community organizations.[44]

We actually have quite a good picture of law practice in the early 1960s, based on detailed studies done in New York by sociologists Erwin Smigel and Jerome Carlin.[45] It was still an era in which the solo practitioner—answerable to no one but himself—was the prototype.[46]

---

of the current state of the bar today recognize that calls for the good old days must not ignore the positive effects of having greater diversity and opportunity in the profession. *See, e.g.,* SOL M. LINOWITZ WITH MARTIN MAYER, THE BETRAYED PROFESSION: LAWYERING AT THE END OF THE TWENTIETH CENTURY (1994).

41. *E.g., In re* Anastopolo, 366 U.S. 82 (1961).

42. *See, e.g.,* MODEL CODE OF PROF'L RESPONSIBILITY DR 2-103(D).

43. *See, e.g.,* Goldfarb v. Virginia State Bar, 421 U.S. 773 (1975).

44. The story of this golden age period is told especially well in SOL M. LINOWITZ WITH MARTIN MAYER, THE BETRAYED PROFESSION: LAWYERING AT THE END OF THE TWENTIETH CENTURY (1994), and MARY ANN GLENDON, A NATION UNDER LAWYERS: HOW THE CRISIS IN THE LEGAL PROFESSION IS TRANSFORMING AMERICAN SOCIETY (1994).

45. ERWIN O. SMIGEL, THE WALL STREET LAWYER: PROFESSIONAL ORGANIZATION MAN? (1964) (Smigel worked out of NYU, Indiana University, and the University of Chicago); JEROME CARLIN, LAWYERS' ETHICS: A SURVEY OF THE NEW YORK CITY BAR (1966) (Carlin was both a lawyer and a sociologist, and his study was done as part of the Program on the Legal Profession at Columbia Law School).

46. ERWIN O. SMIGEL, THE WALL STREET LAWYER: PROFESSIONAL ORGANIZATION MAN? 3, 293–99 (1964). Carlin had the most to say about solo practitioners, concluding that they had fewer mentors, had more opportunity to exploit clients, and were more likely to be the subject of professional discipline. JEROME CARLIN, LAWYERS' ETHICS: A SURVEY OF THE NEW YORK CITY BAR 71–73, 101–05, 166–76 (1966).

Lawyers did much of their work for corporations, but they claimed to value a reputation as the conscience of those clients. They valued the chance to spend some of their careers in government or international organizations. Even then, however, some lawyers feared that clients were not asking for professional advice about whether to do something; they were asking only for advice about how to implement the client's preconceived plan. These lawyers were concerned, in short, that law was being transformed from a profession into an arm of business.[47]

Professor Mitt Regan summarizes the prevailing ethos of the "golden age" period as "nobody starves."[48] The going rate for an entry-level Wall Street lawyer in 1963 was $7,500.[49] Firms tended to rotate lawyers through several practice groups within the firm during the first three years of practice, and there was an unwritten sense that, once hired, the lawyer would either become a partner or get another attractive position, perhaps with one of the firm's clients.[50] Even in the golden age, however, associates reported that "they [found] it difficult to do their jobs well and spend what they consider to be enough time with their family."[51] The only firm during that time for which a report was available noted that more than half of its associates left the firm by the end of what was seen as the "educational period," i.e., their first three years.[52]

Today, of course, the world has come a long way from that golden age, and what will ultimately replace it is unclear; but lawyers are rightfully concerned that the new world will be much different. Legal regulation is not vanishing; indeed, as society becomes more complex, the place of law in regulating conduct is likely to increase. What this book

---

47. Erwin O. Smigel, The Wall Street Lawyer: Professional Organization Man? 302–06 (1964).

48. Milton C. Regan, Jr., Eat What You Kill: The Fall of a Wall Street Lawyer 26 (2006) (quoting Paul C. Hoffman, Lions in the Street 2 (1973)). See also Eve Spangler, Lawyers for Hire: Salaried Professionals at Work 29 (1986).

49. Erwin O. Smigel, The Wall Street Lawyer: Professional Organization Man? 58 (1964). In 1953, the figure was $4,000 per year. The figure in 2007 was $160,000, plus bonus.

50. Id. at 64–65.

51. Id. at 75, 102–04.

52. Id. at 78.

predicts is that the interaction of law with increasingly complex economic and social issues will make distinctively legal questions less common and make many of the skills now honed in law schools less relevant.

Rather than needing professionals whose understanding of law dwarfs their understanding of the substantive issues faced by clients, the world will require legally-trained persons to be more fully integrated into the substantive challenges today's clients face. Such a reality may require that more persons, not fewer, have some legal training, but the training of most such persons will almost certainly not be today's three-year graduate program designed to produce an all-purpose legal generalist. Today's lawyers, in turn, will not be unemployable, but for at least significant parts of their careers, they will be required to develop specialized expertise both in an area of substantive law and in the non-legal aspects of their potential clients' problems. If they fail to do so, they will find at almost every turn that clients will take their business to those prepared to deliver what the clients need at a higher level of quality, a lower cost, or both.[53]

Lawyers are not alone in their response to the disconnect between professional aspirations and market realities. Consider your local pharmacist thirty years ago. He probably had a stand-alone business and was seen by customers as a trusted health care advisor. Today, many pharmacists have been reduced to dispensing pills from the corner of a local Walmart and advising customers only by handing out printed warnings about the side-effects of prescription drugs. One can argue that the cost of prescription drugs is coming down as a result, but from the perspective of the pharmacist, the world has gotten worse instead of better.

Or think of your doctor thirty years ago. He or she tended to be practicing independently and doing well financially. Patients thought of their doctor as almost equal with God, and cost control was rarely

---

53. For reasons discussed in later chapters, this book rejects the view of SOL M. LINOWITZ WITH MARTIN MAYER, THE BETRAYED PROFESSION: LAWYERING AT THE END OF THE TWENTIETH CENTURY 26–27 (1994): "The fact is that law simply cannot operate as a business . . . . Consumers have no way to know whether a lawyer can promise (let alone deliver) value for money. . . . Professional services are sold by input rather than by output simply because output is unmeasurable by the consumer."

an issue. Today, doctors seem to deal with insurance companies as much as with patients, and opportunities for independent professional judgment are much too rare. The problem, of course, was that doctors also were not in control of the world around them, and despite rhetoric about professional status, the practice of medicine has been overwhelmed by politics, issues of cost, and the distribution of care.[54]

Developments in the world of lawyers will similarly be driven by the world lawyers and their clients face, not the world lawyers wish they could create. This book tries to paint a picture of the future changes in professional life and self-understanding that individual lawyers and others with legal training will experience. It ultimately concludes that the concept of a lawyer we have known will become a part of history, along with the knights and mercenaries who were hired to fight the battles of others in earlier times.[55]

Not everyone will like the look of the future suggested here, but what lawyers like will be of little relevance. Lawyers are experiencing the effects of long-term trends that lawyers neither created nor can avoid. Ultimately, while lawyer organizations tinker around the edges of rules of professional conduct—they can and should issue calls for more courtesy in lawyers' dealings—ultimately, what American lawyers wish their future to be will be of little relevance to the way their work develops.

---

54. The transformation of the medical profession is chronicled in ELIOT FRIEDSON, PROFESSIONALISM: THE THIRD LOGIC 182–93 (2001); ELLIOTT A. KRAUSE, DEATH OF THE GUILDS: PROFESSIONS, STATES, AND THE ADVANCE OF CAPITALISM, 1930 TO THE PRESENT 36–49 (1996).

55. This is not to say there will not be a continuing effort to increase lawyer professionalism. *See, e.g.,* A.B.A. COMM'N ON PROFESSIONALISM, ". . . . IN THE SPIRIT OF PUBLIC SERVICE:" A BLUEPRINT FOR THE REKINDLING OF LAWYER PROFESSIONALISM (1986); PETER MEGARGEE BROWN, RASCALS: THE SELLING OF THE LEGAL PROFESSION (1989); ROBERT A. KATZMANN, ED., THE LAW FIRM AND THE PUBLIC GOOD (1995); Professionalism Symposium, 52 S.C. L. REV. 443–758 (2001). For a more skeptical view of the concerns expressed in such books and articles, *see* Richard K. Greenstein, *Against Professionalism,* 22 GEO. J. LEGAL Ethics 327 (2009); Thomas D. Morgan, *Toward Abandoning Organized Professionalism,* 30 HOFSTRA L. REV. 947 (2002).

The direction of change seems inevitable, but the rate of change is harder to predict, and the date by which particular changes will occur remains uncertain. This book hopes to help lawyers and lay people alike understand what is going on in the world facing lawyers. Even if the American lawyer's role does not "vanish" immediately, understanding the direction in which change is moving may help individual lawyers—and would-be lawyers—plan their futures.

2. AMERICAN LAWYERS ARE NOT PART OF A PROFESSION

A. THE PROBLEMATIC EMPHASIS ON LAW AS A PROFESSION

References to the "legal profession" are common. Some lawyers use the term in an almost reverential sense. In its draft report on the future of the legal profession, for example, an American Bar Association committee reiterated the A.B.A.'s long-standing position that: "[L]aw is not just another business or industry. It is the foundation upon which our entire society and our system of justice and enlightened self-government are founded. Indeed, without lawyers [creation of our free society] would likely never have occurred!"[1]

Much of the current focus on law as a "professional" function is a legacy of the A.B.A. Commission on Professionalism, created at the urging of Chief Justice Warren Burger in the mid-1980s.[2] The Commission called on law schools to teach professional responsibility more creatively, including incorporating ethics issues into substantive courses.[3] It called on lawyers to place greater emphasis on the role of lawyers as officers of the court.[4] It called on trial courts to impose sanctions on lawyers who abuse the litigation process,[5] and it urged lawyers to engage in pro bono work and not make "wealth a principal

---

1. A.B.A. COMM. ON RESEARCH ABOUT THE FUTURE OF THE LEGAL PROFESSION, WORKING NOTES: DELIBERATIONS ON THE CURRENT STATUS OF THE LEGAL PROFESSION 4 (August 31, 2001). See also, e.g., Sandra Day O'Connor, *Professionalism*, 78 ORE. L. REV. 385 (1999); Harry T. Edwards, *Renewing Our Commitment to the Highest Ideals of the Legal Profession*, 84 N.C. L. REV. 1421 (2006).

2. The Commission, chaired by former A.B.A. President Justin Stanley, was created in December 1984 and announced in February 1985. It issued its report, ". . . . IN THE SPIRIT OF PUBLIC SERVICE:" A BLUEPRINT FOR THE REKINDLING OF LAWYER PROFESSIONALISM (hereafter Professionalism Report), in August 1986. The report is also published at 112 F.R.D. 243 (1986).

3. Professionalism Report at 14–16.

4. Professionalism Report at 28–30.

5. Professionalism Report at 42–43.

goal of law practice."[6] A significant number of state courts followed with commissions or conferences of their own, and these yielded a substantial body of literature about professionalism and professional ideals.[7]

Given the commitment of many to professional rhetoric, it may seem mean-spirited to condemn it. The point of this chapter, however, is that use of the idea of a "profession" to understand the world of lawyers obstructs clear thinking about what lawyers actually do and how they are likely to have to respond to the world they face.[8] Further, the concept of lawyer professional status underlies a view that lawyers can be assumed to perform the same functions, share the same goals, and have common expectations about proper lawyer behavior.[9] Indeed, at

---

6. Professionalism Report at 50–51.

7. Other professionalism reports or programs include SPECIAL COMM. ON PROFESSIONALISM, THE BAR, THE BENCH AND PROFESSIONALISM IN ILLINOIS: PROUD TRADITIONS, TOUGH NEW PROBLEMS, CURRENT CHOICES (1987); A.B.A. SEC. LEGAL EDUC. & ADMISSION TO THE BAR, TEACHING AND LEARNING PROFESSIONALISM (1996); A.B.A., PROMOTING PROFESSIONALISM: A.B.A. PROGRAMS, PLANS & STRATEGIES (1998); CONF. OF CHIEF JUSTICES, A NATIONAL ACTION PLAN ON LAWYER CONDUCT AND PROFESSIONALISM (1999). *See also* JACK L. SAMMONS, JR., LAWYER PROFESSIONALISM (1988); Roy T. Stuckey, *Introduction to Professionalism Symposium*, 52 S.C. L. REV. 443 (2001).

There are similarly strong traditions seeing law as a professional activity in other nations. The Council of Bars and Law Societies of Europe (CCBE), for example, coordinates the work of national bar associations throughout Europe. As discussed later, however, in a number of other countries such as England and Australia the old vestiges of self-regulatory professional status are rapidly disappearing.

8. Others have expressed concern about the use of professionalism rhetoric. *See, e.g.*, Rob Atkinson, *A Dissenter's Commentary on the Professionalism Crusade*, 74 TEX. L. REV. 259 (1995); David Barnhizer, *Profession Deleted: Using Market and Liability Forces to Regulate the Very Ordinary Business of Law Practice for Profit*, 17 GEO. J. LEGAL ETHICS 203 (2004); Timothy P. Terrell & James H. Wildman, *Rethinking "Professionalism,"* 41 EMORY L.J. 403 (1992). *See also* Gillian K. Hadfield, *Legal Barriers to Innovation: The Growing Economic Cost of Professional Control over Corporate Legal Markets*, 60 STAN. L. REV. 1689 (2008).

9. *See, e.g.*, REPORT OF THE TASK FORCE ON LAW SCHOOLS AND THE PROFESSION: NARROWING THE GAP, LEGAL EDUCATION AND PROFESSIONAL DEVELOPMENT—AN EDUCATIONAL CONTINUUM 138–41 (1992) (overview of skills and values that every lawyer should have). One recurring concern is

least part of the anxiety felt by many of the lawyers quoted in Chapter 1 appears to arise from recognizing that lawyers have no such common understanding and have not responded in large numbers to calls to action made in the name of restoring a sense of professionalism.

In my view, lawyers in American are not now a profession and—over most of their history—they have never been one.[10] While many characteristics attributed to professionals represent praiseworthy personal traits to which any moral person should aspire, the characteristics are ultimately those of individuals, not groups. This chapter tries to remove the professional lens through which the practice of law has been viewed. At least part of the current professionalism campaign has been an effort to deny or resist the "commercial" pressures lawyers face. By contrast, I believe lawyers will be able to understand their problems and opportunities only by seeing the world clearly and without the distortion the label "professional" introduces.

B. TWO APPROPRIATE USES OF THE TERM "PROFESSIONAL"

It should be acknowledged at the outset that the terms profession and professional are used almost promiscuously in our society, with little agreed-upon definition. Not all uses are troubling. One use of the terms describes people who are sufficiently skilled at what they do that others are willing to pay for their services. Thus, today we speak of professional athletes, professional musicians, professional beauticians, and even professional bill collectors. There is nothing inherently wrong with that common view of professionalism; it would be churlish to object to the sense of pride and dignity the term "professional" gives to many kinds of work.[11]

---

with respect to free legal services for the poor, a frequently articulated professional obligation that is largely ignored by many lawyers today. *See, e.g.,* DEBORAH L. RHODE, ACCESS TO JUSTICE (2004); Douglas L. Colbert, *Professional Responsibility in Crisis*, 51 HOWARD L.J. 677 (2008) (expressing concern that few lawyers helped with the aftermath of Hurricane Katrina).

10. Significant portions of this chapter were previously published as Thomas D. Morgan, *Toward Abandoning Organized Professionalism*, 30 HOFSTRA L. REV. 947 (2002).

11. Eliot Friedson, *Professionalism as Model and Ideology, in* ROBERT L. NELSON, DAVID M. TRUBEK & RAYMAN L. SOLOMON, EDS., LAWYERS' IDEALS/LAWYERS'

There is also nothing wrong with using the term "professional" to describe moral and praiseworthy personal conduct. We call a skilled pilot a "true professional" when he keeps his head in an emergency and saves the lives of all on board. We admire the professionalism of doctors who sometimes go to all corners of the world to deliver services with no hope of remuneration. Likewise, lawyers' professionalism codes appropriately call for civility in dealings with others, compliance with court rules, and charging only reasonable fees. The use of the term "professional conduct" is typically applied to admirable personal behavior, whether the people engaging in it would otherwise be seen as part of a profession. Having terms with which to applaud exemplary conduct is important, and the term "professional" works as well as any for the purpose.

C. THE MISTAKE OF TRANSFORMING PROFESSIONALS INTO A PROFESSION

The problem with use of the term "profession" arises when the term is used in its more formal sense by sociologists and other scholars who analyze and evaluate what lawyers do.[12] Ordinarily, most people would not care how scholars think of lawyers, but the sense of

---

PRACTICES: TRANSFORMATIONS IN THE AMERICAN LEGAL PROFESSION 217 (1992). The objective measure of success in this sense of professionalism is whether actual performance by the professional of whatever kind measures up to the level that the public has been led to expect. Estimates of current improvement or decline by lawyers in such professionalism tend to be mixed. Today's best lawyers are probably smarter, know more law, and are harder working than at almost any time in history. Their role in public leadership and their efforts to see that legal services are widely available to all citizens, however, have declined. *See, e.g.,* A.B.A. SEC. LEGAL EDUC. & ADMISSIONS TO THE BAR, TEACHING AND LEARNING PROFESSIONALISM (1996) (collecting reports on many professionalism programs).

12. In the context of lawyers' work, sociologist Eliot Friedson has defined a profession as:

an occupation whose members have special privileges, such as exclusive licensing, that are justified by the following assumptions:

(1) That its practice requires substantial intellectual training and the use of complex judgments;

lawyers as special and inherently different from mere "lay" persons has affected much of lawyers' own analysis of their professional standards, educational requirements, and the appropriate directions their futures should take.[13]

Professor Neil Hamilton provides a clear explanations of the traditional story of the creation of professions and the implication of the story for law and lawyers.

> Since the late 1800s, the peer-review professions in the United States, including the legal profession, have gradually worked out stable social contracts with the public in both custom and law. The public grants a profession autonomy to regulate itself through peer review, expecting the profession's members to control entry into and continued membership in the profession, to set standards for how individual professionals perform their work so that it serves the public good in the area of the profession's responsibility and to foster the core values and ideals of the profession.

---

(2) That since clients cannot adequately evaluate the quality of the service, they must trust those they consult;

(3) That the client's trust presupposes that the practitioner's self interest is overbalanced by devotion to serving both the client's interest and the public good; and

(4) That the occupation is self-regulating—that is, organized in such a way as to assure the public and the courts that its members are competent, do not violate their client's trust, and transcend their own self-interest.

A.B.A. COMM'N ON PROFESSIONALISM, "...IN THE SPIRIT OF PUBLIC SERVICE:" A BLUEPRINT FOR THE REKINDLING OF LAWYER PROFESSIONALISM 10 (1986). Dr. Friedson, a sociologist, was a member of the A.B.A. Commission. His other work, initially centered on the medical profession, includes ELIOT FRIEDSON, PROFESSIONAL POWERS: A STUDY OF THE INSTITUTIONALIZATION OF FORMAL KNOWLEDGE (1986); PROFESSIONALISM REBORN: THEORY, PROPHECY AND POLICY (1994); and PROFESSIONALISM: THE THIRD LOGIC: ON THE PRACTICE OF KNOWLEDGE (2001).

13. Other leading analyses of professions include MAGALI S. LARSON, THE RISE OF PROFESSIONALISM: A SOCIOLOGICAL ANALYSIS (1977), ANDREW ABBOTT, THE SYSTEM OF PROFESSIONS: AN ESSAY ON THE DIVISION OF EXPERT LABOR (1988); WILLIAM M. SULLIVAN, WORK AND INTEGRITY: THE CRISIS AND PROMISE OF PROFESSIONALISM IN AMERICA (2d ed. 2004). The American Bar Foundation is the premier research organization studying lawyers today, and much of its work also presupposes that lawyers represent an important category of "professional" workers.

In return, each member of the profession and the profession as a whole agree to meet certain correlative duties to the public: to maintain high standards of minimum competence and ethical conduct; to serve the public purpose of the profession and to discipline those who fail to meet these standards; to promote the core values and ideals of the profession; and to restrain self-interest to some degree to serve the public purpose of the profession. The term "professionalism" . . . captures the correlative duties of the profession's social contract for each individual professional.[14]

Professor Eliot Friedson explains the concept of professionalism more boldly.

In the case of [professions], neither individual buyers of labor in the market nor the managers of bureaucratic firms have the right to themselves choose workers to perform particular tasks or evaluate their work except within the limits specified by the occupation.[15]

In short, the premise of these descriptions of the legal profession is that, because law and legal issues are largely impenetrable by non-lawyers, responsibility for both has been delegated to the legal profession. For example, as Professor Friedson asserts, professional work "is so specialized as to be inaccessible to those lacking the required training and experience, and [thus] . . . it cannot be standardized, rationalized or . . . commodified."[16]

Simply stating these traditional understandings of a profession should suggest their lack of relevance to the reality facing lawyers today. In the first place, the "social contract" was never a historical event. That in itself is not a sufficient answer, of course; many philosophers and social theorists have justified social institutions by

---

14. Neil Hamilton, *Professionalism Clearly Defined*, 18 PROF. LAW. 4–5 (No. 4, 2008). The professionalism committee of the A.B.A. Section of Legal Education and Admission to the Bar had its own definition: "A professional lawyer is an expert in law pursing a learned art in service to clients and in the spirit of public service; and engaging in these pursuits as part of a common calling to promote justice and common good." REPORT OF THE PROFESSIONALISM COMM., A.B.A. SEC. LEGAL EDUC. & ADMISSIONS TO THE BAR, TEACHING AND LEARNING PROFESSIONALISM 6 (1996).

15. ELIOT FRIEDSON, PROFESSIONALISM: THE THIRD LOGIC: ON THE PRACTICE OF KNOWLEDGE 12 (2001).

16. *Id.* at 17.

imagining a pre-social state of nature in which people would have agreed that creation of particular institutions was wise and fair.[17]

But for a social contract argument to have even theoretical credibility, there must be a sense that people at the time of the alleged contract would have seen it as desirable. The term "profession" might have seemed like a meaningful concept in the middle ages, for example, when local and national economics were organized around multiple guilds, each authorized to do particular work. It might even have remained a recognizable idea in societies in which literacy was not widespread and clients could not read, much less evaluate, a lawyer's work.

In the post-Civil War period, however, and again after World War II, when American lawyers collectively asserted they were a profession, it was not true in anything like the social contract sense.[18] For reasons developed later in this volume, many clients today are able to—and do—evaluate and direct their lawyers. "Commodified" services, in turn, are what many lawyers deliver, and trends suggest the number doing so will only increase. Finally, while state courts acting as licensing bodies still limit some forms of lawyer competition, the overarching reality today is that lawyers are not set apart and special. They are economic actors, specially trained, but driven by all the vices—and virtues—of a capitalist economic system.

If this book is correct, even the term "lawyer" itself will increasingly be seen as imprecise and obsolete. Indeed, if the term is retained at all, it will come to describe a very different kind of occupation. For better or worse, most of tomorrow's lawyers will resemble what we today call business consultants more than they will call to mind Clarence Darrow and Atticus Finch.[19]

---

17. *E.g.*, JOHN LOCKE, SECOND TREATISE ON CIVIL GOVERNMENT, ch. 2 (1689); JOHN RAWLS, A THEORY OF JUSTICE (1971) (imagining an "original position" in which people defined rules of social relationships without knowing the wealth or status with which they would be born).

18. A good analysis of many of these issues can be found in ELLIOTT A. KRAUSE, DEATH OF THE GUILDS: PROFESSIONS, STATES, AND THE ADVANCE OF CAPITALISM, 1930 TO THE PRESENT (1996).

19. The concept of professionalism has been important to critics of what they see lawyers doing. *See, e.g.*, DEBORAH H. RHODE, IN THE INTERESTS OF JUSTICE: REFORMING THE LEGAL PROFESSION (2000); ANTHONY N. KRONMAN, THE LOST LAWYER: FAILING IDEALS OF THE LEGAL PROFESSION (1993);

D. COULD THE WORLD GET ALONG WITHOUT A LEGAL PROFESSION?

It is hard to imagine a civilized society without law. From enforcement of promises, to regulation of violence, to collection of taxes, a complex society uses its legal system to enhance personal liberty and security, permit planning and investment, and punish those who otherwise undermine the public interest. One can properly question complacency about the law's fairness or about the ability of regulatory provisions to draw distinctions among the seemingly-infinite forms human conduct takes,[20] but the idea that law in some form is necessary to help make a modern society run seems beyond doubt.

Given a need for law, it may be hard to imagine not having persons trained to have a special ability to deal with legal issues. Specialists in legal matters surely can help others right wrongs and understand the obligations and opportunities that law creates when the law gets too complex for a non-lawyer to understand. But it does not follow that a system based on law requires lawyers, as we now know them, to run effectively.[21] Roscoe Pound reports that ancient Greek litigants conducted trials without lawyers; parties appeared before commissions

---

Anthony N. Kronman, *Chapman University School of Law Groundbreaking Ceremony,* 1 CHAP. L. REV. 1 (1998). *But see* Timothy P. Terrell & James H. Wildman, *Rethinking "Professionalism,"* 41 EMORY L.J. 403 (1992).

20. There is now a compelling, if largely anecdotal, literature on the excesses of legal regulation. *See, e.g.,* PHILIP K. HOWARD, LIFE WITHOUT LAWYERS: LIBERATING AMERICANS FROM TOO MUCH LAW (2009) (arguing that matters requiring judgment are now governed by legal requirements); ROBERT A. KAGAN, ADVERSARIAL LEGALISM: THE AMERICAN WAY OF LAW 7 (2001) (suggesting that Americans rely excessively on law and litigation to resolve issues); PAUL F. CAMPOS, JURISMANIA: THE MADNESS OF AMERICAN LAW (1998) ("What is clear is that all of us move through a social space that becomes more saturated with rules: regulations that attempt to control the minutiae of our social roles in ever-more obsessive detail." *Id.* at 5.).

21. The best single work on this subject is JEROLD S. AUERBACH, JUSTICE WITHOUT LAW?: RESOLVING DISPUTES WITHOUT LAWYERS (1983). For a general look at the rise of adjudicative processes, *see* Richard E. Messick, *The Origin and Development of Courts,* 85 JUDICATURE 175 (Jan.–Feb. 2002).

of citizens who decided both the law and the facts.[22] Litigants sometimes aired grievances using words authored by others, but professional lawyers were rare, and the Greeks are said to have relied on
community-shaming more than on enforceable judgments as the
ultimate sanctions for wrongful conduct.[23]

Likewise, Rome provided the groundwork for the civil law that
governs much of the world today, but many of those whom we call
Roman lawyers were simply educated citizens (*patronus causarum*) who
gave unpaid courtroom oratory on behalf of friends and associates.[24]
Indeed, a largely non-lawyer system seems to have continued in
Western societies for at least the first millennium of the common era.
It was a period in which the church gave moral force to the law, and
the people who created and organized legal principles tended to be
clerics who were primarily expert in canon (church) law.[25]

---

22. ROSCOE POUND, THE LAWYER FROM ANTIQUITY TO MODERN TIMES
29–33 (1953). *See also* GEOFFREY C. HAZARD, JR. & ANGELO DONDI, LEGAL
ETHICS: A COMPARATIVE STUDY 16 (2004).

23. Robert S. Alexander, *The History of the Law As an Independent Profession
and the Present English System, in* A.B.A. SEC. TORTS & INS. PRAC., THE
LAWYER'S PROFESSIONAL INDEPENDENCE (1984); JOHN MAXCY ZANE, THE
STORY OF LAW 110–13 (2d ed. 1998). *Cf.* ARISTOPHANES, THE WASPS (a play
about a class of professional accusers).

24. JOHN MAXCY ZANE, THE STORY OF LAW 160 (2d ed. 1998); ROSCOE
POUND, THE LAWYER FROM ANTIQUITY TO MODERN TIMES 44–48 (1953). It is
true that "[b]y the end of the first century B.C . . . . a professional lawyer class,
which performed a gamut of services for clients and represented them in
court as well, had come into being . . . . But lo, the causiducus [speaker of
cases] soon earned cynical distrust in Rome." RICHARD W. MOLL, THE LURE
OF THE LAW 8 (1990). *Cf.* GEOFFREY C. HAZARD, JR. & ANGELO DONDI, LEGAL
ETHICS: A COMPARATIVE STUDY 18–20 (2004) (cautioning that "conducting a
historical analysis of the Roman period is a complex undertaking").

25. By the fifth and sixth centuries A.D., the role of procurator had developed in Roman Law, and individuals presented cases on behalf of others. The
litigation was conducted as if the respective procurators were the litigants,
and the result of that litigation was rendered binding on the actual parties by
agreement. ROSCOE POUND, THE LAWYER FROM ANTIQUITY TO MODERN
TIMES 38–40 (1953). By tradition, procurators were not paid, although later
they were permitted to charge fees subject to caps on the amounts. *Id.* at
51–55. For more on this period, *see generally,* JAMES A. BRUNDAGE, THE
MEDIEVAL ORIGINS OF THE LEGAL PROFESSION: CANONISTS, CIVILIANS, AND

Obviously, much has changed over the intervening years—including loss of a sense of community in large parts of the modern world—and the growth of legal specialists has been no accident in complex, secular, commercial societies. Modern societies seem to require persons who can understand the obligations law imposes, facilitate transactions and other interpersonal relationships, plan for distributing the rewards and sharing the burdens of mutual undertakings, resolve disputes associated with the relationships and undertakings, and seek to affect the regulatory structure in which they are conducted.[26]

Further, many important community benefits received by citizens are provided by private clients served by lawyers. Professors Silver and Cross write exuberantly

> Lawyers who are dispirited about the profession should test themselves every so often. Go to a museum, a park, a city street, a bank, or a school—any pleasant place—and try to identify every feature of the surroundings for which lawyers can take some credit. . . . [For example,] look at the workers and wonder how many have pension plans, benefit plans, or employment contracts that lawyers drafted.[27]

COURTS (2008); HAROLD J. BERMAN, LAW AND REVOLUTION: THE FORMATION OF THE WESTERN LEGAL TRADITION (1983); Amelia J. Uelmen, *A View of the Legal Profession from a Mid-Twelfth-Century Monastery*, 71 FORDHAM L. REV. 1517 (2003).

26. Former Harvard Law School Dean Robert Clark calls this work "normative ordering." Robert C. Clark, *Why So Many Lawyers? Are They Good or Bad?*, 61 FORDHAM L. REV. 275, 281 (1992). *See also* Ronald L. Gilson, *Value Creation by Business Lawyers: Legal Skills and Asset Pricing*, 94 YALE L.J. 239 (1984); Frank B. Cross, *The First Thing We Do, Let's Kill All the Economists: An Empirical Evaluation of the Effect of Lawyers on the United States Economy and Political System*, 70 TEX. L. REV. 645 (1992); Steven L. Schwarcz, *Explaining the Value of Transactional Lawyering*, 12 STAN. J.L. BUS. & FIN. 486 (2007). Professor Auerbach calls these developments "the commercialization of community." He cites efforts to use arbitration in lieu of court proceedings as a way of trying to restore the days when law was less dominant in commercial activity. The very slow move to the use of alternative dispute resolution processes, in spite of their apparent cost savings and conflict reduction, may also be seen as part of the decline in a sense of community in American society. JEROLD S. AUERBACH, JUSTICE WITHOUT LAW?: RESOLVING DISPUTES WITHOUT LAWYERS 95–96, 123–37 (1983).

27. Charles Silver & Frank B. Cross, *What's Not to Like About Being a Lawyer?*, 109 YALE L.J. 1443, 1460 (2000).

One can discount the unbridled optimism of that observation and still appreciate that clients looking out for their own interests—and the lawyers helping them—may bring substantial benefits to the public in the course of what the clients do.[28]

E. SOME PERSPECTIVE ON LAWYERS AS A PROFESSION—THE ENGLISH LEGAL TRADITION

Dating the origin of Anglo-American lawyers is somewhat arbitrary, but the best estimate is probably about 850 years ago during the reign of Henry II.[29] Before then, courts in England tended to be convened and conducted by local nobles.[30] Even in the *curia regis* over which the king himself presided, litigants tended to be accompanied by friends and relatives who might speak in their support, but professional advisers were largely unknown.[31]

Henry II set out to consolidate the early decentralized system of local courts into what became the "General Eyre." England was divided into circuits, and judges who had been personally appointed by the king periodically traveled throughout each. At the same time,

---

28. Of course, one may argue that certain interests do not deserve a lawyer's help, and indeed that some corporate interests may not be on the same moral plane as the interests of individuals or the common interest. *See* Geoffrey C. Hazard, Jr., *The Future of Legal Ethics*, 100 Yale L. J. 1239, 1259–62 (1991).

29. Henry II's reign began in 1154. An alternate date sometimes given for the start of a legal profession in Europe is the founding of the law school at Bologna in 1087. *See* John Maxcy Zane, The Story of Law 194 (2d ed. 1998).

30. Paul Brand, The Origins of the English Legal Profession 1 (1992).

31. It is not clear when the law first permitted the use of "pleaders," agents permitted to speak on behalf of the litigant and a precursor to what we now call lawyers. *Id.* at 10–13 (1992). Professor Brand finds no evidence of legal experts and no professional lawyers in England between the time of the Norman Conquest in 1066 and the end of the reign of Henry I in 1135. A monk represented the abbot of Battle in the 1160s, but there is apparently no other litigation through a representative until after 1182. *Id.* at 44.

the Exchequer court at Westminster became a Common Bench with a more general jurisdiction.[32]

Development of the system of royal courts led to other changes. Early litigation was conducted by applying for a royal writ. The applicant was required to prove the elements necessary for grant of the writ, and if granted, the writ would entitle the applicant to particular relief. By the time Henry II died in 1189, there were about fifteen such writs, but a little over a century later, the number had risen to over a hundred.[33]

Selecting the correct writ and stating it in precisely the correct form was critical to a claimant's success. Even if the claimant would have been entitled to judgment under another writ, filing for the wrong writ could result in the claimant taking nothing. In some cases, Chancery might be able to offer some relief for a bad choice, but that was not inevitable. In such a technical system, it was clearly better for a litigant to consult someone who could select and prepare a correct writ in the first instance. Thus were born plaintiffs' lawyers.

Defense lawyers were not far behind. Their role began, sometimes not so much to oppose claimants' cases, as to delay the inevitable. Procedural rules in cases dealing with rights in land, for example, allowed a defendant to claim he was too ill to attend the court sessions.[34] Even after those delays, the defendant could ask for

---

32. Paul Brand, The Origins of the English Legal Profession 14–15 (1992).

33. *Id.* at 33–34 (1992). During the reign of King John (1199–1216), apparently some men did act for others in court proceedings, but they were likely only precursors to professional attorneys. *Id.* at 50–54. By 1219, early in the reign of Henry III, it was possible to appoint a lawyer to appear before the Common Bench. *Id.* at 45. However, it was apparently also possible for a litigant to disavow what a representative said on the litigant's behalf. *Id.* at 47–48. Shorter but excellent accounts of the development of the legal profession can be found in Jonathan Rose, *The Legal Profession in Medieval England: A History of Regulation*, 48 Syracuse L. Rev. 1 (1998), and Jonathan Rose, *The Ambidextrous Lawyer: Conflict of Interest and the Medieval and Early Modern Legal Profession*, 7 U. Chi. Legal Roundtable 137 (2000).

34. The Statute of Westminster II in 1285 permitted citizens to appear in court through an attorney and not to have to appear in person. Jonathan Rose,

a postponement to have an inspection of the property, and he was then permitted to assert excuses from attendance three more times.[35] Courts ultimately recognized the injustice of these unsubstantiated delays and began to investigate the honesty of the claims, but the system became complex enough that a defendant who wanted to engage in maximum delay could profit from the help of legal counsel.[36] When a system of "recognized exceptions," i.e., defenses that had to be pled, replaced the practice of general denial, the need for specialized assistance increased.[37]

As early as the reign of King John (1199–1216), names of persons authorized to plead in court on behalf of others were recorded, and judges tended to be appointed from among the persons listed. In 1275, the Statute of Westminster I imposed formal regulation on "Serjeant-Countors" who appeared in the King's courts, and a regulatory London Ordinance soon followed in 1280.[38]

The Legal Profession in Medieval England: A History of Regulation, 48 SYRACUSE L. REV. I, 15 (1998).

35. PAUL BRAND, THE ORIGINS OF THE ENGLISH LEGAL PROFESSION 34–35 (1992).

36. Id. at 35–37 (1992). Early in the development of lawyers, it was seen as necessary to regulate them. In 1259, for example, legislation made it illegal for a serjeant-at-law to act for a litigant in return for a share of the land at stake. Id. at 67. And in 1264, serjeants were prohibited from acting as essoiners, the persons who acted to delay decisions in real property disputes. Id.

37. Id. at 40–42 (1992). Professor Brand explains:
The ordinary litigant might well have been able to manage a straight denial leading to battle or the grand assize or wager of law or the verdict of a jury, but he was at a distinct disadvantage in the making of exceptions. This was a technical matter requiring the skills of a professional lawyer attuned both by prior study and by his own experience to discovering defects in writs and counts and to presenting exceptions in the correct order . . . . And because such exceptions needed to be rebutted by the arguments of the plaintiff or his legal representative, the use of exceptions, indeed the positive encouragement of that use by the courts, also created opportunities for professional lawyers in the service of plaintiffs.
Id. at 42.

38. Carol Rice Andrews, Standards of Conduct for Lawyers: An 800-Year Evolution, 57 SMU L. REV. 1385, 1395 (2004). Both standards, along with a description of some of the early cases, are set out in Jonathan Rose, The Legal Profession in Medieval England: A History of Regulation, 48 SYRACUSE L. REV. 1,

Professor Baker says that by 1329, entry into the role of lawyer was "closed" in the sense that judges had identified a group of lawyers who would be permitted to appear before them.[39] It is worth noting that, although the judges were appointed by the Crown and monarchs could appoint lawyers to appear on the Crown's behalf, lawyers generally were under the supervision and regulation of the courts in which they appeared, not direct regulation by the Crown.[40]

By 1500, "pleaders" were distinguished from "attorneys." Both were considered officers of the court, but pleaders could advocate for clients and charge fees,[41] while early attorneys were simply those who stood in for—and made admissions on behalf of—litigants who did not want to travel to a distant court.[42] Pleaders had to serve an apprenticeship, and did so as members of one of the Inns of Court. The Inns doubled as educational bodies, and their ability to admit or deny admission to membership allowed them to regulate the total number of pleaders.[43]

122–32 (1998). *See also* Judith L. Maute, *Alice's Adventures in Wonderland: Preliminary Reflections on the History of the Split English Legal Profession and the Fusion Debate (1000–1900 A.D.)*, 71 FORDHAM L. REV. 1357, 1366 (2003).

39. J.H. BAKER, THE ORDER OF SERJEANTS AT LAW 6 (1984).

40. *Id.* at 14–16 (1984).

41. Robert S. Alexander, *The History of the Law As an Independent Profession and the Present English System, in* THE LAWYER'S PROFESSIONAL INDEPENDENCE (A.B.A./TIPS 1984). *See also* GEOFFREY C. HAZARD, JR. & ANGELO DONDI, LEGAL ETHICS: A COMPARATIVE STUDY 25 (2004) (noting that by the sixteenth century, throughout Europe, "it became a practical impossibility for the ordinary litigant in a major legal dispute to represent himself effectively").

42. Carol Rice Andrews, *Standards of Conduct for Lawyers: An 800-Year Evolution*, 57 SMU L. REV. 1385, 1391 (2004). On the other hand, unlike lawyers today, pleaders were not agents whose admissions could bind a litigant. *Id.*

43. During the apprenticeship, pleaders were sometimes called "utter barristers," a forerunner of the term "barrister" that now has replaced both "pleader" and "serjeant" in general use. *See* Judith L. Maute, *Alice's Adventures in Wonderland: Preliminary Reflections on the History of the Split English Legal Profession and the Fusion Debate (1000–1900 A.D.)*, 71 FORDHAM L. REV. 1357, 1366 (2003). *See also* The Rt. Hon. Sir David Maxwell-Fyfe, K.C., M.P., *The Inns of Court and the Impact on the Legal Profession in England*, 4 SW. L.J. 391 (1950).

By 1600, the pleaders had become "barristers," and a gulf had arisen between barristers and attorneys.[44] "Attorneys" and "solicitors" could not join the Inns and could only appear for clients in the lower courts,[45] and attorneys were subject to regulation by Parliament.[46] Ultimately, the distinction between solicitors and attorneys was abandoned, and the "solicitor" title has survived in England while the "attorney" or "lawyer" titles have been the ones used in the United States.

F. THE EARLY DAYS IN AMERICA AND THE REJECTION OF ENGLISH LAW AND LAWYERING

While many American lawyers still consider what they do as derived from the English tradition, that is largely not true. Indeed, many colonists had fled the English system of justice, and English attempts to interfere with the administration of justice in the colonies only tended to confirm the view of many colonists that English law was hostile to all the colonists held dear.[47]

---

44. Parliament acted to regulate attorneys and solicitors in 1605. Professor Maute believes that the legislation was likely initiated by the serjeants-at-law. Judith L. Maute, *Alice's Adventures in Wonderland: Preliminary Reflections on the History of the Split English Legal Profession and the Fusion Debate (1000–1900 A.D.)*, 71 FORDHAM L. REV. 1357, 1361 (2003). Professors Anderson & Tollison credit Sir Edward Coke with bringing about the barristers' centrality in litigation. Gary M. Anderson & Robert D. Tollison, *Barristers and Barriers: Sir Edward Coke and the Regulation of Trade*, 13 CATO J. 49 (1993).

45. ROSCOE POUND, THE LAWYER FROM ANTIQUITY TO MODERN TIMES 82–93 (1953). Because attorneys could not join barristers in the Inns of Court after about the mid-sixteenth century, they formed a "Society of Gentlemen Practitioners," out of which grew what is now called the Law Society. Judith L. Maute, *Alice's Adventures in Wonderland: Preliminary Reflections on the History of the Split English Legal Profession and the Fusion Debate (1000–1900 A.D.)*, 71 FORDHAM L. REV. 1357, 1367 (2003). *See also* HARRY KIRK, PORTRAIT OF A PROFESSION: A HISTORY OF THE SOLICITOR'S PROFESSION, 1100 TO THE PRESENT DAY (1976).

46. Carol Rice Andrews, *Standards of Conduct for Lawyers: An 800-Year Evolution*, 57 SMU L. REV. 1385, 1403 (2004).

47. ROSCOE POUND, THE LAWYER FROM ANTIQUITY TO MODERN TIMES 130–38 (1953). *See also* LAWRENCE M. FRIEDMAN, A HISTORY OF AMERICAN

Large parts of America similarly began as lawyer-free zones "whose Edenic visions of New World possibilities consigned lawyers to a role only slightly above the Biblical serpent."[48] No lawyers came over on the Mayflower, and the first lawyer who arrived in Massachusetts was disbarred for jury tampering.[49] Clergy acted as the judges in many of the colonies, and while the Maryland, Virginia, and South Carolina colonies tolerated lawyer practice, they set such restrictive limits on lawyers' fees that few could make a living.[50]

Professor Jerold Auerbach suggests that American societies without lawyers succeeded because they were communities whose values were not adequately captured in civil law. "Communities that rejected legalized dispute settlement were variously defined: by geography, ideology, piety, ethnicity, and commercial pursuit."[51] Quakers in Philadelphia, Jews in New York, Amish in Iowa, Chinese on the west coast, and

---

LAW 34–36, 46–48 (1985); MAXWELL BLOOMFIELD, AMERICAN LAWYERS IN A CHANGING SOCIETY, 1776–1876, at 34 (1976); KERMIT L. HALL, THE MAGIC MIRROR: LAW IN AMERICAN HISTORY 22–23 (1989).

48. JEROLD S. AUERBACH, JUSTICE WITHOUT LAW?: RESOLVING DISPUTES WITHOUT LAWYERS 8 (1983).

49. Richard B. Morris, *The Legal Profession in America on the Eve of the Revolution, in* HARRY W. JONES, ED., POLITICAL SEPARATION AND LEGAL COMMUNITY 5 (1976). *See also* LAWRENCE M. FRIEDMAN, A HISTORY OF AMERICAN LAW 94–97 (1985). Professor Friedman importantly reminds readers, however, that each colony was different, and generalizations about colonial experience are inevitably oversimplified. *Id.* at 36–37, 98–99.

50. Richard B. Morris, *The Legal Profession in America on the Eve of the Revolution, in* HARRY W. JONES, ED., POLITICAL SEPARATION AND LEGAL CONTINUITY 4–11 (1976). *See also* Carol Rice Andrews, *Standards of Conduct for Lawyers: An 800-Year Evolution,* 57 SMU L. REV. 1385, 1414–23 (2004). Even in England, the lawyer's reputation may be estimated to a certain extent by the titles of frequent tracts which were printed in London, like *The Downfall of Unjust Lawyers, Doomsday Drawing Near with Thunder and Lightning for Lawyers* (1645); *A Rod for Lawyers Who Are Hereby Declared Robbers and Deceivers of the Nation; Essay Wherein is Described the Lawyers, Smugglers and Officers Frauds* (1675). CHARLES WARREN, HISTORY OF THE HARVARD LAW SCHOOL, Vol. 1, at 3 (1908), *quoted in* ORIE L. PHILLIPS & PHILBRICK McCOY, CONDUCT OF JUDGES AND LAWYERS: A SURVEY OF PROFESSIONAL ETHICS, DISCIPLINE AND DISBARMENT 189 (1952).

51. JEROLD S. AUERBACH, JUSTICE WITHOUT LAW?: RESOLVING DISPUTES WITHOUT LAWYERS 4 (1983).

Mormons in Utah all tried for periods of time to settle disputes and regulate other relationships without civil law and lawyers.[52] Even groups such as merchants and freed slaves established panels to help resolve disputes with the assistance of persons who understood their problems better than civil judges might.[53] Despite the variety of such societies "they used [non-legal] processes because they shared a common commitment to the essence of communal existence: mutual access, responsibility and trust. . . . Utopian Christians and mercenary merchants shared the understanding that law begins where community ends."[54]

Some of this had changed by 1700. The early systems of administering justice had given way to a system of secular courts established in the colonies and lawyers who were being admitted to practice before them. Further, colonial legislation was still subject to review by the Privy Council, and the British had set up a regional system of colonial courts.[55] Lawyers were seen by many as a necessary evil in America, but more aligned with large landowners than with less financially successful citizens.[56] The number of lawyers in eighteenth-century America was

> extremely, and artificially, small. There were only 15 lawyers in Massachusetts in 1740—one for every 10,000 inhabitants. Even in 1775 there were only 71. So few trained lawyers were qualified to practice

---

52. JEROLD S. AUERBACH, JUSTICE WITHOUT LAW?: RESOLVING DISPUTES WITHOUT LAWYERS 19–68, 82–83 (1983). "'As for the *Business* of an *Attorney*,' wrote evangelical preacher George Whitefield, 'I think it *unlawful* for a Christian, or at least *exceeding dangerous: Avoid it therefore*, and glorify God in some *other Station*.'" *Id.* at 41. "Brigham Young described lawyers as 'a stink in the nostrils of every Latter-Day Saint.'" *Id.* at 55. Even in more recent times, some have urged that evangelical Christians take a similar court-avoidance approach. *See, e.g.*, LYNN R. BUZZARD, TELL IT TO THE CHURCH (1982).

53. JEROLD S. AUERBACH, JUSTICE WITHOUT LAW?: RESOLVING DISPUTES WITHOUT LAWYERS 43–45, 57–59 (1983).

54. *Id.* at 4–5 (1983). Professor Auerbach continued: "Throughout the twentieth century social theorists have insisted that a formal legal system, with a trained professional class of legal experts, is the superior form of civilized social organization." *Id.* at 11. However, "colonists who rejected law made a self-conscious choice. They were not a primitive people whose stage of social evolution had yet to reach the 'higher' level of legal development." *Id.* at 19.

55. LAWRENCE M. FRIEDMAN, A HISTORY OF AMERICAN LAW 49–56 (1985).

56. *Id.* at 95–97 (1985).

before the New York Supreme Court that . . . [a]pparently it was possible to "fee" all the attorneys, that is, hire the whole New York bar, leaving one's opponent high and dry.[57]

Lawyers today take pride in the number of lawyers who led the new nation. Lawyers rose from near outcasts to positions of public prominence when British Parliamentary Acts came for enforcement in colonial courts, and it was lawyers who were first called upon to articulate the "natural rights" reasons that the laws were unenforceable.[58] When the Revolution began, however, a large percentage of lawyers—especially those who had studied in England—decided to cast their lot with Britain;[59] Forty percent of Massachusetts lawyers were loyal to England, and 200 left the country because they were British loyalists.[60]

One of the rhetorical themes of the American Revolution was what is now called "civic republicanism," the idea that all persons are created equal and have equal rights but also obligations to pursue the common good. Lawyers tended to see law as embodying that sense of the common good and themselves as having special insights,

---

57. *Id.* at 100 (1985). Another writer notes:
The rise of the legal profession can be clearly dated from John Adams' boyhood. . . . [Previously,] to be a lawyer was to incur social opprobrium. In 1698, for example, in Connecticut, they were included in discriminatory legislation in company with drunkards and keepers of brothels. In 1730, in Rhode Island, a law was enacted excluding them from membership in the legislature. In that same year the number allowed to practice in the courts of New York was limited to eight, although there were thirty in the city, many of extremely bad reputation. In very mid-century, however, their rise was rapid.
JAMES TRUSLOW ADAMS, THE ADAMS FAMILY 16 (1930), *quoted in* ORIE L. PHILLIPS & PHILBRICK MCCOY, CONDUCT OF JUDGES AND LAWYERS: A SURVEY OF PROFESSIONAL ETHICS, DISCIPLINE AND DISBARMENT 188–89 (1952).

58. Richard B. Morris, *The Legal Profession in America on the Eve of the Revolution, in* POLITICAL SEPARATION AND LEGAL CONTINUITY 18–23 (Harry W. Jones ed., 1976).

59. *Id.* at 23–27 (1976). *See also* MAXWELL BLOOMFIELD, AMERICAN LAWYERS IN A CHANGING SOCIETY, 1776–1876, at 139 (1976) (one-fourth of pre-war practitioners left the country).

60. LAWRENCE M. FRIEDMAN, A HISTORY OF AMERICAN LAW 303–04 (1985).

governing obligations, and status.[61] Not everyone agreed, in part because the Revolution had affected Americans in different ways. After the Revolution, economic times were hard, and law and lawyers were often seen as on the side of creditors trying to collect debts that their fellow Americans were hard put to pay.[62] Legal proceedings granting all sides due process can be costly, and lawyers and the legal system tend to protect property holders against have-nots. That was as true in the nation's early years as it is today.[63]

Indeed, as the new nation emerged from its revolutionary birth, its lawyers no longer limited themselves to recording deeds and handling modest claims. "The leaders of the Bar in the period after 1790 are not the land conveyancers of the earlier period, but for the first time, the commercial lawyers."[64] Marine insurance claims, for example, became a major area of practice in Boston, New York, and Philadelphia. Lawyers assisted merchants by helping develop a practice of resolving cases on questions of law and reducing judges' deference to jury decisions in commercial disputes. Arbitration of disputes that removed the role of juries altogether also evolved

---

61. See, e.g., Russell G. Pearce, Lawyers as America's Governing Class: The Formation and Dissolution of the Original Understanding of the American Lawyer's Role, 8 U. CHI. L. SCHOOL ROUNDTABLE 381, 384–92 (2001); Robert W. Gordon, The Independence of Lawyers, 68 B.U. L. REV. 1 (1988); Russell G. Pearce, Rediscovering the Republican Origins of the Legal Ethics Codes, 6 GEO. J. LEGAL ETHICS 241 (1992); Rob Atkinson, Reviving the Roman Republic: Remembering the Good Old Cause, 71 FORDHAM L. REV. 1187 (2003).

62. ROSCOE POUND, THE LAWYER FROM ANTIQUITY TO MODERN TIMES 177–87 (1953). The common law itself became unpopular; indeed, there was a call to introduce French law. Id. In Massachusetts, during Shay's Rebellion, there were uprisings against courts and lawyers who seemed too zealous in the pursuit of debtors. LAWRENCE M. FRIEDMAN, A HISTORY OF AMERICAN LAW 303 (2d ed. 1985). See also MAXWELL BLOOMFIELD, AMERICAN LAWYERS IN A CHANGING SOCIETY, 1776–1876, at 30–40 (1976).

63. Geoffrey C. Hazard, Jr., The Future of Legal Ethics, 100 YALE L.J. 1239, 1266–77 (1991). See also Norman W. Spaulding, The Myth of Civil Republicanism: Interrogating the Ideology of Antebellum Legal Ethics, 71 FORDHAM L. REV. 1397 (2003); cf. Norman W. Spaulding, Reinterpreting Professional Identity, 74 U. COLO. L. REV. 1 (2003).

64. MORTON J. HOROWITZ, THE TRANSFORMATION OF AMERICAN LAW, 1780–1860, at 140–41 (1977).

rapidly in that period.[65] Another development was the use of "struck juries" or "merchant juries" designed to bring together a more knowledgeable group of jurors hearing commercial cases, but by the early 1800s, those juries' decisions were subject to lawyer demands for close judicial review as well.[66]

This increase in the role of lawyers aiding merchants had a positive effect on lawyer wealth. Lemuel Shaw and Daniel Webster, for example, earned what in today's dollars would be high six-figure incomes. Overall, however, American lawyers would probably not have seen themselves as primarily advocates for the rich.[67] They apparently saw themselves as moderating what could otherwise be wide swings of mood and policy in a democracy.[68]

It was in this sense of seeing American lawyers as relatively worldly figures in an otherwise-backwoods society that Alexis de Tocqueville offered this widely quoted description.

> The special knowledge that lawyers acquire in studying the law assures them a separate rank in society; they form a sort of privileged class among [persons of] intelligence. Each day they find the idea of this superiority in the exercise of their profession; they are masters of a necessary science, knowledge of which is not widespread; they serve as arbiters between citizens, and the habit of directing the blind passions of the litigants toward a goal gives them a certain scorn for the judgment of the crowd. Add to this that they naturally form a body. It is not that they agree among themselves . . . but community of studies and unity of methods bind their minds to one another as interest could unite their wills.[69]

---

65. *Id.* at 142–45, 150–55. Merchants did not like juries. Three procedural devices were developed to keep merchant cases away from juries. First was the "special case" that allowed submitting points of law to the court alone. Second was award of new trials that were contrary to the weight of the evidence; this gave courts the power to avoid jurors' mistakes. Third was development of the system of instructing juries rather than letting them decide both the facts and the law. *Id.*

66. *Id.* at 155–59.

67. LAWRENCE M. FRIEDMAN, A HISTORY OF AMERICAN LAW 306 (1985).

68. Geoffrey C. Hazard, Jr., *The Future of Legal Ethics*, 100 YALE L.J. 1239, 1274–75 (1991).

69. ALEXIS DE TOCQUEVILLE, DEMOCRACY IN AMERICA, VOL. I, Part 2, ch. 8 (1835) (Harvey C. Mansfield & Delba Winthrop, eds. & trans. 2000), p. 252.

That part of de Tocqueville's assessment sounds as if he is describing law as an honored, set-apart profession. What he says next, however, is far less flattering to modern ears.

> Hidden at the bottom of the souls of lawyers one therefore finds a part of the tastes and habits of aristocracy. They have its instinctive penchant for order, its natural love of forms; they conceive its great disgust for the actions of the multitude and secretly scorn the government of the people.[70]

Indeed, in the years after de Tocqueville's visit in the 1830s, the "people" reciprocated some of the disgust he found to have been felt by lawyers. States eased barriers to becoming a lawyer.[71] Educational standards became low or non-existent. If Abraham Lincoln could become a celebrated lawyer after studying by the fireside, presumably so could anyone else. Professor Lawrence Friedman explains:

> [W]ith the rise of Jeffersonian and Jacksonian democracy, the leading political party opposed the idea of government by experts. . . . [Thus,] it would have been surprising if a narrow, elitist [legal] profession grew up—a small exclusive guild. No such profession developed. There were tendencies in this direction during the colonial period; but after the Revolution the dam burst, and the number of lawyers . . . has never stopped growing. In Massachusetts, in 1740, there were only about 15 lawyers (the population was about 150,000). A century later, in 1840, there were 640 lawyers in the state—ten times as many in ratio to the population.[72]

Roscoe Pound called the period from 1836 to 1870 the "Era of Decadence" and attributed many of its problems to the decline of lawyers' professional status.[73] Paul Carrington describes it as the era of the "Barnburners" and says that "[W]herever Barnburners gained power, they dismantled the ramparts of privilege, and often among the first among the privileged regulatory protections stripped away

---

70. *Id.*

71. Roscoe Pound, The Lawyer From Antiquity to Modern Times 225–39 (1953).

72. Lawrence M. Friedman, A History of American Law 304 (2d ed. 1985).

73. Roscoe Pound, The Lawyer From Antiquity to Modern Times 221–49 (1953).

were licensing requirements in medicine and law."[74] Professor Friedman continues:

> It was a society where many people, not just the noble or the lucky few, needed some rudiments of law, some forms or form-books, some know-how about the mysterious ways of courts or governments. . . . In many ways, then, loose standards were inevitable. Perhaps they even enhanced the vigor of the bar. *Formal* standards tended to disappear; but the market for legal services remained, a harsh and sometimes efficient control. It pruned away deadwood; it rewarded the adaptive and the cunning. Jacksonian democracy did not make every man a lawyer. It did encourage a scrambling bar of shrewd entrepreneurs.[75]

G. THE AMERICAN BAR ASSOCIATION AND THE RENEWED RHETORIC THAT LAW IS A PROFESSION

Professionalism advocates tend to date the "social contract" between lawyers and the public as arising late in the nineteenth century because the sense that lawyers were a separate and superior class had largely disappeared in the early to middle part of that century. Even then, lawyers continued to be regulated by state courts throughout the century, and they typically swore an oath to engage only in ethical conduct.[76] Furthermore, an effort to preserve lawyers' sense of themselves as moral leaders infuses the two best-known nineteenth-century accounts of lawyers' ethics—those by lawyer-academics David Hoffman of Maryland and George Sharswood of Pennsylvania.[77]

---

74. Paul D. Carrington, Stewards of Democracy: Law As a Public Profession 19–20 (1999). ·

75. Lawrence M. Friedman, A History of American Law 317–18 (2d ed. 1985).

76. Indeed, New York's original Field Code of 1848 contained a section listing eight ethical duties of a lawyer. This period is discussed well in Carol Rice Andrews, *Standards of Conduct for Lawyers: An 800-Year Evolution*, 57 SMU L. Rev. 1385, 1424–26 (2004).

77. Their books are David Hoffman, A Course of Legal Study (1836), and George Sharswood, A Compend of Lectures on the Aims and Duties of the Profession of the Law (1854). In addition, Professor Andrews notes several other writers who also tried to interject ethical conduct into practice. *See* Carol Rice Andrews, *Standards of Conduct for Lawyers: An 800-Year Evolution*, 57 SMU L. Rev. 1385, 1432–34 (2004). *See also*

But overall, most nineteenth-century lawyers tended to focus on acquiring and performing legal work in a world where many competitors also wanted to practice law. The lawyer's role depended more on what client realities required than on inherent characteristics associated with being a lawyer.[78]

A decade or so after the Civil War, American lawyers refocused their efforts toward meeting legal needs in a world where large new business entities were becoming the order of the day. In some cases, the legal work required much more than going to court; it required creation of new legal institutions such as the modern corporation.[79] The most prominent of the corporate law firms arose in New York,[80]

M. H. Hoeflich, *Legal Ethics in the Nineteenth Century: The "Other Tradition,"* 47 U. Kan. L. Rev. 793 (1999).

78. As Professor Friedman puts it, "lawyers in the United States were upwardly mobile men, seizers of opportunities. The American lawyer was never primarily a learned doctor of laws; he was a man of action and cunning, not a scholar. He played a useful role, sometimes admired, but rarely loved." Lawrence M. Friedman, A History of American Law 304 (2d ed. 1985). Professor Friedman goes on to say that the English distinctions between barristers and solicitors "exerted a certain fascination, but failed to leave a permanent mark on the American bar." *Id.* at 315.

The contrast in the careers of lawyers is reflected in the contemporaneous careers of Charles Sumner who had a commercial practice and Abraham Lincoln whose practice included representing individual interests. The two careers are discussed in Paul D. Carrington, *A Tale of Two Lawyers*, 91 Nw. U. L. Rev. 615 (1997). The contemporary form of this distinction between individual and commercial lawyers has been chronicled and analyzed in John P. Heinz and Edward O. Laumann, Chicago Lawyers: The Social Structure of the Bar (1982), and John P. Heinz, Robert L. Nelson, Rebecca L. Sandefur and Edward O. Laumann, Urban Lawyers: The New Social Structure of the Bar (2005).

79. *See, e.g.,* Kermit L. Hall, The Magic Mirror: Law in American History 212–14 (1989). *See also* Milton C. Regan, Jr., Eat What You Kill: The Fall of a Wall Street Lawyer 17 (2004).

80. The best known account of this development is R.T. Swaine, The Cravath Firm and Its Predecessors: 1819–1948 (1948). *See generally* Wayne K. Hobson, *Symbol of the New Profession: Emergence of the Large Law Firm, 1870–1951, in* The New High Priests: Lawyers in Post–Civil War America (Gerard W. Gawalt ed., 1984). Hobson reports that "368 firms in 78 cities . . . at some time during the 1872–1915 period reached large-firm size," defined as five or more total lawyers. *Id.* at 6. Hobson considered any firm

although such firms evolved in other large cities as well. The "lead-ing" lawyers in those cities formed bar associations, membership in which was intended to distinguish those lawyers from the rabble who also practiced law.

Richard Rovere's description of lawyers William Howe and Abraham Hummel, with their office across from the jail and their large sign soliciting the business of jail inmates, gives a tangy flavor of the period.

> There were several cases on record in which the bench felt called upon to rebuke Howe for insinuating to the jury that the incarceration or execu-tion of a defendant who, to the best of the court's knowledge, was single and childless when he was arrested would bring tragedy into the lives of so many people seated about the courtroom; and there is one instance of a stern reprimand from a judge who felt that a jury was somehow being imposed upon when, just as Howe reached the family motif in his summation, a young lady on the front bench found it the appropriate moment to bare her breast to the infant in her arms and look tenderly in the direction of the prisoner at the bar.[81]

At least nominally in response to this kind of unseemly practice, in 1870, "the 'decent part' of the profession"[82] created the Association

---

with over eleven lawyers to have been a "law factory" during this period. *Id.* at 17. *See also* LAWRENCE M. FRIEDMAN, A HISTORY OF AMERICAN LAW 636–39 (2d ed. 1985).

81. RICHARD H. ROVERE, HOWE & HUMMEL: THEIR TRUE AND SCANDALOUS HISTORY 57–58 (1985 ed). Professor Friedman's account is consistent.

> Lawyers came early to the frontier boom towns, eager to turn a quick dollar. Lawyers who placed money and collected on notes often turned to banking and merchandising to earn a better living. For others, politics was the best way to scramble up the greasy pole. In these small communities, one of the biggest businesses was government. Politics was bread-and-butter work. For lawyers, county, state, territorial and federal jobs were sources of income and, in addition, advertisements for themselves.

LAWRENCE M. FRIEDMAN, A HISTORY OF AMERICAN LAW 646 (2d ed. 1985).

82. LAWRENCE M. FRIEDMAN, A HISTORY OF AMERICAN LAW 648–50 (2d ed. 1985). *See also* Robert W. Gordon, *"The Ideal and the Actual in the Law": Fantasies and Practices of New York City Lawyers, 1870–1910, in* THE NEW HIGH PRIESTS: LAWYERS IN POST–CIVIL WAR AMERICA 51 (Gerard W. Gawalt ed., 1984); ROSCOE POUND, THE LAWYER FROM ANTIQUITY TO MODERN TIMES: WITH PARTICULAR REFERENCE TO THE DEVELOPMENT OF BAR ASSOCIATIONS IN THE UNITED STATES (1953).

of the Bar of the City of New York. Later that same decade, Yale law professor Simeon E. Baldwin led a call for a national bar association.[83] Baldwin organized a group of leading lawyers from around the country to sign a "Call for a Meeting" to be held August 21, 1878, in Saratoga, New York. The invitation was only sent to "a few members of the Bar in each state," and the stated purpose, beyond social events, was to help "assimilate the laws of the different states, in extending the benefit of true reforms and in publishing the failure of unsuccessful experiments in legislation." About 100 lawyers came to that first meeting of what was called the American Bar Association.[84]

Association aspirations in the first twenty-five years of the American Bar Association's existence were quite modest and only rarely invoked the idea of a profession.[85] At the time of its founding

---

83. Baldwin, a Yale law professor, later became Chief Justice and then Governor of Connecticut. Earlier, in 1849, a much broader group called the American Legal Association had been established, and in 1850 its founder, John Livingston, published the names and addresses of all known practicing lawyers and judges in the United States, a total of 21,979. The organization never really got traction, however, and it collapsed in 1854. *See* MAXWELL BLOOMFIELD, AMERICAN LAWYERS IN A CHANGING SOCIETY, 1776–1876, at 154–55 (1976); LAWRENCE M. FRIEDMAN, A HISTORY OF AMERICAN LAW 633 (2d ed. 1985).

84. EDSON R. SUNDERLAND, HISTORY OF THE AMERICAN BAR ASSOCIATION AND ITS WORK 3–4 (1953). *See also* John A. Matzko, *"The Best Men of the Bar": The Founding of the American Bar Association, in* THE NEW HIGH PRIESTS: LAWYERS IN POST–CIVIL WAR AMERICA 75 (Gerard W. Gawalt ed., 1984).

85. Edson R. Sunderland, author of the official A.B.A. history, takes pains to reports that

> [t]here was no suggestion in any of the published letters, nor in the reported remarks of anyone who spoke at the conference sessions, that the purpose of the proposed organization was to strengthen or safeguard the position or privileges of the bar by any other means than raising its standards of proficiency and ethical conduct and improving its capacity to render adequate service to the public.

EDSON R. SUNDERLAND, HISTORY OF THE AMERICAN BAR ASSOCIATION AND ITS WORK 13 (1953). But in a letter of October 29, 1878 (within sixty days of creation of the A.B.A.), Elihu Root described the dire economic state of the legal profession:

> There never has been a worse time within my experience for a young man to undertake to make a beginning as a lawyer in New York. The community has been feeling poorer and poorer for a number of years. The law business

in 1878, the American Bar Association had 289 members. Ten years later, it had 752 members, and by 1902, its membership was only 1,718. By 1914, membership had grown to 8,000 members, but average attendance at the annual meeting during the first twenty-five years of the A.B.A.'s existence was 158.[86]

Part of the membership growth resulted from American Bar Association efforts to hold its annual meetings around the country. Early meetings consisted of prominent lawyers reading prepared papers. Roscoe Pound's 1906 paper, "The Causes of Popular Dissatisfaction with the Administration of Justice,"[87] a highly influential contribution to law reform, for example, was presented in St. Paul, Minnesota.[88] But no matter how they tried to increase their sense of respectability, lawyers representing large corporations and their owners were subjected to intense criticism. President Theodore Roosevelt told Harvard graduates in 1905:

> We all know that . . . many of the most influential and most highly remunerated members of the Bar in every centre of wealth make it their special task to work out bold and ingenious schemes by which their very wealthy clients, individual or corporate, can evade the laws which are made to regulate in the interest of the public the use of great wealth. Now, the great lawyer who employs his talent and learning in . . . enabling a very wealthy client to override or circumvent the law is doing all that in him lies to encourage the growth in this country of a spirit of dumb anger against all laws and of disbelief in their efficacy.[89]

---

and the proceeds of law business have been contracting steadily and the contraction has forced out of practice and into clerkships a great many lawyers of experience and ability, and has at the same time forced all lawyers in practice to greater economy . . . .
PHILIP C. JESSUP, ELIHU ROOT, Vol. 1, at 108.

86. ROSCOE POUND, THE LAWYER FROM ANTIQUITY TO MODERN TIMES 270–72 (1953).

87. The speech can be found at 29 A.B.A. Rep. 395 (Part I, 1906). For interesting background on Pound, see JOHN FABIAN WITT, PATRIOTS AND COSMOPOLITANS: HIDDEN HISTORIES OF AMERICAN LAW 213–34 (2007).

88. EDSON R. SUNDERLAND, HISTORY OF THE AMERICAN BAR ASSOCIATION AND ITS WORK 128–33 (1953).

89. Theodore Roosevelt, IV Presidential Addresses and State Papers 407 (1910), quoted in James M. Altman, Considering the A.B.A.'s 1908 Canons of Ethics, 71 FORDHAM L. REV. 2395, 2304 (2003). The work of such lawyers is analyzed, and President Roosevelt's charge verified, in Robert W. Gordon,

AMERICAN LAWYERS ARE NOT PART OF A PROFESSION

By 1908, the A.B.A. still represented only about 2 percent of the nation's lawyers, but in response to this criticism and in order to further convey its desire to "raise standards," the A.B.A. adopted its first Canons of Ethics. Based on an 1887 Code of Ethics of the Alabama State Bar Association,[90] and in turn on standards proposed by George Sharswood, the Canons served as a model for state lawyer standards and were subsequently adopted by courts around the country.[91] The A.B.A. recommended that the Canons be taught in all law schools and that all bar applicants be examined on them.[92]

Canon 32 perhaps best states the sense of the lawyer's role the A.B.A. wanted to convey in response to President Roosevelt's critique:

> No client, corporate or individual, however powerful, nor any cause, civil or political, however important, is entitled to receive nor should any lawyer render any service or advice involving disloyalty to the law whose

---

"The Ideal and the Actual in the Law": Fantasies and Practices of New York City Lawyers, 1870–1910, *in* THE NEW HIGH PRIESTS: LAWYERS IN POST–CIVIL WAR AMERICA (Gerard W. Gawalt ed., 1984).

90. *See, e.g.*, CAROL RICE ANDREWS, ET AL., GILDED AGE LEGAL ETHICS: ESSAYS ON THOMAS GOODE JONES' 1887 CODE AND THE REGULATION OF THE PROFESSION (2003).

91. The draft Canons were sent to all the members of the A.B.A., and over 1000 replies were received. Each Canon was debated by the Association one by one, and only Canon 13 on contingent fees was altered at all. There are a number of excellent articles about this period, although some tend to be relatively uncritical. *E.g.*, Russell G. Pearce, *Rediscovering the Republican Origins of the Legal Ethics Codes*, 6 GEO. J. LEGAL ETHICS 241 (1992); Susan D. Carle, *Lawyers' Duty to Do Justice: A New Look at the History of the 1908 Canons*, 24 LAW & SOC. INQUIRY 1 (1999); James M. Altman, *Considering the A.B.A.'s 1908 Canons of Ethics*, 71 FORDHAM L. REV. 2395 (2003); Carol Rice Andrews, *Standards of Conduct for Lawyers: An 800-Year Evolution*, 57 SMU L. REV. 1385 (2004). The professional standards under the Canons are given concrete application in AMERICAN BAR FOUNDATION AND AMERICAN BAR ASSOCIATION, OPINIONS OF THE COMM. ON PROFESSIONAL ETHICS WITH THE CANONS OF PROF. ETHICS ANNOTATED AND CANONS OF JUDICIAL ETHICS ANNOTATED (1967 ed.).

92. EDSON R. SUNDERLAND, HISTORY OF THE AMERICAN BAR ASSOCIATION AND ITS WORK 110–12 (1953). The Committee on Professional Ethics and Grievances was created in 1919, and in 1922, it was granted the power to issue ethics opinions. *Id.* at 113.

ministers we are, or disrespect to the judicial office, which we are bound to uphold . . . . When rendering any such improper service or advice, the lawyer invites and merits stern and just condemnation. Correspondingly, he advances the honor of his profession and the best interests of his client when he renders service or gives advice tending to impress upon the client and his understanding exact compliance with the strictest principles of moral law.[93]

Dean Wigmore seized on the concept of law as a "profession" when he said in 1915:

The law as a pursuit is not a trade. It is a profession. It ought to signify for its followers a mental and moral setting apart from the multitude,–a priesthood of Justice.

* * *

How the present attitude has come about is easy to see. . . . In a country where all men started even and each man had to earn his living,–where tradition and privilege were cast aside,–. . . the law took its place with other livelihoods; and its gainful aspect became emphasized. And then . . . came the commercial expansion following the Civil War; and the lawyer was more and more drawn into the intimate relations as adviser of the business man. And now, in the large cities, the commercial standards have spread to the Law, and the profession has been merged into the trade.

Nevertheless, that is all an error. That is, the inherent nature of things demands always that the law shall be a profession.[94]

By 1916, the number of A.B.A. members had climbed to 10,636.[95] Membership was essentially level during World War I, but by 1924,

---

93. A.B.A. CANONS OF ETHICS, Canon 32 (1908).

94. John H. Wigmore, Preface to ORRIN N. CARTER, ETHICS OF THE LEGAL PROFESSION xxi (1915). The year earlier, Louis Brandeis had published his own important book, "BUSINESS A PROFESSION" (1914), that called upon business itself to place the public interest above profit. *See also* JOHN R. DOS PASSOS, THE AMERICAN LAWYER AS HE WAS–AS HE IS–AS HE 'CAN BE (1907).

95. In 1916, A.B.A. President Elihu Root sought to give state and local bar associations a greater role in A.B.A. meetings. Up until then, representatives had been able to attend but had no formal role. The Conference of Bar Association Delegates thus became a Section of the A.B.A. EDSON R. SUNDERLAND, HISTORY OF THE AMERICAN BAR ASSOCIATION AND ITS WORK 87–90 (1953).

membership had risen to 22,024.[96] In 1923, A.B.A. President John W. Davis called for a federal union between the A.B.A. and state bar associations so that the A.B.A. could speak "with the accredited voice of the united bar of the entire country" and give all bar organizations "a broader sense of professional solidarity and responsibility."[97]

When we think of today's American Bar Association, with over 400,000 members and a national lobbying network, it is easy to forget that even after President Davis's call, it took until 1936 for the A.B.A. to organize itself into the broad national organization that we now know.[98] Even in 1936, the A.B.A. still had only 28,228 members, of whom only about 10 percent attended the annual meeting. In 1936, instead of having the Assembly of all A.B.A. members continue to vote on policy issues, the A.B.A. created a House of Delegates and a Board of Governors.[99]

The circumstances the A.B.A. confronted in 1936 are sometimes forgotten. The Depression was in its darkest days, and the Roosevelt administration had backed "Codes of Fair Competition," prepared by tripartite institutions of labor, management, and government, but that otherwise had little apparent legal basis. Many lawyers (and their corporate clients) were anxious about the New Deal and sought to make law and lawyers independent of what they saw as the work of political institutions. Just two years earlier, Supreme Court Justice Harlan Fiske Stone had warned:

> We meet at a time when, as never before in the history of the country, our most cherished ideals and traditions are being subject to searching criticism.

* * *

---

96. *Id.* at 97–98. Membership grew to 26,246 in 1927 and 42,121 in 1950, while annual meeting attendance averaged 1,170 between 1902 and 1936, and 2,221 between 1936 and 1950. *Id.* at 40.

97. *Id.* at 173.

98. By 1950, A.B.A. membership had increased to 42,121, of whom 3,233 came to the annual meeting. *Id.* at 221.

99. *Id.* at 176–77. The Assembly could only prepare resolutions to be considered by the other bodies. It also could elect five delegates to the House. New Sections were created, as well as new committees, among them the Standing Committee on Professional Ethics and Grievances whose job it was to propose standards of professional conduct and issue opinions on ethics questions. *Id.* at 183–89.

[W]e may rightly look to the Bar for leadership in the preservation and development of American institutions. Specially trained in the field of law and government, invested with the unique privileges of his office, experienced in the world of affairs, and versed in the problems of business organization and administration, to whom, if not to the lawyer, may we look for guidance in solving the problems of a sorely stricken social order?

Throughout the history of Anglo-American civilization, the professional groups have been among the most significant of those non-governmental agencies which promote the public welfare. Although in smaller measure, . . . their function has been not unlike that of the medieval guilds. . . . While it has not inherited the completely independent status of the English bar, to no other group in this country has the state granted comparable privileges or permitted so much autonomy. No other is so closely related to the state, and no other has traditionally exerted so powerful an influence on public opinion and public policy.[100]

Giving authority to the new House of Delegates, which included state bar associations and other potentially influential professional groups, provided the A.B.A. with hope that it could help marshal public influence behind common positions.[101] Among the first things the transformed American Bar Association aggressively—and successfully—opposed was President Roosevelt's court packing plan.[102] During World War II, professional issues were a relatively low priority

---

100. Harlan F. Stone, *The Public Influence of the Bar*, 48 HARV. L. REV. I, 1–5 (1934).

101. EDSON R. SUNDERLAND, HISTORY OF THE AMERICAN BAR ASSOCIATION AND ITS WORK 173–76. Among the other groups represented in the House of Delegates were the American Law Institute and the American Judicature Society. The meeting at which these changes were adopted is reported in great detail in 22 A.B.A. J. 660 (1936).

102. *See, e.g.*, A.B.A. President Frederick H. Stinchfield, *The Supreme Court Issue*, 23 A.B.A. J. 233 (1937); Sylvester C. Smith, Jr., *The Present Situation in the Fight to Save the Court*, 23 A.B.A. J. 401 (1937). The same volume of the A.B.A. Journal contains a discussion by a member of the House of Delegates about the need to increase lawyer income by reducing the number of new lawyers. John Kirkland Clark, *Limitation of Admission to the Bar*, 23 A.B.A. J. 48 (1937). For an account of other causes in which the A.B.A. became involved, *see* Rayman L. Solomon, *Five Crises or One: The Concept of Legal Professionalism, 1925–1960, in* LAWYERS' IDEALS/LAWYERS' PRACTICES: TRANSFORMATIONS IN THE AMERICAN LEGAL PROFESSION 144 (Robert L. Nelson, David M. Trubek & Rayman L. Solomon, eds., 1992).

in the country, but in the post-war period, the A.B.A. resumed its conservative political leanings and supported loyalty oaths and other parts of the anti-Communist movement.[103]

A close second among A.B.A. concerns was the economic health of lawyers themselves.[104] After the war, many lawyers were attracted to the bar by the belief that they could make good money. Some lawyers were continuing a family tradition, but bar leaders sneered that for "some families, principally of recent European extraction, the existence of a lawyer in the family is deemed to add greatly to its social prestige."[105] To make such social climbing more difficult, focus in the early 1950s was placed on increasing standards for bar admission. Three years of law school were required of all students, although many states still required only two pre-law years of college.[106]

H. THE SIGNIFICANCE OF THE SURVEY OF THE LEGAL PROFESSION

The key development in the effort to make lawyers a "professional" institution, however, was the A.B.A.'s now almost-forgotten "Survey of the Legal Profession," conceived as World War II was coming to a end. Thousands of lawyers had gone into military service, leaving their families and closing or suspending their offices. What would the lawyer-soldiers find when they returned home, both in terms of the substantive law and the circumstances of their practice?

Originally proposed by the A.B.A. Section of Legal Education and Admission to the Bar, the Survey of the Legal Profession examined such issues by inquiring into the "much wider problem of finding out what lawyers actually do in present-day society and whether they are adequately

103. Jerold S. Auerbach, Unequal Justice: Lawyers and Social Change in Modern America 231–59 (1976).

104. A.B.A. Special Comm., The Economics of the Legal Profession (1938).

105. Homer D. Crotty, *Who Shall Be Called to the Bar?*, 20 B. Examiner 173, 176 (1951).

106. *Id.* at 180–86 (1951).

meeting the needs of the public."[107] Lawyers recruited to conduct the Survey were a "Who's Who" of the American bar. The project's first Director was Arthur T. Vanderbilt, dean of New York University's law school. When Dean Vanderbilt resigned to become Chief Justice of New Jersey, he was succeeded by Boston lawyer Reginald Heber Smith, long revered as the soul of the U.S. legal aid movement.

Results of the Survey were published in over 150 books and articles. Harvard's Dean Roscoe Pound wrote the book on the history of lawyers and bar associations.[108] Chief Judge Orie Phillips of the Tenth Circuit wrote the volume on lawyer compliance with the Canons of Ethics.[109] Dean Albert J. Harno of Illinois wrote the book on legal education,[110] and Professors Zechariah Chaffee, Jr.,[111] Maynard Pirsig,[112] and Elliott Cheatham[113] all conducted important studies for the Survey. In the Survey, the A.B.A. tried to restore (or create) the idea of law as a profession, an effort it had pressed in 1878 and again in 1936. Dean Pound tried to articulate what being a profession meant.

> There is much more in a profession than a traditionally dignified calling. The term refers to a group of men pursuing a learned art as a common

---

107. Reginald Heber Smith, *Survey of the Legal Profession: Its Scope, Methods and Objectives, in* ROSCOE POUND, THE LAWYER FROM ANTIQUITY TO MODERN TIMES, at vii (1953). Although not an "official" survey publication, the best collection of survey findings is ALBERT P. BLAUSTEIN & CHARLES O. PORTER, THE AMERICAN LAWYER: A SUMMARY OF THE SURVEY OF THE LEGAL PROFESSION (1954).

108. ROSCOE POUND, THE LAWYER FROM ANTIQUITY TO MODERN TIMES: WITH PARTICULAR REFERENCE TO THE DEVELOPMENT OF BAR ASSOCIATIONS IN THE UNITED STATES (1953).

109. ORIE L. PHILLIPS & PHILBRICK McCOY, CONDUCT OF JUDGES AND LAWYERS (1952).

110. ALBERT J. HARNO, LEGAL EDUCATION IN THE UNITED STATES (1953). We return to his book in Chapter 5 of these materials.

111. Zechariah Chaffee, Jr., *Changes in the Law During Forty Years*, 32 B.U. L. REV. 46 (1952) (describing differences in practice faced by modern lawyers as a result of the creation of the Workers' Compensation system and the rise of administrative agencies).

112. Maynard E. Pirsig, *A Survey of Judicial Councils, Judicial Conferences, and Administrative Directors*, 47 THE BRIEF 181 (1952).

113. Elliott E. Cheatham, *The Inculcation of Professional Standards and the Functions of the Lawyer*, 21 TENN. L. REV. 812 (1951).

calling in the spirit of a public service—no less a public service because it may incidentally be a means of livelihood. Pursuit of the learned art in the spirit of a public service is the primary purpose. Gaining a livelihood is incidental, whereas in a business or trade it is the entire purpose.[114]

Notice carefully the phrase Pound used—"a common calling in the spirit of a public service." When that language was borrowed by the A.B.A.'s Commission on Professionalism in 1986, it was misquoted; the word "a" was omitted.[115] Pound did not say lawyers were to act "in the spirit of public service," as the 1986 Commission asserted. Pound said lawyers were to act in the spirit of *a* public service. Pound, who cut his professional teeth in the Progressive Era of the late nineteenth century, knew that "*a* public service" of the kind he was describing was a formerly private business put under public regulation—that is, what we today call a public utility.

Far from being a call for a shift in lawyers' personal attitudes, then, Pound's was a demand that lawyers be treated as if they were analogous to electric companies or railroads. That is, Pound demanded that lawyers be given a monopoly right over law and legal remedies in exchange for individual lawyers giving up the right to high personal wealth. Pound explained:

> [I]f an engineer discovers a new process or invents a new mechanical device he may obtain a patent and retain for himself a profitable monopoly. If, on the other hand, a physician discovers a new specific for a disease or a surgeon invents a new surgical procedure they each publish their discovery or invention to the profession and thus to the world. If a lawyer has learned something useful to the profession and so to the administration of justice through research or experience he publishes it in a legal periodical or expounds it in a paper before a bar association or in a lecture to law students. It is not his property. He may publish it in a copyrighted book and so have rights to the literary form in which it is expounded. But the process or method or developed principle he has worked out belongs to the world.[116]

---

114. Roscoe Pound, The Lawyer From Antiquity to Modern Times 5 (1953).

115. I can personally testify that the misquotation was intentional. I was the Reporter for the Commission on Professionalism, and the quotation as used was personally rewritten by the chair, Justin Stanley, who said he thought Pound's quotation sounded better without the "a."

116. Roscoe Pound, The Lawyer From Antiquity to Modern Times 5–6 (1953). In an epilogue to his book in the Survey of the Legal Profession,

While focused in part on the significance of law to the public, simultaneously and in at least equal measure, the Survey of the Legal Profession reflected a concern about the economic health of the post-war legal profession. As one author candidly described the problem:

> The large number of students in the law schools presents a difficult problem of placing the young law graduates after they are admitted to practice and is symptomatic of the possible serious overcrowding of the bar in the future. The problem is not likely to become lessened so long as government aid is available to veterans. As one law dean has put it, the question some day will arise as to whether the veteran will go on relief or enroll in law school.[117]

A 1952 study done in cooperation with the Martindale-Hubbell law directory counted the number of lawyers at just over 204,000, of whom about 177,000 were in private practice.[118] Less than three percent of that number were women.[119] Survey Director Smith was more concerned, however, that "[t]he brutal fact is that the lawyers of

---

Dean Pound confided a fear that lawyers were becoming candidates for organization into trade unions. He called for lawyers to be part of an organized bar "bred to a professional tradition." In particular, he called for lawyers to be independent of political forces and to stand against big government. *Id.* at 353–62. To be sure, Pound's politics were not universally shared. Other prominent lawyers like Reginald Heber Smith were concerned that if lawyers did not assume greater responsibilities to see that law met the needs of ordinary citizens, the government would "socialize" the profession and do it for them. Reginald Heber Smith, *Legal Service Offices for Persons of Moderate Means*, 1949 Wis. L. Rev. 416, 444 (1950). In like manner, Henry Stimson argued that lawyers existed to preserve the bill of rights. If they ever simply became the servants of business, the future of liberties would be gloomy indeed. Sol M. Linowitz with Martin Mayer, The Betrayed Profession: Lawyering at the End of the Twentieth Century 1 (1994).

117. Homer D. Crotty, *Who Shall Be Called to the Bar?*, 20 B. Examiner 173, 175 (1951).

118. Albert P. Blaustein, *The Legal Profession in the United States: A 1952 Statistical Analysis*, 38 A.B.A. J. 1006, 1007 (1952). The study recognized inherent problems determining which law school graduates are in fact practicing law, but concluded there was no better data than that provided by Martindale-Hubbell listings.

119. *Id.* The study acknowledged that the actual figure might have been higher because names were tabulated as men unless designated Miss or Mrs.

the United States have been as indifferent to their own [economic] interests as they have been jealous of, and faithful to, the interests of their clients."[120] As partial proof of that phenomenon, a related study noted that "[a]lthough the incomes of lawyers have increased by 46 per cent from 1929 to 1949, the incomes of doctors have increased by 125 per cent in this period."[121]

A remarkable volume, "The 1958 lawyer and his 1938 dollar," asserted that the average lawyer in 1954 earned less than $7,382, a figure said to be less than "a living wage."[122] To change their economic fortunes, lawyers were urged to disregard the fact that they "hesitate to utilize techniques that smack of commercial enterprise."[123] Even without compromising professional standards, the volume asserted, "we can learn much from our business brother."[124] The key to lawyer economic success, the volume went on, lay in increasing the lawyer's return from each hour worked. The concept sounds familiar to modern lawyers, even if the numbers do not.

> There are only approximately 1300 fee-earning hours per year unless the lawyer works overtime. Many of the 8 hours per day available for office work are consumed in personal, civic, bar, religious and political activities, general office administration and other non-remunerative matters . . . [so] chargeable time will average 5 hours per day [for 260 days per year].[125]

Lawyers were urged to set a target income for themselves and divide it by 1300 to set their hourly rate. Not all cases would support that rate, the authors noted, but in that case, the lawyer "must secure additional business and increase his number of working hours, the

---

120. Reginald Heber Smith, *Forward to Robert M. Segal & John Fey, The Economics of the Legal Profession: An Analysis by States*, 39 A.B.A. J. 110, 111 (1953).

121. Robert M. Segal & John Fey, *The Economics of the Legal Profession: An Analysis by States*, 39 A.B.A. J. 110, 113 (1953). Another important finding of the study was that the demand for legal services in particular states is more closely related to economic activity in those states than it is to population. That point was later confirmed in B. Peter Pashigian, *The Determinants of the Demand for and Supply of Lawyers*, 20 J.L. & ECON. 53 (1977).

122. A.B.A. SPECIAL COMM. ON ECONOMICS OF LAW PRACTICE, THE 1958 LAWYER AND HIS 1938 DOLLAR 9 (1958).

123. *Id.* at 6.

124. *Id.*

125. *Id.* at 10.

greater number of chargeable hours at the present hourly rate giving him the desired gross."[126] In the case of a law partnership, the report observed, "the estimated earning power of the younger men should include an anticipated profit to be realized [by the partners] from their services."[127]

At the same time, a parallel dimension of the Survey of the Legal Profession was its renewal of the vision of lawyers as the principal custodians of American law and the American way of life. Reginald Heber Smith's introduction to Dean Pound's volume asserted the centrality of the lawyer's role in American society.

> Under a government of laws the lives, the fortunes, and the freedom of the people are *wholly dependent* upon the enforcement of their constitutional rights by an independent judiciary and by an independent bar.
>
> The legal profession is a public profession. Lawyers are public servants. They are the stewards of all the legal rights and obligations of all the citizens.[128]

At first reading, the sentiment sounds almost self-deprecating. In context, however, it was another assertion that the content as well as the administration of the law is the province of lawyers. Dean Pound explained:

> Under our polity many political questions are as well legal and many legal questions are also political. Thus our constitutional polity is so legal as to be dependent upon lawyers for interpretation, application and maintenance against official absolutism and *legislative encroachment.*[129]

---

126. *Id.*

127. *Id.* at 14.

128. Reginald Heber Smith, *Survey of the Legal Profession: Its Scope, Methods and Objectives, in* ROSCOE POUND, THE LAWYER FROM ANTIQUITY TO MODERN TIMES: WITH PARTICULAR REFERENCE TO THE DEVELOPMENT OF BAR ASSOCIATIONS IN THE UNITED STATES, at vii (1953) (emphasis added). Professor Gillian Hadfield has found a similar sentiment in an address by Edward Phelps to the second annual meeting of the A.B.A. in 1879: "We . . . are charged with the safekeeping of the constitution itself." Gillian K. Hadfield, *Legal Barriers to Innovation: The Growing Economic Cost of Professional Control over Corporate Legal Markets,* 60 STAN. L. REV. 1689, 1697 (2008).

129. ROSCOE POUND, THE LAWYER FROM ANTIQUITY TO MODERN TIMES: WITH PARTICULAR REFERENCE TO THE DEVELOPMENT OF BAR ASSOCIATIONS IN THE UNITED STATES, at xxvi (1953) (emphasis added).

What Pound and other A.B.A. leaders forgot, of course, is that law is a public value and is not the property of lawyers. One of recent history's great ironies is that leaders of the A.B.A. at the time of the Survey of the Legal Profession were generally highly conservative. The power they sought to give common law courts to suppress legislative change, however, came into effect just as the Supreme Court moved the law in ways leaders of the bar did not imagine possible. In 1954—the year after Dean Pound's volume—the Supreme Court decided *Brown v. Board of Education*,[130] rejecting the school district's defense presented by John W. Davis, the earlier proponent of a larger, more assertive legal profession. *Baker v. Carr*,[131] with its one-person, one-vote mandate, represented the next revolution, followed soon by *Gideon v. Wainwright*[132] on the right to counsel and *Miranda v. Illinois*[133] on the right to a lawyer during police questioning. Surely there are few clearer examples of the law of unintended consequences than those that arose from the efforts of bar leaders in the early 1950s.

I. WHAT MAKES THE PROFESSIONALISM IDEAL SURVIVE?

Seen in historical context, the American view of law as a profession is at most a little more than a century old and, more realistically, a project of the 1950s and 1980s. Far from representing a social contract, the professionalism label has largely been applied by lawyers to themselves in an effort to achieve political influence and economic advancement. It was the use of the "learned profession" exemption to the antitrust laws, for example, that until 1975 allowed state and local bars to set minimum fees for lawyers to charge and thereby try to avoid price competition.[134]

---

130. 349 U.S. 294 (1955).

131. 369 U.S. 186 (1962).

132. 372 U.S. 335 (1963).

133. 384 U.S. 436 (1966).

134. The effort came to an end after the Supreme Court decision in *Goldfarb v. Virginia State Bar*, 421 U.S. 773 (1975), held that legal services were part of "trade or commerce" and thus that the "profession" label provided lawyers no antitrust exemption. *Cf.* Mark D. Bauer, *The Licensed Professional*

What then keeps the idea of professionalism alive and encourages calls for its restoration? In part, it is surely that professional status is flattering to many lawyers, and appeals in the name of professionalism are taken more seriously as a result. But it is also true that many elements of professionalism represent personal qualities or styles of behavior that appropriately appeal to lawyers' aspirations to live good lives and act in ways that serve the public interest.

Even acknowledging the diversity among lawyers' practices, inherent in the claim that law is a profession is the belief that certain values distinguish lawyers from other service providers. The values can be described in various ways, but four recur in most lists. They are (1) keeping information entrusted to the lawyer confidential, (2) pressing each client's position with independence and commitment, (3) giving all citizens access to justice regardless of their ability to pay, and (4) creating a legal system that contributes to individual and social justice.[135]

These values are unquestionably important to clients individually and to society generally, and if sensitivity to such values were unique to the profession of lawyers—or impossible to preserve without professional rhetoric—the case for seeing lawyers as a special class of service providers might be strong. However, lawyers have no unique claim to these values. Most are consistent with the ideals of citizens generally, and some are legally enforced against all "agents," of whom lawyers are simply a sub-category.[136]

Exemption in Consumer Protection: At Odds with Antitrust History and Precedent, 73 TENN. L. REV. 131 (2006).

135. Dean Kronman uses four different categories to define what makes law a profession, i.e., law is (1) a public calling and lawyers assume duties to the public interest, (2) a generalized craft, not highly specialized, (3) a role that relies on wise judgment, and (4) an activity with a sense of history. Anthony T. Kronman, *The Law as a Profession, in* ETHICS IN PRACTICE: LAWYERS' ROLES, RESPONSIBILITIES, AND REGULATION 29–34 (Deborah L Rhode ed., 2000).

136. *See generally* Deborah A. DeMott, *The Lawyer as Agent,* 67 FORDHAM L. REV. 301 (1998); RESTATEMENT (THIRD) OF THE LAW GOVERNING LAWYERS, ch. 2, Introductory Note. (The client-lawyer relationship is "derived from the law of agency. It concerns a voluntary relationship in which an agent, a lawyer, agrees to work for the benefit of a principal, a client.").

1. Confidentiality of Client Information

When a client tells something to a lawyer, the information must go no farther. Lawyers disagree about many things, but there is no more common understanding lawyers share.[137] The confidentiality obligation is in part embodied in the lawyer-client privilege that prohibits a court from requiring disclosure of a confidential communication between a client and his lawyer made in the course of seeking or providing legal advice. Lawyer ethical standards go beyond the privilege, however, to require that lawyers not disclose any information they receive from any source—not simply the client—if it is related to the representation of the client. Even if a lawyer's disclosure of facts learned while doing research in a client's case could prevent an innocent non-client from going to prison, for example, the lawyer must remain silent unless the client consents to disclosure.[138]

Lawyers are proud of the confidential ear they can provide to clients, even conceding that there are sometimes adverse consequences to others. The promise of confidentiality allows a client to be completely honest and tell the lawyer unpleasant or potentially incriminating facts. It is revelation of such facts that allows the lawyer to provide a more complete defense, negotiate settlement of a controversy, or advise the client to adopt a different course of action that will not violate the law. While the net social consequences of confidentiality can never be accurately calculated, lawyers and courts have concluded that the value of cases fairly tried and illegal conduct avoided exceeds the possible negative consequences of confidentiality.

What many lawyers fail to see, however, is that "professional" status has nothing to do with the obligation of confidentiality. Lawyers

---

137. It is an understanding with constitutional underpinnings. Americans have a Fifth Amendment right not to be forced to incriminate themselves in a criminal trial. If a lawyer could be asked what a client had told the lawyer, prosecutors could obtain from the lawyer what they could not demand from the client. Fisher v. United States, 425 U.S. 391 (1976). *See also* MONROE H. FREEDMAN & ABBE SMITH, UNDERSTANDING LAWYERS' ETHICS 186 (3d ed. 2004); David E. Seidelson, *The Attorney-Client Privilege and the Client's Constitutional Rights*, 6 HOFSTRA L. REV. 693 (1978).

138. *Cf., e.g., Symposium, Executing the Wrong Person: The Professionals' Ethical Dilemmas*, 29 LOYOLA L.A. L. REV. 1543 (1996). The lawyer rules have since been changed when the innocent person is facing death. *See* MODEL RULES OF PROF'L CONDUCT R. 1.6(b)(1).

are not unique or even unusual in having such obligations. Doctors and clergy are confidential listening ears, and so are investment advisors, social workers, secretaries, and accountants.[139] Indeed, potentially all persons acting as what the law calls "agents" are required to protect confidentiality of information of the persons for whom they work. The Restatement of Agency explains the general principle to be that:

> Unless otherwise agreed, an agent . . . [may not] use or communicate information confidentially given him by the principal or acquired by him during the course of or on account of his agency . . . to the injury of the principal, on his own account or on behalf of another, although such information does not relate to the transaction in which he is then employed, unless the information is a matter of general knowledge.[140]

Lawyers can take pride in the value they put on protecting confidential information, but that value simply does not reflect or justify special professional status for lawyers.

2. Committed Advocacy on a Client's Behalf

The second value, committed advocacy, is perhaps the most widely known. Television and movies tend to glorify advocates, and deep in the imagination of many lawyers is a picture of themselves defending an innocent client that all the world wants to hang. When a client is alone and the full resources of the state are arrayed against him, the

---

139. Accountants produce public audits, so it might seem that corporations will not trust auditors with sensitive information. But corporations must give accurate information to their accountants, whether they want to or not, and the fact is that accountants, too, have a duty of confidentiality. It is the company's—the accountant's client's—duty to disclose bad news, not the accountant's duty. An accountant may not be a party to a client's fraud any more than a lawyer can, but it is not a breach of confidentiality that sends a signal to financial markets that something is wrong at a company. Instead, it is the accountant's refusal to issue a report, or his or her withdrawal from the audit assignment, that raises the red flag. In that sense, an auditor's role is much like a lawyer's duty of "noisy withdrawal" in cases where fraud may be involved. *See, e.g.*, Remarks of Roger L. Page, Deloitte & Touche, LLP, to the A.B.A. Commission on Multidisciplinary Practice, March 11, 1999.

140. RESTATEMENT SECOND, AGENCY § 395. *See also* § 388, cmt. c (agent's duty to account for profits made by use of principal's confidential information).

lawyer's imagination suggests, it is only the lawyer-advocate who will assure that justice will be done.

The image is compelling, but once again, that image has to do with the lawyer's role, not the lawyer's status. Some lawyers do act as advocates, but effective advocacy is not limited to lawyers. Accountants vigorously advocate tax positions on behalf of clients during IRS audits and before the Tax Court. Non-lawyer patent agents loyally advocate their clients' positions before the U.S. Patent and Trademark Office. Non-lawyers provide specialized advocacy before courts and administrative agencies. Indeed, lawyers' arguments about the significance of advocacy as a professional activity are circular. One of the primary reasons we do not see more non-lawyer advocacy is because the rules of most courts reserve the function for lawyers.

It is not even clear that dedicated advocacy—even if it were associated with professional status—is necessarily a virtue. Lawyers working by the hour have a financial incentive to keep people fighting rather than solving their problems.[141] In an earlier day, lawyers did not brag about litigation or their role in it. Conflict was to be avoided. Lawyers saw themselves as able to work out differences through cooperation.[142] The suggestion that lawyers are uniquely able to pursue their clients' interests because they have licenses to go to court, then, is not much of a public value on which to rest a claim to special status.

3. Preservation of the Rule of Law and Independence From Clients

The first two "core values," then, simply acknowledge that lawyers have a fiduciary obligation to put their clients' interests ahead of

---

141. On the nature of today's litigation and the alleged litigation explosion, see, e.g., Marc S. Galanter, *Reading the Landscape of Disputes: What We Know and Don't Know (and Think We Know) About Our Allegedly Contentious and Litigious Society*, 31 UCLA L. Rev. 4 (1983).

142. *See* DAVID LUBAN, LAWYERS AND JUSTICE: AN ETHICAL STUDY 50–103 (1988); DEBORAH L. RHODE, IN THE INTERESTS OF JUSTICE: REFORMING THE LEGAL PROFESSION 81–115 (2000). *See also* SOL M. LINOWITZ WITH MARTIN MAYER, THE BETRAYED PROFESSION: LAWYERING AT THE END OF THE TWENTIETH CENTURY 2 (1994); MICHAEL H. TROTTER, PROFIT AND THE PRACTICE OF LAW: WHAT'S HAPPENED TO THE LEGAL PROFESSION, ch. 8 (1997).

their own rather than deal with clients at arm's length.[143] The final two values—assuring broad access to legal services, and preserving the rule of law generally—address public benefits. Even these public roles of a lawyer, however, do not justify a unique "professional" label.

One can argue that the "core value" of preserving the rule of law is special and implies that a lawyer's duty to try to assure that his clients obey the law is as great as the duty to protect his clients against abuses the legal system can impose.[144] The historical argument along these lines is that the nation's founders saw lawyers as disinterested in their clients' commercial success. Thus, arguably, some things became matters of law that political leaders did not want subject to partisanship or self-interest.[145] In an address in 1910 to the American Bar Association, for example, Woodrow Wilson said:

> You are not a mere body of expert business advisers in the field of civil law, or a mere body of expert advocates for those who get entangled in the meshes of the criminal law. You are servants of the public, of the state itself. You are under bonds to serve the general interest, the integrity and enlightenment of law itself, in the advice you give individuals.[146]

Professors Robert Gordon and William Simon have tried to "redeem" this view of professionalism in a way that fits their own ideals. Each has argued that lawyers should maintain a critical independence from their

---

143. *See, e.g.,* Homer D. Crotty, *Who Shall Be Called to the Bar?*, 20 B. EXAMINER 173, 179 (1951) (quoting the autobiography of George Wharton Pepper). The term given to having a duty to put the client's interest ahead of the lawyer's is called a "fiduciary" duty or relationship.

144. *See, e.g.,* Robert W. Gordon, *The Independence of Lawyers*, 68 B.U. L. REV. 1 (1988).

145. *See, e.g.,* PAUL G. HASKELL, WHY LAWYERS BEHAVE AS THEY DO 85–92 (1998); SOL M. LINOWITZ WITH MARTIN MAYER, THE BETRAYED PROFESSION: LAWYERING AT THE END OF THE TWENTIETH CENTURY 4, 9–18 (1994) (rule of law is diminished when lawyers see their role as to help clients get what they want rather than what they are entitled to); Kenneth M. Rosen, *Lessons on Lawyers, Democracy, and Professional Responsibility*, 19 GEO. J. LEGAL ETHICS 155 (2006) (law schools have a duty to teach lawyers their role in preserving democratic institutions).

146. *Quoted in* ORIE L. PHILLIPS & PHILBRICK MCCOY, CONDUCT OF JUDGES AND LAWYERS: A SURVEY OF PROFESSIONAL ETHICS, DISCIPLINE AND DISBARMENT 57 (1952).

society in 1876.[158] Sadly, however, many legal service programs for the poor have had as much to do with the interests of lawyers as the interests of clients. Concerns about meeting the legal needs of "persons of moderate means" arose at the end of World War II as soldiers who had received free legal services while in the military came home and needed to buy houses, start businesses, and the like. The expressed concern was about how to meet their needs. "Lawyer reference plans" (now lawyer referral services) were one response; legal services offices were another.[159]

In 1951, the depression was a recent reality and lawyers had returned from World War II. Pro bono services were justified as part of both the battle against communism, i.e., a way to show the poor that the rule of law was their friend,[160] and as an effort to see lawyers fully occupied in professional activity.[161] The legal aid movement was funded heavily by what we would today call the United Way, not primarily by voluntary services of lawyers,[162] and in the context of the time, the movement was seen mainly as a way to give experience to law students and practical training to young lawyers who had

---

158. *See, e.g.,* EMERY A. BROWNELL, LEGAL AID IN THE UNITED STATES (1951) (part of the Survey of the Legal Profession); JOHN MACARTHUR MAGUIRE, THE LANCE OF JUSTICE: A SEMI-CENTENNIAL HISTORY OF THE LEGAL AID SOCIETY 1876–1926 (1928); REGINALD HEBER SMITH, JUSTICE AND THE POOR (1919).

159. Reginald Heber Smith, *Legal Service Offices for Persons of Moderate Means,* 1949 WIS. L. REV. 416, 417–24 (1950).

160. *E.g.,* "It is a fundamental tenet of Marxian Communism that law is a class weapon used by the rich to oppress the poor through the simple device of making justice too expensive . . . . Nothing rankles more in the human heart than a brooding sense of injustice. Illness we can put up with; but injustice makes us want to pull things down." *Introduction by Reginald Heber Smith* to EMERY A. BROWNELL, LEGAL AID IN THE UNITED STATES: A STUDY OF THE AVAILABILITY OF LAWYERS' SERVICES FOR PERSONS UNABLE TO PAY FEES xiii (1951).

161. Returning lawyer veterans were denied the G.I. Bill because the government reasoned they were already trained. Reginald Heber Smith, *Legal Service Offices for Persons of Moderate Means,* 1949 WIS. L. REV. 416, 437–44 (1950).

162. ALBERT P. BLAUSTEIN & CHARLES O. PORTER, THE AMERICAN LAWYER: A SUMMARY OF THE SURVEY OF THE LEGAL PROFESSION 86–90 (1954).

---

clients' values, an independence facilitated by the sense that lawyers as professionals are inherently different from other kinds of advisers.[147]

As a later writer described this point of view:

[T]he ideal of the "independent professional" as public servant haunts the minds of many American lawyers, not just their academic critics. The independent professional displays expert judgment while remaining relatively unspecialized and is thus familiar with the wide range of legal issues into which his clients' diverse endeavors draw him. He cultivates collegiality with professional peers without being diverted from his own life plan. He maintains independence from clients' interests while retaining and enhancing their business. He devotes serious attention to pro bono and periodic public service without enduring economic sacrifice, doing both "good" and "well" while not striving directly to do either. In this conception of the lawyer, practitioners are understood as integral components of a society's legal system who happen to be compensated by private payment, not as part of the market for human services whose services happen to involve interactions with the legal system.[148]

The problem with such a view, of course, is that lawyers cannot truly be independent of their clients. Quite apart from their status as fiduciaries who are legally required to pursue their client's interests, they have value to their clients only as they serve the clients' interests. People do not retain a lawyer to preserve the rule of law; they retain a lawyer for an instrumental purpose, i.e., to get a useful service.[149] Lawyers have been assisting parties in corporate affairs at least as

---

147. *See* Robert W. Gordon & William H. Simon, *The Redemption of Professionalism?, in* LAWYERS' IDEALS/LAWYERS' PRACTICES: TRANSFORMATIONS IN THE AMERICAN LEGAL PROFESSION (Robert L. Nelson, David M. Trubek & Rayman L. Solomon, eds., 1992), at 230; William H. Simon, *Ethical Discretion in Lawyering,* 101 HARV. L. REV. 1083 (1988); Robert W. Gordon, *The Independence of Lawyers,* 68 B.U. L. REV. 1 (1988); Robert W. Gordon, *Corporate Law Practice as a Public Calling,* 49 MD. L. REV. 255 (1990).

148. Mark J. Osiel, *Book Review: Lawyers as Monopolists, Aristocrats, and Entrepreneurs,* 103 HARV. L. REV. 2009, 2014 (1990).

149. MACKLIN FLEMING, LAWYERS, MONEY, AND SUCCESS: THE CONSEQUENCES OF DOLLAR OBSESSION, ch. 8 (1997). Indeed, much of the conflict in attitudes about the Skadden Arps firm is based on views about the takeover business that they helped thrive. The junk bond firm, Drexel Burnham, was Skadden's largest client, and Michael Milken and junk bonds were an important part of its world. Many saw the law firm as evil because they thought the takeover activity was immoral, while others thought both

long as there have been corporations.[150] Indeed, lawyer creativity in helping businesses find ways to do things differently than they had previously tried has been arguably one of the things that has made economic development as dynamic as it has been.

What observers like to hope happened is that, in the process, lawyers also restrained excesses in which corporate officials would have engaged.[151] Dean Kronman says:

> A lawyer whose only responsibility is to prepare the way for ends that others have already set can never be anything but a deferential servant. The lawyer-statesman is not a servant in this sense. Whether acting as the representative of private interests or as a counselor in matters of state, one important part of what he does is to offer advice about ends. An essential aspect of his work as he and others see it, is to help those on whose behalf he is deliberating come to a better understanding of their own ambitions, interests, and ideals and to guide their choice among alternative goals.[152]

Some lawyers may be statesmen, and some lawyer-statesman-like behavior may occur.[153] Elihu Root is quoted as saying, for example, that "half of what a lawyer must do is tell his client he is a damn fool."[154] But even statements such as Root's provide no evidence that clients take such advice from lawyers seriously. All we really know about lawyers' preserving the rule of law and assuring client compliance with it comes from lawyers. The accuracy of their reports is hardly a basis for granting lawyers a unique status.

Lawyers, as a matter of disposition and training, tend to look backward. From their earliest days as students, they are too often taught the problems of the past instead of looking to the future in which they will live. Professor Chaffee observed that the law student of 1900 was largely unprepared for the revolutions of the twentieth century, i.e., workers' compensation, income taxes, labor relations, and growth of administrative agencies. It is perhaps no accident that lawyers' vision of preserving the rule of law often consisted of resisting such changes.[155] The idea that lawyers are guardians of the law is ultimately a condemnation of democratic ideals. Lawyers must have respect for law and legal institutions, but so should everyone else. Lawyer guardianship is not a promising substitute for citizen involvement in political activity.

4. Making Legal Services Widely Available

Finally, lawyers say that without their willingness to make their services broadly available—regardless of a client's ability to pay—the American legal system would be significantly less able to do justice. Making legal services broadly available is, indeed, a noble objective of lawyers; it is unfortunately not a reality of most lawyers' practice. Indeed, no American jurisdiction imposes any responsibility on lawyers to provide free or reduced-rate legal services.[156] And when the A.B.A. "Ethics 2000" Commission that considered changes in lawyer obligations recently took up a proposal to require such service, the proposal was rejected.[157]

Voluntary legal aid societies around the country have delivered legal services to the poor since at least the founding of the New York

---

were simply ahead of their time. LINCOLN CAPLAN, SKADDEN: POWER, MONEY, AND THE RISE OF A LEGAL EMPIRE, ch. 15 (1993).

150. *See, e.g.*, MORTON J. HOROWITZ, THE TRANSFORMATION OF AMERICAN LAW, 1780–1860, ch. 5 (1977).

151. Some say that, in the past, relationships with clients and within firms were more like family. Now. the pursuit of money has arguably replaced that. SOL M. LINOWITZ WITH MARTIN MAYER, THE BETRAYED PROFESSION: LAWYERING AT THE END OF THE TWENTIETH CENTURY 30–32 (1994). Law practice has become more competitive and lawyers more personally insecure. MICHAEL H. TROTTER, PROFIT AND THE PRACTICE OF LAW: WHAT'S HAPPENED TO THE LEGAL PROFESSION, ch. 12 (1997). Indeed, now, it is probably in the interest of corporate counsel to keep lawyers uncertain about what work will be coming their way. *See generally* MARK STEVENS, POWER OF ATTORNEY: THE RISE OF THE GIANT LAW FIRMS, ch. 3 (1987).

152. ANTHONY T. KRONMAN, THE LOST LAWYER: FAILING IDEALS OF THE LEGAL PROFESSION 15 (1993). *See also id.* at 354–64.

153. There certainly was rhetoric to that effect at the time the A.B.A. first prepared its Canons of Ethics in 1908. *See* Russell G. Pearce, *Rediscovering the Republican Origins of the Legal Ethics Codes*, 6 GEO. J. LEGAL ETHICS 241 (1992); Susan D. Carle, *Lawyers' Duty to Do Justice: A New Look at the History of the 1908 Canons*, 24 LAW & SOC. INQUIRY 1 (1999).

154. ERWIN O. SMIGEL, THE WALL STREET LAWYER 4–7 (1964).

155. Zechariah Chafee, Jr., *Changes in the Law During Forty Years*, 32 B.U. L. REV. 46–53 (1952).

156. *See, e.g.*, MODEL RULES OF PROF'L CONDUCT R. 6.1.

157. *Report of the Comm. on Evaluation of Prof'l Standards*, R. 6.1 (2000).

gone into military service and wanted to brush up on their skills before setting out on their own.[163] Creation of the Legal Services Corporation was in part a government response to a need that lawyers individually had refused to assume.[164] However lawyers might like to claim the core value of furthering access to the legal system, then, their basis for doing so is doubtful.

Professor Deborah Rhode acknowledges lawyers' lack of commitment to many core professional values such as pro bono service, but she calls for creating a "culture of commitment" to making legal services available to all.[165] It is possible that such an appeal to professional tradition will have more effect in the future than it has had in the past, but it is hard to see why. However justified such appeals may seem in the abstract, the pressures of modern practice may be likely to reduce their persuasiveness.

Some lawyers may provide such services out of a sense of self-interest. Skadden Arps generated enormous goodwill for itself by

---

163. Reginald Heber Smith, *Legal Service Offices for Persons of Moderate Means*, 1949 WIS. L. REV. 416, 437–44 (1950).

164. The organized Bar was also concerned that if lawyers did not at least appear to assume such public responsibilities, the government would "socialize" the profession:

> For selfish and unselfish reasons we hope that the new world will be attracted by our form of government and the American way of life so that, in other nations, free peoples will set up democratic regimes and institutions. In order that our general system may make its maximum appeal, and because we are not hypocrites, we are engaged in reexamining our own institutions. We want to keep what is good, and add what is found needed. Law is the foundation of our whole structure. We are determined that it shall be strong. We know that law is not self-enforcing, and that lawyers are essential.

Reginald Heber Smith, *Legal Service Offices for Persons of Moderate Means*, 1949 WIS. L. REV. 416, 444 (1950).

165. *See, e.g.*, Deborah L. Rhode, *Cultures of Commitment: Pro Bono for Lawyers and Law Students, in* DEBORAH L. RHODE, ED., ETHICS IN PRACTICE: LAWYERS' ROLES, RESPONSIBILITIES, AND REGULATION 264 (2000). Professor Rhode also calls on law schools to help inculcate these professional values in their students. Deborah L. Rhode, *The Professional Responsibilities of Law Professors*, 51 J. LEGAL EDUC. 158 (2001); Deborah L. Rhode, *Legal Education: Professional Interests and Public Values*, 34 IND. L. REV. 23, 42–45 (2000).

creating the Skadden fellowships for public interest practice, for example.[166] Other firms view pro bono work as good training for lawyers, and law firms may accept responsibility for such service as a way to attract lawyers as well as to gain a reputation for community service. It is fine to call for lawyers to provide pro bono service, but the idea of "professionalism" seems to add little to the moral claim inherent in that objective.[167]

J. LAW IN AMERICA IS NOT A PROFESSION—AND THAT'S A GOOD THING

Objecting to calling law a profession might seem a lost cause. No one can deny, for example, that the right to practice law is extensively regulated. One must take special training, undergo special testing and be specially licensed to practice law, and the license may be taken away if the lawyer fails to adhere to a jurisdiction's rules of professional conduct. The rules to which lawyers are held, in turn, have been proposed by bar associations composed of lawyers and imposed by judges who are themselves lawyers.[168] The sociologist's definition of a profession would seem to be confirmed.

Furthermore, designation as a profession is a measure of status in which lawyers take pride, and if status were the only thing at stake,

---

166. LINCOLN CAPLAN, SKADDEN: POWER, MONEY, AND THE RISE OF A LEGAL EMPIRE, ch. 14 (1993).

167. SOL M. LINOWITZ WITH MARTIN MAYER, THE BETRAYED PROFESSION: LAWYERING AT THE END OF THE TWENTIETH CENTURY 201–06 (1994). Indeed, it is said that European countries that have broken down the professionalism protection of the bar have done more to restore the public role of lawyers than the more cautious approach in this country. Mark J. Osiel, *Book Review: Lawyers as Monopolists, Aristocrats, and Entrepreneurs*, 103 HARV. L. REV. 2009, 2047–48 (1990). *See also* ROBERT GRANFIELD & LYNN MATHER, EDS., PRIVATE LAWYERS IN THE PUBLIC INTEREST: THE EVOLVING ROLE OF PRO BONO IN THE LEGAL PROFESSION (2009).

168. The regulatory provisions in most states are based on those proposed in the American Bar Association Model Rules of Professional Conduct (2000, as amended). Each state's bar association usually then reviews the A.B.A. proposals, but the state rules are then typically imposed by the state's supreme court.

challenging the label would not be worth the effort. But more is involved. The changes in what today's and future lawyers will do that this book suggests are almost inevitable and are likely to change the way legal services are delivered and thus the way the term "lawyer" has been understood.[169] The changes will be matters of substance, not semantics, and they are likely to affect important ways in which lawyers understand who they are and what role they are likely to play in local and national life.

Much of the concern expressed here is familiar to those who have thought about professions and professionalism,[170] but it is hard to abandon concepts that have become such an integral part of lawyers' self-image. Sociologist Terrence Halliday tries to preserve the professionalism rhetoric by suggesting that the legal profession be seen as a way for lawyers to involve themselves in an "intermediate" institution in an otherwise fragmented society.[171] We all need such institutions, Halliday suggests. Government is too distant and impersonal; institutions like clubs, churches, and professions are needed to help people work together effectively on a smaller scale. Professors Gordon and Simon likewise posit such smaller organizations to "give collegial support to members in developing their own conception of responsible practice."[172]

---

169. Elliott Krause frames it this way: "I am not saying that professions are dying. What is dying is their guild power—as this power is increasingly being replaced by the power of capitalists or the state or both together to control the nature and quality of the professional associations, the professional workplace, the professional marketplace, and the relation of professional groups to the state." ELLIOTT A. KRAUSE, DEATH OF THE GUILDS: PROFESSIONS, STATES, AND THE ADVANCE OF CAPITALISM, 1930 TO THE PRESENT 283 (1996).

170. See, e.g., Timothy P. Terrell & James H. Wildman, Rethinking "Professionalism," 41 EMORY L.J. 403 (1992); Nancy J. Moore, Professionalism Reconsidered, 1987 AM. B. FOUND. RES. J. 773.

171. TERENCE C. HALLIDAY, BEYOND MONOPOLY 16–24 (1987). Halliday cites Émile Durkheim for this idea in France and Magali Larson in the United States. Lawyers, Halliday says, have what is called "technical authority," i.e., influence because of their ability to manipulate legal ideas.

172. Robert W. Gordon & William H. Simon, The Redemption of Professionalism?, in LAWYERS' IDEALS/LAWYERS' PRACTICES: TRANSFORMATIONS IN THE AMERICAN LEGAL PROFESSION 244 (Robert L. Nelson, David M. Trubek

That is certainly a possible role for bar associations. The associations unquestionably act as important networking institutions today, for example, just as they provide continuing education and informed judgment about legal issues for legislatures, courts, and agencies. But to any individual lawyer, a profession of a million-plus lawyers is far too large to be any realistic kind of intermediate institution. Even the A.B.A., with its more than 400,000 members, rarely attracts more than about 3 percent of its membership to a single meeting, and even its most active members do most of their work through sections or section committees.

The legal profession itself is certainly unlikely to be a useful intermediate institution, even if some bar association groups might serve such a role. It may be, instead, that in many cases, law firms have replaced bar associations as the principal intermediate institutions for their members.[173] Many law firms are now as big as most bar associations were at the time Roscoe Pound and others saw the associations as central to professional development. Firm culture is likely to affect individual lawyer behavior far more directly than A.B.A. culture ever will. Indeed, differing firm cultures can constructively compete for the kind of reputation to which they will aspire.[174]

It is clear from the work of Gordon, Halliday, Rhode, and Simon that very good people have tried to make something of the professional rhetoric, but we are a long way from the grandiose claims of Roscoe Pound, Reginald Heber Smith, and others behind the Survey of the Legal Profession. In my view, professionalism in the sense

---

& Rayman L. Solomon, 1987). A similar theme is offered in W. Bradley Wendel, *Nonlegal Regulation of the Legal Profession: Social Norms in Professional Communities*, 54 VAND. L. REV. 1955 (2001).

173. *See, e.g.,* Mark D. Nozette & Robert A. Creamer, *Professionalism: The Next Level,* 79 TULANE L. REV. 1539 (2005); Ted Schneyer, *A Tale of Four Systems: Reflections on How Law Influences the "Ethical Infrastructure" of Law Firms,* 39 S. TEX. L. REV. 45 (1998).

174. Professor Richard Painter speculates that firms may even realize a competitive advantage by developing a reputation for ethical conduct. Richard W. Painter, *Toward a Market for Lawyer Disclosure Services: In Search of Optimal Whistleblowing Rules,* 63 GEO. WASH. L. REV. 221 (1995). *See also* Peter C. Kostant, *Paradigm Regained: How Competition From Accounting Firms May Help Corporate Attorneys to Recapture the Ethical High Ground,* 20 PACE L. REV. 43 (1999).

developed by the A.B.A. during the twentieth century is—and should be seen as—dead.

Looking back at the efforts to achieve professionalism, of course, one must acknowledge that much more was involved than hollow phrases. Efforts to improve the law's fairness, to eliminate invidious discrimination, and to enhance opportunities for all our citizens have occupied the public careers of many of the nation's finest lawyers, often at real personal cost to themselves. We all benefit from the uniform laws, simplified procedures, and important reforms that they have to show for their work, and there is no reason that such work should end.

But the point of this book is that the good work was the work of good people who happened to do some of their good work using legal skills. The Conference of Chief Justices, the association of presiding officers of America's state courts, was correct when it said

> Professionalism ultimately is a personal, not an institutional characteristic. . . . The institutional framework of the legal profession can create a climate in which professionalism can flourish, but individual lawyers must be the ones to cultivate this characteristic in themselves.[175]

Lawyers, like all citizens, have a moral obligation to devote their best efforts to using their skills in ways that contribute to the public interest. Lawyers should, however, remove the lenses of professionalism through which they have been encouraged to see their futures. Their future will not be like their past, and it is time now to look hard at what that future is likely to be.

---

175. CONFERENCE OF CHIEF JUSTICES, A NATIONAL ACTION PLAN ON LAWYER CONDUCT AND PROFESSIONALISM (1999) (*quoted in* Neil Hamilton, *Professionalism Clearly Defined*, 18 PROF. LAW. 7 (No. 4, 2008). Professor Hamilton's own principles of professionalism are similarly directed ultimately at the individual lawyer. They call for (1) growth in personal conscience over the lawyer's career, (2) compliance with all professional duties, (3) striving to internalize even higher standards of professional conduct than the law requires, (4) holding other lawyers to minimum standards and helping them achieve high standards, and (5) a devotion to serving the public interest in justice by volunteering time to render pro bono service and continuing to reflect on the relative importance of wealth and professionalism. *Id.* at 8–14. *See also* Robert F. Cochran, Jr., *Professionalism in the Postmodern Age: Its Death, Attempts at Resuscitation, and Alternate Sources of Virtue*, 14 NOTRE DAME J.L. ETHICS & PUB. POL'Y 305 (2000).

3. THE TRANSFORMATION OF LAW PRACTICE SINCE THE 1970s

In the first two chapters, we have seen lawyers as persons specially trained to bring general legal principles and methods of analysis to bear on concrete issues. This chapter suggests that a transformation of an American lawyer's work and reality began in the last half—and accelerated in the last quarter—of the twentieth century. The transformation continues and affects everything about the world facing clients and their legal advisors.[1] In the words of an A.B.A. committee charged with studying the future of law practice: "We are in the midst of the biggest transformation of civilization since the caveman began bartering. The practice of law and the administration of justice are at the brink of change of an unprecedented and exponential kind and magnitude."[2]

Those words may seem exaggerated. Almost everyone who has been paying attention will acknowledge changes in the abstract, but their speed and nature have led many into the kind of "future shock" that author Alvin Toffler predicted.[3] That "shock," in turn, has

---

1. Several but not all of them are discussed in THOMAS L. FRIEDMAN, THE WORLD IS FLAT: A BRIEF HISTORY OF THE TWENTY-FIRST CENTURY, chs. 2 & 3 (2005). As applied to lawyers, among the most prescient works were Herbert M. Kritzer, *The Professions Are Dead, Long Live the Professions: Legal Practice in a Postprofessional World*, 33 L. & Soc. REV. 713 (1999), and Russell G. Pearce, *The Professionalism Paradigm Shift: Why Discarding Professional Ideology Will Improve the Conduct and Reputation of the Bar*, 70 N.Y.U. L. REV. 1229 (1995).

2. A.B.A. COMM. ON RESEARCH ABOUT THE FUTURE OF THE LEGAL PROFESSION, WORKING NOTES: DELIBERATIONS ON THE CURRENT STATUS OF THE LEGAL PROFESSION 2 (Aug. 31, 2001). The Committee seems never to have expanded its "working notes" into a formal report.

3. ALVIN TOFFLER, FUTURE SHOCK (1970). Toffler observed: "[I]f the last 50,000 years of man's existence were divided into lifetimes of approximately sixty-two years each, there have been 800 such lifetimes. . . . Only during the last six lifetimes did masses of men ever see a printed word. Only during the last four has it been possible to measure time with any precision. Only in the last two has anyone anywhere used an electric motor. And the overwhelming majority of

paralyzed many lawyers into denial of the reality and failure to respond to it. Toffler himself expected such paralysis. Each of us lives our life learning more and more from experience. As we grow older, we expect that experience will allow us to know more and to do familiar things better. In an era of change such as ours, however, experience can become a burden. We expect life to confront us with more of the same, but reality is changing in ways our experience cannot predict and to which we find it hard to adapt.[4] It oversimplifies reality to put discrete labels on the revolutionary changes affecting society in general and lawyers in particular, but several such changes can help convey a sense of the reality that affects everything today's and tomorrow's lawyers will face.

---

all material goods we use in daily life today have been developed within the present, the 800th, lifetime." *Id.* at 15.

4. Toffler uses the term "transience" to describe the psychological feeling of impermanence and anxiety that this accelerating change creates. ALVIN TOFFLER, FUTURE SHOCK 42 & chs. 4–8 (1970). Contemporaneous with Toffler's work, Thomas Kuhn described what periodically happens in science as a shift of paradigms, that is, of fundamental ways of understanding how the world works. If one saw physical reality as Newton did, for example, confirmation of the paradigm he described seemed all around. When enough examples that did not fit his paradigm were accumulated, however, an entirely new paradigm such as quantum physics was required. THOMAS S. KUHN, THE STRUCTURE OF SCIENTIFIC REVOLUTIONS (2d ed. 1970). Some writers who reach insights such as those offered in this book cite Kuhn in calling for a new paradigm to replace the "professional" model for lawyers. *E.g.*, Russell G. Pearce, *The Professionalism Paradigm Shift: Why Discarding Professional Ideology Will Improve the Conduct and Reputation of the Bar*, 70 N.Y.U. L. REV. 1229 (1995); W. Bradley Wendel, *Morality, Motivation and the Professionalism Movement*, 52 S.C. L. REV. 557 (2001).

The A.B.A. Committee quoted earlier used the idea of a "strategic inflection point" suggested in ANDY S. GROVE, ONLY THE PARANOID SURVIVE: HOW TO EXPLOIT THE CRISIS POINTS THAT CHALLENGE EVERY COMPANY (1996). In the Committee's words, "A strategic inflection point is a moment, often unforeseen and more often not perceived until too late, when massive, unprecedented, and fundamentally unforeseen change occurs. All bets are off, and all the rules change . . . . A strategic inflection point is not an incremental or peripheral change. It is a fundamental and revolutionary transformation." A.B.A. COMM. ON RESEARCH ABOUT THE FUTURE OF THE LEGAL PROFESSION, WORKING NOTES: DELIBERATIONS ON THE CURRENT STATUS OF THE LEGAL PROFESSION 3 (Aug. 31, 2001).

A. JUDICIAL ABROGATION OF LAWYER STANDARDS

Throughout much of the so-called golden age of the 1950s and 1960s, lawyers could get away with convincing themselves they were part of a self-regulating profession. That was true, in part, because of what leading lawyers told them. In addition, unauthorized practice prohibitions—often enforced by criminal sanctions—defined work that only lawyers could do.[5] Within that zone of protected activity, rules of professional conduct had been established by bar associations working through state supreme courts whose justices had been lawyers only a few years before. Legislative and executive branch institutions—the traditional sources of public lawmaking—had relatively little authority when it came to regulating lawyers.

Insulation from outside influence on lawyer conduct was never complete, but it seemed nearly so until the 1960s when the United States Supreme Court began systematically to break down the special protections lawyers enjoyed. Most Supreme Court cases about the legal profession since the early 1960s can be described as invalidating the self-regulatory standards that were developed or reinforced as a result of the Survey of the Legal Profession.[6]

In *NAACP v. Button*,[7] for example, the state of Virginia had extended the traditional ban on a lawyer's solicitation of new clients beyond the usual prohibition against hiring ambulance drivers to pass out the lawyer's cards. The state had prohibited contact of potential clients by agents of any person or association that "employs, retains or compensates" any attorney in a judicial proceeding in which the person or organization "is not a party and in which it has no pecuniary right or liability."[8] As applied to the NAACP, the

---

5. The most comprehensive discussion and critique of unauthorized practice provisions is Deborah L. Rhode, *Policing the Professional Monopoly: A Constitutional and Empirical Analysis of Unauthorized Practice Prohibitions*, 34 STAN. L. REV. 1 (1981).

6. *E.g.*, Schware v. Bd. of Bar Examiners, 353 U.S. 232 (1957) (state may not deny bar admission based on communist party membership); Bhd. of R.R. Trainmen v. Va. *ex rel.* Va. State Bar, 377 U.S. 1 (1964) (state may not prohibit union's referring members to lawyers); Goldfarb v. Va. State Bar, 421 U.S. 773 (1975) (lawyer minimum fee schedules violate federal antitrust law).

7. 371 U.S. 415 (1963).

8. VA. CODE ANN. § 54-78 (1950).

provision would have prohibited lawyers from cooperating with efforts to organize citizens to challenge racial segregation in the public schools.[9]

The state asserted that lawyers' attempts to obtain legal work are not speech protected by the First Amendment, but the Supreme Court brushed the argument aside. "[L]itigation is . . . a means for achieving the lawful objectives of equality of treatment . . . for the members of the Negro community in this country,"[10] Justice Brennan wrote for the Court. Whatever propriety the A.B.A. Canons and Virginia Rules had as applied to lawyers seeking pecuniary gain, in this context, lawyers' ethical standards enjoyed no immunity from constitutional review.[11]

Of course, *Button* was focused on a challenge to ethical standards that uniquely affected the vindication of civil rights, but the Supreme Court refused to limit it in that way when it decided *Brotherhood of Railway Trainmen v. Virginia ex rel. Virginia State Bar*[12] the very next year. In that case, the union had established a list of lawyers whom it encouraged railway employees or their survivors to consult about job-related deaths or injuries. These were ordinary damage actions from which lawyers sought the "pecuniary gain" found not to be present in *Button*. Union members had traditionally been the victims of incompetent lawyers and aggressive claims adjusters, the Court asserted. The union's program was not "ambulance-chasing," and the union was not itself practicing law; it was simply recommending that, before settling their cases, union members consult counsel whom the union had found to be competent. Use of ethical standards

---

9. Perhaps the Court found it relevant that the Virginia statute had been passed in 1956, just two years after *Brown v. Board of Education*, 347 U.S. 483 (1954), created the legal rights that the NAACP sought to enforce. However, the Court expressly said that it would have reached the same result if the older ABA Canons of Ethics had been the source of the prohibition. 371 U.S. at 429 n.11.

10. 371 U.S. at 429.

11. *Id.* at 439–43. It seems clear that the Court understood what it was doing. Indeed, a vigorous dissent by Justices Harlan, Clark, and Stewart reminded the majority that it had invaded "the domain of state regulatory power over the legal profession." *Id.* at 448–65.

12. 377 U.S. 1 (1964).

to bar such recommendations was held to violate First Amendment rights of both free speech and free association.[13]

The Vietnam War held the nation's attention in the late 1960s, and the legal profession largely slept through some of the early changes transforming its own future. In 1974, the nation was gripped by the unfolding story of Watergate and the fall of a presidential administration. A trial-like Senate hearing was conducted daily on television, and White House Counsel John Dean publicly asked how an administration filled with lawyers could have allowed the Watergate events to occur. In response to concerns about Watergate, the A.B.A. required all law schools—as a condition of their accreditation—to provide instruction in professional responsibility,[14] but the image of lawyers as simultaneously media stars and fallen angels was confirmed.

Even more significant in exposing the legal profession to regulation like that under which almost everyone else works was the Court's 1975 decision in *Goldfarb v. Virginia State Bar*.[15] When he tried to buy a house in Fairfax County, Virginia, Lewis Goldfarb discovered that all the lawyers he consulted proposed to charge him exactly the same fee. The legal issue became the validity of the minimum fee schedule recommended by the Fairfax County Bar Association, a voluntary bar, but one that was recognized by the Virginia State Bar, the group with disciplinary authority over the state's lawyers. Although compliance with the fee schedule was said not to be mandatory, the State Bar had opined that a lawyer's "habitual" failure to comply with a local fee schedule would "raise a presumption" that the lawyer was improperly soliciting cases.[16]

---

13. 377 U.S. at 5–6. Thereafter, in *United Mine Workers of America v. Illinois State Bar Association*, 389 U.S. 217 (1967), the Court gave constitutional protection to a union's practice of employing a salaried lawyer to represent members wanting to prosecute worker's compensation claims before the state's Industrial Commission. *United Transportation Union v. State Bar of Michigan*, 401 U.S. 576 (1971), then said that the Constitution required a state to permit a union to recommend selected lawyers to pursue suits under the Federal Employers' Liability Act and to secure a commitment from those lawyers not to charge a fee in excess of 25 percent of the amount recovered.

14. A.B.A. Standards for Approval of Law Schools, Standard 302(a)(5) and Interpretation 302–9 (2008).

15. 421 U.S. 773 (1975).

16. Va. State Bar Comm. on Legal Ethics, Op. No. 170 (1971).

Unlike the earlier cases, this time the Supreme Court was unanimous.[17] In an opinion by Chief Justice Burger, who later became a critic of "commercialization" of the legal profession, the Court found that the "voluntary" fee schedule had the practical effect of fixing prices for legal services in Fairfax County. More significantly for lawyers who thought themselves sheltered from outside regulation, the Court expressly rejected a contention that, as a "learned profession," the practice of law is not subject to antitrust constraints. "The nature of an occupation, standing alone, does not provide sanctuary from the Sherman Act," the Court said,

> nor is the public-service aspect of professional practice controlling in determining whether § 1 includes professions. . . . Whatever else it may be, the examination of a land title is a service; the exchange of such a service for money is "commerce" in the most common usage of that word. It is no disparagement of the practice of law as a profession to acknowledge that it has this business aspect.[18]

The combination of First Amendment and Sherman Act attacks made it inevitable that the idea that, as a profession, lawyers were self-regulating and thus need look only inward, was gone forever. The *coup de grace* was inflicted two years later in *Bates v. State Bar of Arizona.*[19] Once again, the case involved the prohibition of solicitation. This time, John Bates and Van O'Steen had opened a "legal clinic" in Phoenix and had published a newspaper advertisement describing routine services they would perform, such as uncontested divorces, adoptions, name changes, and simple personal bankruptcies

---

17. Justice Powell, long a member of the Virginia State Bar, did not participate in the decision.

18. 421 U.S. at 787–88. The Court closed: "In holding that certain anticompetitive conduct by lawyers is within the reach of the Sherman Act we intend no diminution of the authority of the State to regulate its professions." *Id.* at 793. However, that qualification has not reduced the significance of the decision. Just three years later, when an engineering association tried to rely on this language to justify its ethical restrain on competitive bidding, the Court quickly brushed aside the special character of professions. *See* Nat'l Soc'y of Prof'l Eng'rs v. United States, 453 U.S. 679 (1978). *See also* Ariz. v. Maricopa County Med. Soc'y, 457 U.S. 332 (1982) (fee schedule for particular doctor services violates antitrust laws).

19. 433 U.S. 350 (1977).

for relatively low fees.[20] The Court's response to arguments that professionalism required prohibition of such advertising was withering.

> We recognize, of course, and commend the spirit of public service with which the profession of law is practiced and to which it is dedicated . . . . But we find the postulated connection between advertising and the erosion of true professionalism to be severely strained. At its core, the argument presumes that attorneys must conceal from themselves and from their clients the real-life fact that lawyers earn their livelihood at the bar. We suspect that few attorneys engage in such self-deception . . . . In fact, it has been suggested that the failure of lawyers to advertise creates public disillusionment with the profession. The absence of advertising may be seen to reflect the profession's failure to reach out and serve the community.[21]

Next, bar associations traditionally have set up unauthorized practice of law committees whose responsibility has been to seek injunctions against those providing services that lawyers believed they alone were entitled to provide. Increasingly, the effectiveness of those efforts also has been reduced, in part because the cases are expensive to bring against well-financed adversaries. When the State Bar of Texas tried to enjoin accounting firm Arthur Andersen from

---

20. 433 U.S. at 354. Earlier, in 1972, Leonard Jacoby and Stephen Meyers had opened their own "legal clinic," but the Arizona courts acted more quickly than those in California, so the *Bates* case reached the Supreme Court first.

21. 433 U.S. at 368–70. "False, deceptive, or misleading" advertising may be regulated, and "limited" disclaimers may be required as to lawyer's claims about themselves. *Id.* at 383–84. However, "truthful advertisement concerning the availability and terms of routine legal services," is protected by the First Amendment. *Id.* at 384. Other cases upholding First Amendment protection of most lawyer advertising include *In re R.M.J.*, 455 U.S. 191 (1982); *Zauderer v. Office of Disciplinary Counsel*, 471 U.S. 626 (1985); *Shapero v. Ky. Bar Ass'n*, 486 U.S. 466 (1988); *Peel v. Attorney Registration & Disciplinary Comm'n*, 496 U.S. 91 (1990). *But see* Florida Bar v. Went For It, Inc., 515 U.S. 618 (1995) (upholding prohibition of targeted direct mail within thirty days of an accident or disaster). *Bates and O'Steen* had also challenged advertising restrictions under the Sherman Act. In this case, however, the Arizona Supreme Court had specifically imposed the bar to lawyer advertising in a court rule. Thus, under the rule of *Parker v. Brown*, 317 U.S. 341 (1943), federal antitrust law had to give way to the state regulation.

providing what were arguably legal services, for example, the Bar ultimately had to give up for lack of funds.[22]

Further, during this same period, until as late as almost 1970, discipline of errant lawyers was carried out largely by committees of other lawyers acting as volunteers. Perhaps not surprisingly, most of their attention was focused on violations of the rules against advertising and lawyer theft from clients, both offenses that are relatively easy to prove. In 1969, however, the A.B.A. adopted a new, detailed Model Code of Professional Responsibility to help states regulate lawyer conduct. The Model Code came out of confidential meetings of its drafting committee, so there was no public debate about its content; but when it came out described as a modern statement of enforceable disciplinary rules and aspirational ethical considerations, it swept the country. Indeed, most state supreme courts adopted it verbatim, without so much as a hearing or debate. The Clark Commission report in 1970 then proposed a professionalized system of lawyer discipline that has now replaced discipline by bar associations.[23]

Just fourteen years later, in 1983, the A.B.A. replaced the Model Code with the equally detailed Model Rules of Professional Conduct. The Model Rules also have been widely adopted by state supreme courts, although often with changes thought desirable by particular states. The Model Rules are required by A.B.A. law school accreditation standards to be at the heart of any discussion of lawyer ethical conduct, but it is the rules adopted by state supreme courts that impose actual lawyer regulation.[24]

---

22. When the State Bar of Texas tried to enjoin sale of a CD-ROM called Quicken Family Lawyer, the state legislature responded within a month with a statute declaring such sales to be legal. Unauthorized Practice of Law Comm. v. Parsons Tech., Inc., 179 F.3d 956 (5th Cir. 1999) (vacating injunction based on the new statute). After an earlier case, *State Bar of Arizona v. Arizona Land Title and Trust Co.*, 366 P.2d 1 (Ariz. 1961), the state of Arizona even amended its constitution to assure real estate brokers the right to fill in the blanks on a real estate sales contract. ARIZ. CONST., art. 26, § 1.

23. The report was A.B.A., PROBLEMS AND RECOMMENDATIONS IN DISCIPLINARY ENFORCEMENT (1970).

24. In 1992, the A.B.A. tried to regulate further the education of new lawyers when a task force called for every law school to develop ten prescribed skills and four prescribed values in each of its graduates. REPORT OF THE TASK FORCE ON LAW SCHOOLS AND THE PROFESSION: NARROWING THE GAP, LEGAL

In 1986, the American Law Institute—acknowledging that legal ethics is more about law than ethics—began to prepare the Restatement of the Law Governing Lawyers. At the same time, civil regulation of lawyers dramatically increased as malpractice suits against lawyers became more common. An important source of the move toward malpractice remedies was the failure of savings and loan associations in the 1980s, often after the mistaken advice of their lawyers that their loan practices were not in violation of federal regulations.[25] As a result of such cases, violation of ethical standards hit lawyers in the pocketbook, and malpractice insurance companies became some of the most important reviewers and regulators of lawyer conduct. In 2002–2003, the A.B.A. again modified the Model Rules, this time in part to conform them to the statements of governing principles found in the Restatement.[26] By now it is clear that the legal profession no longer exists in a protective bubble, and legal ethics is no longer the business of lawyers alone.[27]

EDUCATION AND PROFESSIONAL DEVELOPMENT–AN EDUCATIONAL CONTINUUM (1992). Robert MacCrate, a New York lawyer and former A.B.A. President, chaired the Task Force.

25. *See, e.g., In re* Am. Cont'l Corp./Lincoln Sav. & Loan Secs. Litig., 794 F. Supp. 1424 (D. Ariz. 1992).

26. For more on the similarities and differences between the Law Governing Lawyers Restatement and the Model Rules of Professional Conduct, *see* THOMAS D. MORGAN, LAWYER LAW: COMPARING THE ABA MODEL RULES OF PROFESSIONAL CONDUCT WITH THE ALI RESTATEMENT (THIRD) OF THE LAW GOVERNING LAWYERS (2005).

27. Additional Supreme Court cases consistent with this proposition include *In re Griffiths*, 413 U.S. 717 (1973) (requiring bar applicants to be U.S. citizens denies equal protection); *Supreme Court of N.H. v. Piper*, 470 U.S. 274 (1985) (requiring bar applicants to reside in state violates the privileges and immunities clause); *Supreme Court of Va. v. Friedman*, 487 U.S. 59 (1988) (only allowing state residents to be admitted "on motion," i.e., without taking a bar exam, also violates the privileges and immunities clause). On the other hand, some lower court decisions have upheld a few of the old restrictive rules, *e.g.,* Tolchin v. Supreme Court of N.J., 111 F.3d 1099 (3d Cir. 1997) (upholding requirement that licensed lawyer maintain an office in the state); Parnell v. Supreme Court of Appeals of W. Va., 110 F.3d 1077 (4th Cir. 1997) (upholding rule requiring a local lawyer to "sponsor" any applicant for pro hac vice admission).

B. THE DRAMATIC GROWTH IN THE NUMBER OF LAWYERS

It was not until 1963–1964 that law school enrollments equaled those immediately after World War II, but they have been growing ever since.[28] Many students choosing careers in the 1960s were probably moved by the courts' role in civil rights and were likely to have seen a career in law as a chance to make a difference in society. Legislatures were left behind as agents of social change. Courts and lawyers had become the key players, and the idea of a society without lawyers was long forgotten.

Over the last thirty-five years, the American bar has grown more rapidly and changed more profoundly than in any comparable-length period in history. Academic year 1972–73 was the year of the most dramatic growth in the number of U.S. law students. The number of students enrolled in law school in that year was approximately 30 percent of the total number of U.S. lawyers in the same year.[29] As a result, the total number of U.S. lawyers went on to double during the decade of the 1970s.[30] Growth in applications was in part from returning Vietnam war veterans, but the largest source of the increase could be attributed to a new interest in law school among women and members of minority groups—both of which had previously been greatly under-represented among lawyers.[31] Since the 1970s, student

---

28. NEW YORK STATE BAR ASS'N COMM. ON THE LAW GOVERNING FIRM STRUCTURE AND OPERATION, PRESERVING THE CORE VALUES OF THE AMERICAN LEGAL PROFESSION 7 (April 2000).

29. John C. York & Rosemary D. Hale, *Too Many Lawyers? The Legal Services Industry: Its Structure and Outlook*, 26 J. LEGAL EDUC. 1 (1973). In round numbers, there were just over 300,000 lawyers, and 100,000 students were in law school. Indeed, the authors were so alarmed by the growth that they predicted that "up to half of the graduates in the near future may have to seek employment in fields where traditionally legal training is not a prerequisite." *Id.* at 31.

30. The most carefully collected data on the legal profession remains BARBARA A. CURRAN, ET AL., THE LAWYER STATISTICAL REPORT: A STATISTICAL PROFILE OF THE U.S. LEGAL PROFESSION IN THE 1980S (1985), and BARBARA A. CURRAN & CLARA N. CARSON, THE LAWYER STATISTICAL REPORT: THE U.S. LEGAL PROFESSION IN THE 1990S (1994).

31. The data is analyzed in Richard L. Abel, *The Transformation of the American Legal Profession*, 20 LAW & SOC'Y REV. 7 (1986), and Barbara A.

interest in becoming lawyers has remained strong, and one effect has been an almost quadrupling of the size of the legal profession from about 300,000 in 1970 to almost 1,200,000 lawyers today.[32]

As a result, one inescapable reality facing today's lawyers is the greatly increased number of fellow lawyers chasing the same work.[33] The demand for lawyers has also increased, although not proportionately. University of Chicago economist Peter Pashigian convincingly showed that the most important stimulus for the need for legal services is not the growth in population or the degree of regulation, not the receptivity of courts to new legal theories, and indeed not anything internal to the legal system. Instead, demand for legal services correlates most closely with growth in Gross Domestic Product, the level of economic activity in the country generally.[34]

The nation's gross domestic product in constant dollars has grown at about the same rate as the number of lawyers in times of prosperity. The effect of recessions in the late 1970s, early 1990s, early 2000s, and now again in the late 2000s—while production of lawyers remained constant and high—has produced a significant "surplus"

Curran, *American Lawyers in the 1980s: A Profession in Transition*, 20 LAW & SOC'Y REV. 19 (1986). For reasons no one seems to have been able to explain fully, the number of white males in law school each year has remained almost constant since 1973.

32. At least this is the number of persons with active law licenses. A.B.A. *Nat'l Lawyer Population by State*, at http://www.abanet.org/marketresearch/2009_NATL_LAWYER_by_State.pdf. One of the chronic problems in determining the actual number of practicing lawyers is delayed data on lawyer deaths and retirements and the fact that even many people with law licenses are not practicing law.

33. *See, e.g.* BARBARA A. CURRAN & CLARA N. CARSON, THE LAWYER STATISTICAL REPORT: THE U.S. LEGAL PROFESSION IN THE 1990S (1994). Unfortunately, the American Bar Foundation has not continued to produce comparable data on the number and distribution of lawyers.

34. *See* B. Peter Pashigian, *The Market for Lawyers: The Determinants of the Demand for and Supply of Lawyers*, 20 J.L. & ECON. 53 (1977); B. Peter Pashigian, *The Number and Earnings of Lawyers: Some Recent Findings*, 1978 A.B.F. RES. J. 51 (1978); B. Peter Pashigian, *Regulation, Preventive Law, and the Duties of Attorneys, in* THE CHANGING ROLE OF THE CORPORATE ATTORNEY (William J. Carney ed., 1982).

of lawyers that understandably makes the pressure to continue to attract clients feel more intense today than it did forty years ago.[35]

Derek Bok issued his famous critique of the ubiquitous role of lawyers in 1983.

> The net result of these trends is a massive diversion of exceptional talent into pursuits that often add little to the growth of the economy, the pursuit of culture, or the enhancement of the human spirit. I cannot press this point too strongly . . . . [T]he supply of exceptional people is limited. Yet far too many of these rare individuals are becoming lawyers at a time when the country cries out for more talented business executives, more enlightened public servants, more inventive engineers, more able high-school principals and teachers.
>
> . . . A nation's values and problems are mirrored in the ways in which it uses its ablest people. In Japan, a country only half our size, 30 percent more engineers graduate each year than in all the United States. But Japan boasts a total of less than 15,000 lawyers, while American universities graduate 35,000 *every year*. It would be hard to claim that these differences have no practical consequences. As the Japanese put it, "Engineers make the pie grow larger; lawyers only decide how to carve it up."[36]

But despite President Bok's call for concern, lawyer growth has continued. Indeed, the Japanese have now copied the United States and expanded their law schools and numbers of licensed lawyers,

---

35. My own work in the mid-1990s to update the Pashigian numbers indicated that even by then, growth in the supply of lawyers was at least 15 percent greater than the growth in demand. Thomas D. Morgan, *Economic Reality Facing 21st Century Lawyers*, 69 WASH. L. REV. 625 (1994). In 2008–2009, for example, the number of lawyers increased by about 4 percent while the economy grew at a negative 3.5 percent rate and produced in that year alone, an additional almost 7.5 percent lawyer surplus. It is no wonder current lawyers are being laid off and new lawyers' jobs are being deferred.

Growth in numbers of lawyers this extensive and this rapid has also had an inevitable effect of reducing the level of informal sanctions that characterized earlier efforts to enforce appropriate—what used to be called "professional"—conduct. One is much more likely to treat a fellow lawyer well when one expects to meet that lawyer again, but the informal penalties for boorishness go down when the numbers of lawyers makes it less likely a pay-back time will ever come.

36. Derek C. Bok, *"A Flawed System": Report to the [Harvard] Board of Overseers*, 85 HARVARD MAGAZINE 38, 41 (May–June 1983).

rather than the other way around.[37] China and India similarly have encouraged their numbers of lawyers to grow in an effort to promote their economic growth.[38] England and other European nations have similarly increased their numbers of practitioners.

C. THE IMPACT OF GLOBALIZATION ON LAWYERS AND LAW PRACTICE

As the world's supply of lawyers grows, the world has been getting smaller and more interdependent. Using Thomas Friedman's metaphor, today the "world is flat."[39] It is not the presence of international exports and imports that is new; global merchants have been at work throughout history. What "globalization" describes is the unprecedented reduction of tariffs, the growth in the volume of international commerce, and the fact that imported products and exported work are no longer seen as exotic or special.[40]

---

37. *See, e.g.,* Setsuo Miyazawa, *The Politics of Judicial Reform in Japan: The Rule of Law at Last?, in* RAISING THE BAR: THE EMERGING LEGAL PROFESSION IN EAST ASIA 136–56 (William P. Alford ed., 2007); Yasuharu Nagashima, *The Changing Landscape of the International Practice of Law in Japan, in* THE INTERNATIONALIZATION OF THE PRACTICE OF LAW 151 (Jens Drolshammer & Michael Pfeifer eds., 2001).

38. *See, e.g.,* William P. Alford, *Of Lawyers Lost and Found: Searching for Legal Professionalism in the People's Republic of China, in* RAISING THE BAR: THE EMERGING LEGAL PROFESSION IN EAST ASIA 287–96 (William P. Alford ed., 2007).

39. THOMAS L. FRIEDMAN, THE WORLD IS FLAT: A BRIEF HISTORY OF THE TWENTY-FIRST CENTURY (2005). The book builds on THOMAS L. FRIEDMAN, THE LEXUS AND THE OLIVE TREE: UNDERSTANDING GLOBALIZATION (1999).

40. THOMAS L. FRIEDMAN, THE WORLD IS FLAT: A BRIEF HISTORY OF THE TWENTY-FIRST CENTURY 9–11 (2005). Friedman describes what he calls the "three great eras of globalization." Globalization 1.0, ran from 1492 to 1800 and involved fairly primitive trade. Globalization 2.0 ran from 1800 to 2000 and was characterized by the work of multinational corporations. The current period, Globalization 3.0, is characterized by an ability people have to collaborate without the obvious intervention of multinational entities. *See also* Martin Walker, *Globalization 3.0,* WILSON Q., Autumn 2007, at 16, 20 (dating the 3.0 period from China's accession to the WTO in 2002, the date after which, in the author's view, "the West can no longer set the rules for world trade").

It is a tautology to say that, when confronted with choices, people will select the option they prefer. In this context, the term "prefer" might be defined in several ways, but part of the preference will reflect a judgment of the relative costs of their options and the attractiveness of the results associated with each. In principle, a manufacturer could look where he lives for material suitable to make a product, for example. He could than manufacture the necessary parts himself, assemble the parts into the finished items, and personally search for a potential buyer. There are indeed fine artisans who still work that way, but ordinary products made by single individuals would tend to be so costly that few consumers could afford to buy them.

Instead, most manufacturers tend to buy material from whatever source seems to offer the best combination of price and quality. A Canadian firm might have material readily available, for example, and at close to the lowest price. The same price/quality inquiry would go into selecting someone to make the parts, and the Canadian firm might be asked to ship the material directly to a parts facility in Indonesia. The Indonesian-made parts might then be sent elsewhere for assembly—perhaps in Mexico—and the finished goods could then be sold to consumers through local dealers all over the world.

That hypothetical manufacturer's story is played out every day as the globalized world becomes reality. The transformation from local to global production and distribution has not been mandated by governments; it reflects the fact that individual producers and consumers are now able to make purchase and production decisions from a worldwide selection of choices rather than simply from the personal labor or local choices available to their grandparents. The move to globalization, in turn, is the result of at least three developments.

First is the fact of reduced legal barriers to trade. Governments may not have required globalization, but they have certainly facilitated it. Creation of the World Trade Organization and regional institutions such as NAFTA have led to reduction of trade barriers such as tariffs and subsidies that previously would have made the cost of purchasing globally much higher. Pursuant to such free trade regimes, countries have been limited in their ability to favor their own producers or to prevent their local consumers from buying products made abroad. Thus, transactions that in prior years might not have made economic sense because of burdens on international trade now take place in large numbers.

Second, globalization reflects the fact of lower-cost transactions and transportation. Container ships and cargo jets—and the equipment to load and service them—have dramatically lowered the cost of producing and purchasing from all over the world. As a result, manufacturers and other businesses now find it possible to pursue a "just in time" delivery policy and still get their parts and finished products from almost anywhere, trading off costs and benefits of speed as seems most beneficial for their own customers. Management consultant Tom Peters describes what has happened dramatically:

> [W]hen a timber ship pulled into [the London] docks in 1970, it took 108 guys some five days to unload it. That's 540 man days . . . . At about that time, something happened . . . called *"containerization."* Thirty years later, at the turn of the [21st] century . . . , when a timber ship pulled into the same docks in the same city . . . it took eight guys one day to unload it . . . . [T]he revolution that happened in Blue-Collar Work is coming soon in a slightly different costume to a white-collar profession near you.[41]

Third, globalization has brought parts of the world into the marketplace that were not significant players before and created new centers of economic influence.[42] China after World War II was largely closed economically; now it has over one billion citizens whom producers have overwhelming incentives to see as potential employees and customers. Some predictions say that "within 20 years the Chinese economy will surpass that of the United States, and in another 10 or 15 years after that India's economy will have outdone them both."[43]

Indeed, Russia, Brazil, India, Dubai—and even locations that used to be dismissed as the "third world"—are now becoming global economic players.

> In the grand sweep of history, the triumph of globalization has been one of the greatest achievements of the human race. The new world economy has quickly hauled hundreds of millions out of abject poverty. . . . They

---

41. TOM PETERS, REIMAGINE!: BUSINESS EXCELLENCE IN A DISRUPTIVE AGE 50 (2003). Peters quotes Jeff Immelt, CEO of General Electric, as saying that 75 percent of GE's "administrative and back-office jobs would be 'digitized' (accomplished by microprocessors and computer-telecom networks) within . . . 3 years."

42. FAREED ZAKARIA, THE POST-AMERICAN WORLD (2008).

43. Martin Walker, *Globalization 3.0*, WILSON Q., Autumn 2007, at 16.

can afford to have dreams as well as possessions and to think about the years to come with some confidence rather than dread.[44]

Sometimes, the wages paid workers there seem low to Americans, but they are enough to lift many countries' citizens out of extreme poverty.[45] Estimates are that as recently as 1985, the globalized economic world consisted of about 2.5 billion people, mostly living in North America, Europe, and Japan. Now, the integrated world economy is more like 6 billion people. Even focusing only on people educated to the level of most Americans, the number of potentially competing workers has about doubled.[46]

Not everyone views the trend toward globalization as benign. Some fear a race to the bottom in safety, environmental, and labor standards as countries compete to attract economic engines of possible business expansion.[47] Tainted dog food and lead-based paint on products from China have put experience behind the fears. Concern is also high that competitive pressure to attract business may cause states and nations to lure their people into dead-end jobs and even undercut the ability of democratic governments to promote

---

44. *Id.*

45. Joseph Stiglitz reminds us, however, that the benefits of globalization are not uniform in underdeveloped countries, and he criticizes policies of the World Bank and International Monetary Fund that lure countries into borrowing money they cannot pay back and adopting policies that he believes leave many of their citizens in poverty. JOSEPH E. STIGLITZ, GLOBALIZATION AND ITS DISCONTENTS 10–88 (2003).

46. THOMAS L. FRIEDMAN, THE WORLD IS FLAT: A BRIEF HISTORY OF THE TWENTY-FIRST CENTURY 182–83 (2005) (relying on a 2004 study by Harvard economist Richard Freeman). *See also* Martin Walker, *Globalization 3.0*, WILSON Q., Autumn 2007, at 16 (asserting that the United States will be a significant loser vis-à-vis China, India, and Europe in a globalized economy; "[t]he West no longer leads the world in capital accumulation and as a result no longer dominates global investment and finance." *Id.* at 19.).

47. *See, e.g.*, JOSEPH E. STIGLITZ, GLOBALIZATION AND ITS DISCONTENTS 85 (2003). ("Lower wages *might* lead some firms to hire a few more workers; but the number of newly hired workers may be relatively few, and the misery caused by the lower wages on all the other workers might be very grave."). *See also* GEORGE SOROS, GEORGE SOROS ON GLOBALIZATION (2002). For a contrary view, *see* Fareed Zakaria, *It's the Economy, Mr. President*, WASHINGTON POST, Nov. 20, 2006, at A17.

social justice.[48] The shaky capital markets experienced around the world in 2008 and 2009 have tended to confirm that bad credit practices in advanced countries can upset the lives of people throughout the rest of the world.[49]

An inevitable, and to many another negative, impact of globalization is that the markets in which lawyers and their clients now work produce a degree of competitive pressure unknown when markets were more narrow and balkanized. In a small town, people specialize in particular economic activities, but people know each other and have to get along in the long run, so intensity of competition in most fields is relatively low. Expand the area of competitive activity to a state or nation, and competitive pressures increase. But expand the arena to a world of millions of companies and billions of employees, and there is always someone ready to produce a better product for a lower price. There is no longer anywhere a lawyer or her clients may hide.

Economists argue persuasively that intense competition among producers will ultimately benefit consumers everywhere. In the meantime, however, lawyers' clients experience global competition in the form of an often excruciating need to control costs. Some call this the "Walmart effect" because it is seen so clearly in the pressure that Walmart puts on suppliers to lower their prices by wringing every last fraction of a cent out of costs.[50] Others look at businesses

---

48. A widely cited expression of these concerns in the context of suggesting that globalization is inevitable is MICHAEL HARDT & ANTONIO NEGRI, EMPIRE (2000). The authors use the term "empire" to describe a corporate world they see as unconstrained by the laws of nation-states, and they use the term "smooth" to describe what Friedman later called the "flat" world. *Id.* at xii–xiii. Professors Hardt and Negri followed EMPIRE with MULTITUDE: WAR AND DEMOCRACY IN THE AGE OF EMPIRE (2004). *See also* LAURENT COHEN-TANUGI, THE SHAPE OF THE WORLD TO COME: CHARTING THE GEOPOLITICS OF A NEW CENTURY (2008).

49. *See, e.g.,* JOSEPH E. STIGLITZ, GLOBALIZATION AND ITS DISCONTENTS (2003); DAVID M. SMICK, THE WORLD IS CURVED (2008).

50. *See, e.g.,* CHARLES FISHMAN, THE WAL-MART EFFECT (2006). Fishman tells the story of Walmart requiring producers of deodorant not to package the containers in boxes.

The nation has saved hundreds of millions of dollars since the deodorant box disappeared . . . [and] one billion deodorant boxes didn't end up in

that have laid off whole tiers of middle management and now use robots on the shop floor to do work once done by skilled craftsmen.[51]

The possibility of terrorist violence, issues about the availability of energy, and concerns about global warming and financial sluggishness all suggest that the rate of globalization may slow. Inevitably, it will be hard to predict the rate of globalization's spread. But the direction of the trend toward a "flat world" seems inevitable, if only because it is possible. Making the transition to participation in a global economy will be hard on many business owners and employees, but it will be necessary in order to keep many businesses alive at all.[52]

As should be obvious, lawyers who were trained in local law and licensed by state courts will not be able to ignore the effects of globalization on their own activities.[53] First, globalization will require

---

landfills each year. It's all unseen, all unnoticed, and all good. Unless, of course, you were in the paperboard box making business. . . . [For those manufacturers], those were rough times. *Id.* at 2. Walmart has now hired pharmacists, *id.* at 41–44, to run what at one time were independent professional facilities. Who is to say they might not try to have lawyers set up an office in a Walmart store?

51. Friedman quotes a friend as saying, "It is like they have cut all the fat out of business, but fat is what gives meat its taste. The leanest cuts of meat don't taste very good." THOMAS L. FRIEDMAN, THE WORLD IS FLAT: A BRIEF HISTORY OF THE TWENTY-FIRST CENTURY 220 (2005). Charles Fishman says the "Wal-Mart economy describes the nagging sense that there might be some unseen but terrible cost to be paid for 'always low prices.' The Wal-Mart economy is a place where the jobs are traps: low wages, miserly benefits, stultifying work, no respect, no future." CHARLES FISHMAN, THE WAL-MART EFFECT 9 (2006).

52. Professors Hardt and Negri note that labor and other input providers may appear to win wage concessions or other benefits, but in a world economy, the gains will be transitory and may even result in losses as capital moves toward lower-cost, less-regulatory parts of the world. MICHAEL HARDT & ANTONIO NEGRI, EMPIRE 252 (2000). But management consultant Tom Peters reports that while 44 million U.S. jobs were lost to globalization and change in general between 1980 and 1988, during the same period, the economy *created* 73 million new jobs, many of them well paying. The challenge for lawyers concerned about seeing their clients among those losing jobs is to help them also become among those who gain new and better jobs. TOM PETERS, REIMAGINE!: BUSINESS EXCELLENCE IN A DISRUPTIVE AGE 41 (2003).

53. As usual, Professor Laurel Terry is out in front in studying these developments. *E.g.*, Laurel S. Terry, *The Legal World is Flat: Globalization and Its*

lawyers to understand the legal principles that allow clients' international commerce to proceed. Indeed, a client engaged in e-commerce may do virtual business everywhere in the world simultaneously, and a lawyer who continues to focus only on what used to be important will neither serve her clients well nor retain her clients long. The day has come and gone when national borders—and *a fortiori* state borders—likely have any real significance in deciding how a transaction should be structured or a matter litigated.

Further, companies involved in global commerce hire or send employees all over the world. Those employees will create family relationship, taxation, and other financial issues that were largely unknown to previous generations of lawyers. No lawyer can be expert in all law everywhere, but even the drafter of a will today must assume that some of the beneficiaries or some of the property could be in other states or nations. Greenacre could as easily be in Sydney as in Syracuse, and lawyers will have to develop skill and imagination that reflects what the new complexity means for twenty-first century clients. Professional contacts—or law firm partners—around the world will be essential.

Finally, American lawyers' professional standards are likely to be affected by globalization as the General Agreement on Trade in Services (GATS) tends to break down barriers that today limit lawyers to practice in their home countries. GATS is not yet an accomplished fact, but the clear intention seems to be that French lawyers will be permitted to open a practice in the United States just as the European Union permits French lawyers to practice in Germany. When that happens, of course, it seems inevitable that a state such as California will have to also allow New York lawyers to open a practice in San Francisco.[54]

Effect on Lawyers Practicing in Non-Global Law Firms, 28 Nw. J. INT'L L. & BUS. 527 (2008).

54. For additional information, *see, e.g.*, Laurel S. Terry, *GATS' Applicability to Transnational Lawyering and its Potential Impact on U.S. State Regulation of Lawyers*, 34 VAND. J. TRANSNAT'L L. 989 (2001); Laurel S. Terry, *But What Will the WTO Disciplines Apply To?: Distinguishing Among Market Access, National Treatment and Article VI:4 Measures When Applying the GATS to Legal Services*, 2003 PROF. LAW. 83 (Symposium Issue 2004). *See also* Carol Silver, *Winners and Losers in the Globalization of Legal Services: Situating the Market for Foreign Lawyers*, 45 VA. J. INT'L L. 897 (2005) (discussing the increase in

That development, in turn, is magnified by changes occurring in lawyer regulation in other parts of the world. English lawyers, for example, have recently experienced the most radical changes in regulation in their careers. As a result of the Legal Services Act of 2007,[55] the number of activities that only a lawyer may do has been reduced,[56] a law firm may have non-lawyer investors,[57] and the lawyer-client privilege extends to communications with people who are not lawyers.[58] Australian law firms are permitted to become corporations that sell their stock to the general public, and at least one has done so.[59] The European Union is considering similar changes in lawyer regulation.[60] If American lawyers ignore the fact that their direct competitors play by different rules, they will have only themselves to blame when clients take advantage of these changes and seek the same or better professional services at lower cost elsewhere.

It would be a mistake, of course, to assume that globalization will occur equally rapidly in every line of commerce. "High-touch" personal services are likely to continue to be delivered locally. Part of the challenge in considering the impact of globalization on lawyers, then, will lie in distinguishing which lawyer roles are more like the making of machine parts and which require a local touch. Thomas Friedman says:

> [N]o matter what your profession—doctor, lawyer, architect, accountant—
> if you are an American, you better be good at the touchy-feely service stuff,

---

programs at U.S. law schools for foreign lawyers, many of whom hope to practice with U.S. firms).

55. Legal Services Act of 2007, 2007 Chapter 29.

56. Legal Services Act of 2007, 2007 Chapter 29, § 12.

57. Legal Services Act of 2007, 2007 Chapter 29, Schedule 13.

58. Legal Services Act of 2007, 2007 Chapter 29, § 190.

59. The law firm is Slater & Gordon, and its $35 million issue of shares began trading on the Australian Securities Exchange on May 21, 2007. *See, e.g.,* Andrew Grech & Kirsten Morrison, *Slater & Gordon: The Listing Experience,* 22 GEO. J. LEGAL ETHICS 535 (2009). The New South Wales legislation under which the firm incorporated is THE LEGAL PROFESSION ACT 2004, supplemented by the *Legal Profession Regulations 2005.*

60. Laurel S. Terry, *The European Commission Project Regarding Competition in Professional Services,* 29 NW. J. INT'L L. & BUS. 1 (2009).

because anything that can be digitized can be outsourced to either the smartest or the cheapest producer, or both.[61]

But the fact is that not all lawyer work is alike, and not all is high-touch. Indian accounting firms are already doing the tax returns of many Americans under subcontracts from U.S. accounting firms,[62] and outsourcing of legal work to India has also already begun.[63] Indeed, as Indian wages rise, we can expect white-collar work to be outsourced to even lower-wage areas. Again, Friedman puts this reality in his usual colorful way:

> There is no future for vanilla for most companies in a flat world . . . . For most companies, the commercial future belongs to those who know how to make the richest chocolate sauce, the sweetest, lightest whipped cream, and the juiciest cherries to sit on top, or how to put them all together in a sundae.[64]

That principle is as applicable to lawyers as it is to any other worker. American lawyers, law firms, and legal education will all experience a need to become known as among the best in the world—or at least in their part of the world—at some important, distinctive tasks.

D. MODERN INFORMATION TECHNOLOGY AND THE TRANSFORMATION OF LAWYERS' WORK

Another factor contributing to globalization—and accelerated by it—is the revolution in computer storage and communications

---

61. Thomas L. Friedman, The World is Flat: A Brief History of the Twenty-First Century 13–14 (2005).

62. *Id.* at 12–15 (2005).

63. *See, e.g.,* David Hechler, *When Your Patent Work Goes to India*, Legal Times, Jan. 19, 2009, at 19; Julie Kay, *India Work Grows, With Glitches*, Nat'l L.J., Dec. 8, 2008, at 1. The American Bar Association has discussed lawyers' obligations in outsourcing in its A.B.A. Comm. on Ethics and Prof'l Responsibility, Formal Op. 08-451 (Aug. 5, 2008) ("There is nothing unethical about a lawyer outsourcing legal and nonlegal services, provided the outsourcing lawyer renders legal services to the client with the 'legal knowledge, skill, thoroughness and preparation reasonably necessary for the representation,' as required by [Model] Rule 1.1.").

64. Thomas L. Friedman, The World is Flat: A Brief History of the Twenty-First Century 91 (2005).

technology that has occurred over roughly the same period as the rest of the revolution involving lawyers.[65] While world-spanning telephone cables have been around for over a century, it was in about 1980 that commercial satellites made large-scale, worldwide transmission of telephone and television signals relatively inexpensive.[66] The Internet, in turn, became a ubiquitous reality around 1995. Now, people of even modest means can call anywhere in the world on a wireless device, and we are close to a time when voice-over-Internet service will make communication nearly free.

The transformation of information technology has led to a variety of effects. First, in less than a decade, lawyers have gone from marketing their services locally through newspaper ads and Yellow Pages to global marketing on the worldwide Web. Some have chosen clever Web addresses such as "lawyersforless.net,"[67] "thegunslinger.com,"[68] and "voiceoftheinjured.com."[69] Others have created the Web-equivalent of attractive brochures with color pictures of the firm's lawyers and dramatic pictures of them in action. Each new article or speech by a firm lawyer can be transmitted to clients or potential clients to keep a lawyer's name constantly in the forefront of their awareness, and lawyers can broadly trumpet each new victory to a worldwide audience.

---

65. The leading analyst in this field is England's Richard Susskind. His most recent book is THE END OF LAWYERS?: RETHINKING THE NATURE OF LEGAL SERVICES (2008). Earlier works in the same spirit are RICHARD SUSSKIND, THE FUTURE OF LAW: FACING THE CHALLENGES OF INFORMATION TECHNOLOGY (1996), and RICHARD SUSSKIND, TRANSFORMING THE LAW (2000).

66. Professors Hardt & Negri argue that, far from improving the lot of working people, the availability of cheap and instantaneous communication simply makes it easier for employers to shift production to parts of the world where costs are lower. MICHAEL HARDT & ANTONIO NEGRI, EMPIRE 296–300 (2000).

67. The firm, based in Greenwich, Connecticut, is Lawyersforless.net, LLC. *See* http://lawyersforless.net/.

68. This is the office of Irvine, California, lawyer Steven R. Young. *See* http://www.thegunslinger.com/.

69. This is used by a Clearwater, Florida, law firm. *See* http://www.voiceoftheinjured.com/.

Second, lawyers—and non-lawyers—now have a capacity for legal research that is quick and current. There is no easy excuse for overlooking a new statute or recent case. Many lawyers still prefer to read law out of books, but almost no lawyers can afford to stock books about the law across the nation and around the world. Now, technological advances have put the world's largest library on every lawyer's desktop, albeit at a high price.[70] Reverence for the research methods of the past will not change the direction of this new reality.

Third, the capacity for data storage, retrieval, and analysis now available has caused lawyers to cast their net more widely during pretrial discovery and to manage larger and larger quantities of documents. Facts and the relationships among them that once would have required weeks or months to understand can now be identified almost instantaneously.[71] None of this technology is cheap, nor is the work involved in entering and retrieving it, but the payoffs can be substantial. The information can even be provided in multimedia form—a deposition can be circulated as a video file, for example, or in a transcript produced instantly by voice-recognition software.[72] Corresponding advances in projection technology make it possible for the dullest document to appear to a jury to leap from the page as if it were even better than a smoking gun.

Fourth, the new information technology has made a lawyer's world more hectic. A client-lawyer exchange that once took days or weeks now can be almost instantaneous, so lawyers are potentially always on call. "[T]he line between workplace and nonworkplace diminishes to the vanishing point, where the lawyer often cannot tell whether he is really at work or not, since he occupies a sort of netherworld between work/leisure and office/home."[73] Client needs that might

---

70. The principal suppliers are Westlaw (www.westlaw.com) and LexisNexis (www.lexisnexis.com).

71. *E.g.*, THE ECONOMIC PAYOFF FROM THE INTERNET REVOLUTION (Robert E. Litan & Alice M. Rivlin eds., 2001).

72. *See* RICHARD SUSSKIND, THE END OF LAWYERS?: RETHINKING THE NATURE OF LEGAL SERVICES 192–210 (2008); RICHARD SUSSKIND, THE FUTURE OF LAW: FACING THE CHALLENGES OF INFORMATION TECHNOLOGY xiii (1998).

73. DOUGLAS LITOWITZ, THE DESTRUCTION OF YOUNG LAWYERS: BEYOND ONE L 117 (2006). *See also* DEBORAH L. RHODE, IN THE INTERESTS OF JUSTICE: REFORMING THE LEGAL PROFESSION 29 (2000).

never have been perceived, except by chance, can now demand responses at what Bill Gates calls "the speed of thought."[74] A possible benefit may be that the ability to engage in virtual meetings could reduce the time lawyers spend in travel, but however all this plays out, once again, the technological developments cannot be undone by sentimental calls for a return to lawyers' golden age.

Fifth, and in the long run most important, information technology promises to transform lawyer work that used to be seen as complex, unique, and worthy of substantial fees into a series of "commodites"— simple, repetitive operations that will be provided to clients by the lowest bidder.[75] Technology available on the simplest personal computer today can allow a lawyer to copy a 100-page document used in one transaction and change the names and terms for use in the next. Obviously, the result will be a disaster if the document is not equally relevant to the new situation, so the malpractice risk created by the ease of copying can be substantial.[76] Knowing what changes are needed to fit a new situation will always be a big part of the professional's service, but the benefits of standardizing forms in transactions promises to be enormous.

---

74. BILL GATES, BUSINESS @ THE SPEED OF THOUGHT: SUCCEEDING IN THE DIGITAL ECONOMY (1999). At the same time, however, the capacity to store information means that there will inevitably be more information available to evaluate. Lawyers are likely to find this technology, then, both a blessing and a curse.

75. RICHARD SUSSKIND, THE END OF LAWYERS?: RETHINKING THE NATURE OF LEGAL SERVICES 27–57 (2008). See also the remarks of Michael Harnish, a law firm Chief Information Officer, in GARY A. MUNNEKE, CONFERENCE INSIGHTS: SEIZE THE FUTURE: FORECASTING AND INFLUENCING THE FUTURE OF THE LEGAL PROFESSION 30–31 (1999).

76. See, e.g., Andrew Beckerman-Rodau, Ethical Risks From the Use of Technology, 31 RUTGERS COMPUTER & TECH. L.J. 1 (2004); Catherine J. Lanctot, Attorney-Client Relationships in Cyberspace: The Peril and the Promise, 49 DUKE L.J. 147 (1999); Natacha D. Steimer, Cyberlaw: Legal Malpractice in the Age of Online Lawyers, 63 GEO. WASH. L. REV. 332 (1995). A form of liability sometimes overlooked may be copyright infringement. See, e.g., Davida H. Isaacs, The Highest Form of Flattery? Application of the Fair Use Defense Against Copyright Claims for Unauthorized Appropriation of Litigation Documents, 71 MO. L. REV. 391 (2006).

The transformation of standardization from a shortcut to a virtue probably began in the real estate industry with the development of the standard form real estate contract. Professor Ahdieh explains the benefits of the use of standard or "boilerplate" terms: "Contrary to the rhetoric sometimes used to describe bargaining, the ultimate goal is not to win but to agree."[77] Standard provisions reduce transaction costs without eliminating the possibility of negotiating something different. Depending on the standard clauses proposed, parties can seek advantage but minimize misunderstanding because boilerplate terms are "focal points" that have meanings parties know from prior experience. In bargaining, even small departures from boilerplate terms can make agreement more difficult as the "changes raise the question, 'Why?'"[78]

Similarly, the increased use of forms can help assure that the drafter will not forget important provisions such as those necessary for desirable tax treatment.[79] Form commercial documents can also provide increased security that representations and warranties are those regularly expected in commercial transactions.[80] Even in litigation, form complaints can help assure that each element of a claim has been properly pled. But the result of document standardization is that it is now an open secret that an increasing amount of what lawyers do is no longer a complex task requiring expertise worthy of premium pay. Much of what lawyers do is what most merchants do, i.e., sell commodities that ultimately command only a price set in competition with many potential sellers.[81]

Sixth, and in some ways most frustrating for lawyers, is the fact that much of the information lawyers have traditionally sold is now freely available on the Internet. Books about law have been around

---

77. Robert B. Ahdieh, *The Strategy of Boilerplate*, 104 MICH. L. REV. 1033, 1036 (2006).

78. *Id.* at 1046.

79. There are a number of Web sites that offer legal documents, some with additional services and some without. *See, e.g.*, legalzoom.com, uslegal-forms.com, legaldocs.com, and lawdepot.com.

80. The parties communicating need not be lawyer and client. Deal rooms, for example, allow multiple participants—even on opposing sides of a transaction—to propose edits for documents in real time.

81. *See, e.g.*, RICHARD SUSSKIND, THE END OF LAWYERS?: RETHINKING THE NATURE OF LEGAL SERVICES 27–33, 100–05 (2008).

for years, but technology now makes the information ubiquitous.[82] It may be provided free at Web sites ranging from Wikipedia to specialized blogs, and the effect is to render a great deal of formerly exotic legal information broadly accessible.[83] Prepared by thousands of authors, these alternative information sources threaten the knowledge monopoly on which lawyers have depended for a steady client base.[84] Clearly, lawyers will tend to be able to assimilate and apply information from these sources more quickly and accurately than many clients can, but the breakthrough is that a lawyer's knowledge is no longer a black box that clients cannot penetrate.[85]

Information may be provided in a form available to all or only to those who have directly or indirectly paid a fee for the access. So far, the free or open-source approach has been much more pervasive than most Americans might have imagined. What would make people provide valuable information to the world at no cost? Probably part of the motivation is public service and a desire to educate others, but at least another part of the motivation may be the potentially considerable rewards of personal publicity and the benefits of peer review that come when other contributors point out flaws in an original idea.[86] Whether free or not, however, ubiquitous help from information

---

82. *Id.* at 69–93.

83. For more about this phenomenon, *see* ORI BRAFMAN & ROD A. BECKSTROM, THE STARFISH AND THE SPIDER: THE UNSTOPPABLE POWER OF LEADERLESS ORGANIZATIONS (2006).

84. *See, e.g.,* DON TAPSCOTT & ANTHONY D. WILLIAMS, WIKINOMICS: HOW MASS COLLABORATION CHANGES EVERYTHING 11 (2006) ("credentialed knowledge producers share the stage with 'amateur' creators who are disrupting every activity they touch"); CASS R. SUNSTEIN, INFOTOPIA: HOW MANY MINDS PRODUCE KNOWLEDGE 156–60 (2006).

85. Management consultant Tom Peters quotes Michael Lewis as saying, "Parents, bosses, stockbrokers, even military leaders are starting to lose the authority they once had. . . . There are all these roles that are premised on access to privileged information. What we are witnessing is a collapse of that advantage, prestige and authority." TOM PETERS, REIMAGINE!: BUSINESS EXCELLENCE IN A DISRUPTIVE AGE 67 (2003).

86. *See, e.g.,* DON TAPSCOTT & ANTHONY D. WILLIAMS, WIKINOMICS: HOW MASS COLLABORATION CHANGES EVERYTHING 11 (2006) (four major principles underlie these developments: "openness, peering, sharing, and acting globally"); THOMAS L. FRIEDMAN, THE WORLD IS FLAT: A BRIEF HISTORY OF THE TWENTY-FIRST CENTURY 83 (2005).

services increasingly will be available to individuals planning their own affairs, drafting their own documents, and even appearing pro se in litigation, just as software helps millions of former accounting clients prepare their own tax returns.

Up to now, lawyer responses to such developments have largely been self-defeating. In Texas, an unauthorized practice of law challenge was brought against sale of the Quicken Family Lawyer CD-ROM for use by people trying to draft their own legal documents.[87] From the standpoint of lawyers, use of such tools might seem amateurish and risky, but to many potential clients, the cost-saving seems sensible. Notwithstanding lawyer views, the Texas legislature promptly took the side of client freedom and made clear that the sale or use of such computer software does not involve the unauthorized practice of law.[88] Clients' desire to avoid lawyer services might bother lawyers, but that desire is a reality lawyers ignore at their peril.[89]

Pressure will be substantial to replace lawyers with people who can quickly help clients find what they need on the Internet and, at most, review a filled-in form before it is filed.[90] As the example

---

87. The case was *Unauthorized Practice of Law Committee v. Parsons Technology, Inc.*, No. 99-10388,1999 WL 47235 (N.D. Tex. 1999), vacated and remanded, 179 F.3d 956 (5th Cir. 1999).

88. The case is discussed in THOMAS D. MORGAN AND RONALD D. ROTUNDA, PROBLEMS AND MATERIALS ON PROFESSIONAL RESPONSIBILITY, at 622 (10th ed. 2008).

89. The A.B.A.'s usual response is consistent with what Alvin Toffler calls "obsessive reversion" in the face of rapid change

> to previously successful adaptive routines that are now irrelevant and inappropriate. The Reversionist sticks to his previously programmed decisions and habits with dogmatic desperation. The more change threatens from without, the more meticulously he repeats past modes of action. . . . Shocked by the arrival of the future, he offers hysterical support for the not-so-status quo, or he demands, in one masked form or another, a return to the glories of yesteryear.

ALVIN TOFFLER, FUTURE SHOCK 320 (1970).

90. The role is sometimes called an "infomediary." *See also* remarks of John Landry, Vice President of IBM, in GARY A. MUNNEKE, CONFERENCE INSIGHTS: SEIZE THE FUTURE: FORECASTING AND INFLUENCING THE FUTURE OF THE LEGAL PROFESSION 27 (1999). The process is analogous to what is called "disintermediation" in financial markets, i.e., the ability to skip whole tiers of intermediaries who had been able to control access to important information.

illustrates, even where the need for lawyers is not replaced by free information, the character of legal services is likely to change. Rather than retaining a lawyer to take a matter from beginning to end, clients are likely to buy only parts of a traditional representation—reviewing a complaint rather than drafting it, for example, or trying a case for which others have done most of the discovery. Disaggregating legal services in this way is likely often to be in the client's interest, and lawyers will have to consider responding accordingly.[91]

In any event, whether the client is a corporation or an individual, clients can be expected to seek assistance from multiple sources ready to provide them using publicly available information rather than the proprietary form created and sold by lawyers alone. Clients ultimately will do what they conclude is in their interest, but the opportunities created by the ubiquitous availability of technology will irreversibly transform those client opportunities.

Finally, and closer to science fiction, the world may not be far from future development of "expert systems" that can begin to do even basic legal reasoning and analysis. For as long as computers are restricted to dealing with language rather than abstracts concepts, human beings are likely to be better at discerning patterns in apparently disparate information. There seems little doubt, however, that in areas of the law where words are regularly used in patterns, expert systems may indeed be possible and may once again reduce the need for live lawyers.[92] The "golden age" for lawyers truly is no more.

See, e.g., James W. Jones & Bayless Manning, *Getting at the Root of Core Values: A "Radical" Proposal to Extend the Model Rules to Changing Forms of Law Practice*, 84 MINN. L. REV. 1159, 1181–82 (2000).

91. See, e.g., remarks of Michael Harnish, a law firm Chief Information Officer, *in* GARY A. MUNNEKE, CONFERENCE INSIGHTS: SEIZE THE FUTURE: FORECASTING AND INFLUENCING THE FUTURE OF THE LEGAL PROFESSION 30–31 (1999); DON TAPSCOTT & ANTHONY D. WILLIAMS, WIKINOMICS: HOW MASS COLLABORATION CHANGES EVERYTHING 97–108 (2006). Others, however, suggest that professionals bring practical judgment to a question that unfortunately will be consistently undervalued in such a process. WILLIAM F. MAY, BELEAGUERED RULERS: THE PUBLIC OBLIGATION OF THE PROFESSIONAL 45–49 (2001); ANTHONY T. KRONMAN, THE LOST LAWYER: FAILING IDEALS OF THE LEGAL PROFESSION (1993).

92. This is an important message of RICHARD SUSSKIND, TRANSFORMING THE LAW: ESSAYS ON TECHNOLOGY, JUSTICE AND THE LEGAL MARKETPLACE

E. THE GROWTH OF LAW FIRMS AS PREMIER PRACTICE ORGANIZATIONS

So far in this chapter, we have looked at four changes wrought in an American lawyer's life by an expansion in the number of lawyers, the prohibition of many anti-competitive professional practices, the globalization of lawyer work, and the transformation of that work by new forms of information technology. Next we look at four more ways that changes in the way lawyers work and the way clients seek legal help have changed the American lawyer's life.

Many people's mental picture of a lawyer may be that of a single individual in court at a client's side. For several hundred years, that picture was fairly accurate. Traditionally, lawyers saw themselves as independent, even lonely. Each had personal clients, and each was personally accountable for his or her own conduct. Until recently, for example, English barristers could work out of the same office, or "chambers," but none could be a partner of another barrister, not even one who was a member of his or her chambers.

American lawyers have never been similarly prohibited from forming firms, but throughout most of the country's history, firms tended to think relatively small.[93] As recently as 1960, fewer than forty U.S. law firms had more than fifty lawyers each.[94] In 1968, only

---

161–220 (2000). Project eLISA, for example, is described as an IBM program on artificial intelligence that aims to help machines learn and reason in much the same way lawyers reason, i.e., to figure out which facts are important. TOM PETERS, REIMAGINE!: BUSINESS EXCELLENCE IN A DISRUPTIVE AGE 53 (2003).

93. Until fairly recently, over half of all American lawyers practiced as solo practitioners or in small groups that shared expenses but did not otherwise operate as a firm. In a million-person profession, the number of solo practitioners remains significant in absolute terms, but their proportion of the profession has fallen to well below 50 percent. CARROLL SERON, THE BUSINESS OF PRACTICING LAW: THE WORK LIVES OF SOLO AND SMALL FIRM ATTORNEYS 4–6 (1996).

94. MARC GALANTER & THOMAS PALAY, TOURNAMENT OF LAWYERS: THE TRANSFORMATION OF THE BIG LAW FIRM 22 (1991). See also Marc Galanter & Thomas Palay, Why the Big Get Bigger: The Promotion-to-Partner Tournament and the Growth of Large Law Firms, 76 VA. L. REV. 747, 749 (1990).

twenty firms had over one hundred lawyers.[95] Richard Abel reports that "[b]etween 1975 and 1987, the number of firms with at least 100 lawyers multiplied more than fivefold (from 47 to 245) and the number of lawyers in those firms grew nearly eightfold (from 6558 to 51,581)."[96]

Many of the large firms were in New York, and most had adopted the so-called "Cravath model" of organization. The firms had relatively few partners but many associates who hoped to become partners.[97] At any given time, an associate tended to do most of his work for a particular partner, but assignments changed and associates tended to get experience in several areas of the firm. On average during the 1960s, New York firms made partnership decisions around the eighth or ninth year.[98] Lawyers recorded the number of hours they worked on a matter, but firms tended to use the reports to compare the diligence of individual lawyers and not as an exclusive basis for billing clients.

Most firms had a managing partner, typically along with an executive committee, although the actual authority of management varied among firms.[99] Some firms hired non-lawyer managers to handle routine administrative tasks. Large firms outside New York had many of the same characteristics, although the pace was slower, the clients less powerful, and the chances of making partner were greater.[100]

---

95. ROBERT L. NELSON, PARTNERS WITH POWER: THE SOCIAL TRANSFORMATION OF THE LARGE LAW FIRM 2 (1988) (citing ERWIN SMIGEL, THE WALL STREET LAWYER 358–59 (1969)).

96. RICHARD L. ABEL, AMERICAN LAWYERS 9–10 (1989).

97. See, e.g., JEROLD S. AUERBACH, UNEQUAL JUSTICE: LAWYERS AND SOCIAL CHANGE IN AMERICA 22–26 (1976); MARC GALANTER & THOMAS PALAY, TOURNAMENT OF LAWYERS: THE TRANSFORMATION OF THE BIG LAW FIRM 9–19 (1991).

98. ERWIN O. SMIGEL, THE WALL STREET LAWYER: PROFESSIONAL ORGANIZATION MAN? 92–93 (1964). Professor Charles Reich has written a charming personal account of life at the Cravath firm in the 1950s. See N.Y. LAWYER, Dec. 17, 2007, published at http://www.nylawyer.com/display.php/file=/news/07/12/121707f.

99. Id. at 237–50.

100. Id. at 183–89. The Cravath model spread beyond New York, and about this same time, the "national" law firm was born. A young Omaha lawyer named Robert J. Kutak recognized that local government agencies all

As late as 1988, only one firm, the worldwide Baker & McKenzie, had as many as 1,000 lawyers,[101] but even then, Robert Nelson could write confidently that "[t]he large law firm sits atop the pyramid of prestige and power within the American legal profession."[102] And whatever firms might say about their collegial aspirations, power, both within and outside New York, rested with lawyers who brought in the business clients.[103]

By 2006, Baker & McKenzie had over 3,500 lawyers, DLA Piper had over 3,300, and a total of twenty firms had crossed the 1,000-lawyer mark.[104] In 2008, thirteen U.S. law firms had gross revenues exceeding $1 billion, and fifty-eight firms had revenue exceeding $500 million.[105] In 2008, revenue per lawyer at sixty-one of the largest 100 American law firms exceeded $750,000.[106]

But size is not an unmixed blessing. At least two-thirds of American lawyers now practice in firms and other organizations, many of which have become less collegial and more bureaucratic.[107] Growth of the modern law firm was largely unplanned, and for some, it has been unwelcome. Frequently, it has been described as law's transition from a profession to a business, but the process has been more complex than that, and the law/business labels are not alternatives.

At bottom, of course, the source of the movement toward large-firm practice has been financial. Large-firm lawyers have long prospered, and now they prosper even more. Only half of all American lawyers earn more than about $115,000 per year; but until recently,

---

over the country were issuing securities to fund local projects. He focused his firm's work on responding to that specialized need, and the Kutak Rock firm opened offices in Denver, Atlanta, Washington, D.C., and elsewhere so as to have lawyers physically close to the demand. Other firms soon followed.

101. The NLJ 250, NAT'L L.J., Sept. 26, 1988, at S-4.

102. ROBERT L. NELSON, PARTNERS WITH POWER: THE SOCIAL TRANSFORMATION OF THE LARGE LAW FIRM 1 (1988). Dr. Nelson is currently Director of the American Bar Foundation.

103. ERWIN O. SMIGEL, THE WALL STREET LAWYER: PROFESSIONAL ORGANIZATION MAN? 200–02 (1964).

104. The NLJ 250, NAT'L L.J., Nov. 13, 2006, at S-18.

105. The AM LAW 100, AM. LAW., May 2009, at 151–52.

106. The AM LAW 100, AM. LAW., May 2009, at 159–60.

107. ROBERT L. NELSON, PARTNERS WITH POWER: THE SOCIAL TRANSFORMATION OF THE LARGE LAW FIRM 4 (1988).

graduates with the best records at top law schools were paid $160,000 or more per year at large firms right out of law school with no experience. By definition, half of American lawyers earn less than the median $115,000 per year, some after many years' experience, and starting salaries at firms are down, but at many big-city firms, average partner income still exceeds $1 million per year.[108]

1. How Lawyers Charge for Their Services

"A lawyer's time and advice are his stock in trade."[109] Abraham Lincoln's pithy insight remains the way lawyers have traditionally thought about the services they deliver. Unlike merchants who sell physical items, a lawyer's "product" has traditionally consisted of advice and litigation that take time during which the lawyer cannot also work on the problems of others.

It is a commonplace of economics that a person will not pay more for a service than the person believes it is worth. For example, unless a very important principle is at stake, no one will pay a lawyer a hundred dollars to litigate a dispute concerning ten dollars. The problem in choosing a billing methodology, then, has been to help the client both know what it will pay and monitor the service the client is receiving, while at the same time assuring lawyers that they will be fairly compensated for their work.

a. **Fixed Fees** Traditionally, legal services were sold at fixed fees that reflected uncomplicated tasks and relatively clear value. Thus, drafting a will might involve adapting a form to incorporate the client's information, and the client would be charged $100. An uncomplicated adoption would take a little longer because a court visit would be involved, but the time could be predicted and the job might be priced at $500. Defense of a drunk driving charge might require more experience and courtroom time, but lawyers could set a fee of $1,000 that clients would gladly pay to reduce the chance of serving time in jail.

Indeed, for many years, "going rates" were sufficiently well known that they were incorporated into schedules published by local bar associations. However, it was widely assumed that greater competition

---

108. The AM LAW 100, Am. Law., May 2009, at 177.

109. Fred Shapiro, ed., Oxford Dictionary of American Legal Quotations 257 (1993).

would both lower fees and make legal services available to a wider range of clients. As noted earlier, the Supreme Court declared that minimum fee schedules violate the antitrust laws,[110] and widespread use of fixed fees went out of favor at about the same time.

b. Fixed Retainers For many years, corporations and wealthy families were often billed the ultimate kind of fixed fee—an annual retainer to cover all the work they would require during a year. Such arrangements yoked lawyer and client in a way that required mutual loyalty.[111] If the client went elsewhere for a given service, the client would bear the cost because it had already paid its regular lawyer's retainer. Similarly, the law firm had a lot riding on providing good service. A client that was dissatisfied this year could pay the often-substantial retainer to another lawyer in the future. Obviously, fixed annual retainers only make sense if both lawyer and client can accurately predict workload and if a single law firm can meet all the client's need for services. As the complexity of modern life has increased, and as clients have preferred to give parts of their legal work to several different firms, the predictability of the workload has declined sharply. Thus, the use of fixed annual retainers has now largely disappeared, at least in large firm practice.

c. Hourly Rate Billing At least in part because of uncertainty about the work involved to resolve complex matters, lawyers and clients have moved to the system of hourly-rate billing that has dominated most areas of practice in recent years. Every business deal is a little different and will turn on the unique needs and personalities of the principals on each side. Every damage claim against a client will involve a different incident than the client's last claim. Indeed, effects of the same incident on different people will be different. The time it

---

110. The case was *Goldfarb v. Virginia State Bar*, 421 U.S. 773 (1975).

111. Sol Linowitz recalled the days when clients had law firms on retainer to do all their work for an overall fee. *See* Sol M. Linowitz with Martin Mayer, The Betrayed Profession: Lawyering at the End of the Twentieth Century 94–100 (1994). Linowitz also discusses an effort by future Supreme Court Justice John M. Harlan to break the system of lockstep pay progression and to get paid more than his colleagues at Cleary Gottlieb. *Id.* at 102–04 (1994). Similar concern about the transformation of the modern law firm are expressed in Michael H. Trotter, Profit and the Practice of Law: What's Happened to the Legal Profession (1997).

takes to resolve each matter successfully has been seen as arguably a reasonable measure of how much value the lawyer's services contributed to the solution.

Furthermore, in many cases, billing by the hour has been instituted by clients who want to be able to monitor what the lawyer did and determine how complex a matter really was. Such clients have been willing to take the risk that a matter would be more difficult and costly than average in exchange for the reward of a lower fee in an easy case. In addition, the requirement of detailed bills promised clients a way to verify how the law firm was staffing the case and whether its handling of the case had been inefficient.

What proponents of hourly rate fees tended to ignore, of course, is that a lawyer paid by the hour has little incentive to bring a matter to a close. In the name of quality representation, the lawyer has every incentive to research every point thoroughly and pursue every factual lead no matter what its value.[112] Indeed, when such research can be done by young lawyers for whom every task is a new experience, a firm paid by the hour has an incentive to staff the matter with lawyers who will benefit from getting an education at the client's expense. Worse yet, because the client has no real way to verify a lawyer's self-reporting of hours, there is always a real possibility that some of the reported hours will be falsified.[113]

d. Percentage and Contingent Fees The challenge of writing a simple will might not vary much from client to client, but the work involved in administering a large estate is likely to be greater than the work required to administer a small one. To moderate the incentive to do time-consuming but unproductive work under an hourly-rate system, a different step away from the use of a fixed fee or retainer

---

112. *See, e.g.*, RALPH NADER & WESLEY J. SMITH, NO CONTEST: CORPORATE LAWYERS AND THE PERVERSION OF JUSTICE IN AMERICA 232–55 (1996); George B. Shepherd & Morgan Cloud, *Time and Money: Discovery Leads to Hourly Billing*, 1999 U. ILL. L. REV. 91.

113. There is a substantial literature on dishonest reporting of hours worked, *e.g.*, WILLIAM G. ROSS, THE HONEST HOUR: THE ETHICS OF TIME-BASED BILLING BY ATTORNEYS (1996); Lisa Lerman, *Unethical Billing Practices*, 50 RUTGERS L. REV. 2151 (1998); Lisa Lerman, *Lying to Clients*, 138 U. PENN. L. REV. 659 (1990); Nathan Koppel, *Lawyer's Charge Opens Window on Bill Padding*, WALL ST. J., Aug. 30, 2006, at B-1.

was the percentage fee, under which the lawyer charged a portion of the value of the matter at issue. It did not take clients long to realize, however, that while working on a large estate or closing a high-value transaction would require more work than would be required for a smaller one, a percentage fee tends to overcompensate the lawyer for the difference in effort. Multiplying the value of a client's deal by ten does not normally require ten times the work or justify a ten-fold increase in the fee.

But what if fees could measure results instead of simply the lawyer's effort? Suppose a combination of the lawyer's brains and effort actually increased the value to the client of the lawyer's work? Add the promise that, if there were no such increased value, the client would owe the lawyer nothing, and surely the client would be happy to pay the lawyer a portion of the value the lawyer added. From that logic was born the contingent fee, one of the most common ways that lawyers now charge in personal injury litigation and increasingly for commercial litigation as well.[114]

But contingent fees have also been controversial. First, when a lawyer becomes an investor in the client's case, the argument goes, the lawyer may be tempted to press an untenable claim. That argument is weakened, of course, by the fact that the lawyer will get paid only if the client wins. If a claim is obviously baseless, the lawyer will take nothing, a result that will certainly not create an incentive to file false claims. Given a defendant's incentive to settle even a bad case to save the costs of litigation, however, the argument may have more force than first appears.

A second concern about contingent fees is the same as about percentage fees. A person who suffers permanent brain injury, for example, or who loses an arm or leg, is likely to recover a substantial judgment no matter what lawyer is involved. It does not take a great advocate to represent a client with such horrific injuries that a jury can understand them without help. Charging a uniform percentage of the judgment, no matter what the inherent value of the case, almost certainly tends to give excessive rewards to lawyers in horrific injury, but

---

114. Even English courts, once suspicious about contingent fees, have now come around and permit such fees.

otherwise simple, matters.[115] On the other hand, there is usually no way to be sure what the client would have received without a lawyer's help. From almost any perspective, use of the contingent fee as a way of rewarding a lawyer for value added necessarily is no more than an ideal.

2. The Matter of Leverage

Whatever system of billing is chosen, a key part of today's law firm business model—and the source of most high partner income—is the principle of "leverage." Assume, for example, that a young lawyer is paid $160,000 per year.[116] Imagine that the lawyer is expected to bill about 1,600 hours per year.[117] Imagine that her firm charges $175 per hour for her services and expends $160,000 in overhead, over and above her salary, to make her productive. That lawyer's firm will lose money on her work. Billing 1,600 hours at $175 per hour will produce revenue of $280,000 per year. On the other hand, the firm's assumed out-of-pocket expenditures on this lawyer total $320,000.

A $25 per hour rate increase to $200 per hour would produce an extra $40,000 annually and reach the break-even point, but if raising rates were that easy, the firm would likely have done so earlier. Increasing the number of hours the firm requires the lawyer to bill,

---

115. There is a substantial literature on contingent fees, *e.g.*, LESTER BRICKMAN, MICHAEL HOROWITZ & JEFFREY O'CONNELL, RETHINKING CONTINGENCY FEES: A PROPOSAL TO ALIGN THE CONTINGENCY FEE SYSTEM WITH ITS POLICY ROOTS AND ETHICAL MANDATES (1994); Marc Galanter, *Anyone Can Fall Down a Manhole: The Contingency Fee and Its Discontents*, 47 DEPAUL L. REV. 457 (1998); John F. Grady, *Some Ethical Questions About Percentage Fees*, 2 LITIGATION 20 (Summer 1976); Herbert M. Kritzer, *The Wages of Risk: The Returns of Contingency Fee Legal Practice*, 47 DEPAUL L. REV. 267 (1998); Herbert M. Kritzer, *Seven Dogged Myths Concerning Contingency Fees*, 80 WASH. U. L. Q. 739 (2002); Peter Melamed, *An Alternative to the Contingent Fee?: An Assessment of the Incentive Effects of the English Conditional Fee Arrangement*, 27 CARDOZO L. REV. 2433 (2006); Robert H. Mnookin, *Negotiation, Settlement and the Contingent Fee*, 47 DEPAUL L. REV. 363 (1998).

116. That may seem high to the average American, but if the lawyer bills 2,000 hours per year, as many do, it comes to $80 per hour—less than the pay of many plumbers and computer technicians.

117. A decision to require billing 1,600 hours per year is itself a big step for a law firm. Remember that in Chapter 2, we saw that the A.B.A. in the 1950s assumed that lawyers could not honestly bill more than 1,300 hours annually.

on the other hand, does not require client acquiescence, and requiring annual billings of 2,000 hours in our example would increase the revenue produced by the lawyer to $350,000 per year even if her billing rate stayed at $175 per hour. Better still for the law firm, at a $250 hourly rate and a 2,000 billable-hour requirement, the associate's revenue production would rise to $500,000, and the law firm partners would share $180,000 profit on her work.

Notice that the associate might still be pleased to be earning $160,000 per year, but her life would have become harder. In order to bill 2,000 hours per year—assuming that at least one hour in four each day is not billable—the lawyer would actually have to be in the office 2,500 hours per year or about 50 hours each week instead of her previous 40 hours. The extra ten hours would have to be found somewhere—in missed dinners while the children are still awake, in weekend days no longer spent with the family, or in an earlier start to each working day.

The figures are arbitrary, but the dynamics of leverage are real, and the example helps explain why increases in numbers of hours lawyers work, as well as in the billing rates law firms charge, have become so pervasive.[118] Indeed, the impact on law firm associates does not tell the whole story. As pressure to increase profits grew—and as existing profits have declined—several firms have "de-equitized" partners and created other non-equity categories to try to increase the number of people producing leverage and decrease the number consuming it.[119]

---

118. The actual number of billable hours required and billed may be somewhat lower than some articles suggest. A broad survey by the National Association for Law Placement (NALP) in 2004 revealed that at large law firms, the mean number of required hours was 1,930, and the mean number of hours billed was 2,059. Susan Saab Fortney, *The Billable Hours Derby: Empirical Data on the Problems and Pressure Points*, 33 FORDHAM URBAN L.J. 171, 176 (2005). Some firms require more hours, of course, and it is apparent that lawyers feel a need to bill more than the firms' minimums. Studies suggest that size of a firm itself is not correlated with profitability, nor is leverage alone. The number of associates in a firm does correlate with profitability, and the number of partners negatively correlates with it, so big firms with many associates are the most profitable. S.S. Samuelson and L.J. Jaffe, *A Statistical Analysis of Law Firm Profitability*, 70 B.U. L. REV. 185 (1990).

119. Non-equity-holders look like associates in the leverage model. Douglas McCollam, *Life on the Bubble*, AM. LAW., July 2001, at 132. *See also* Nathan

3. The Law Firm as a Tournament

Another effort to explain the growth of large firms has applied what economists call "tournament theory" to law firm growth. Young lawyers entering a firm, the theory says, want to become partners because only partners split the firm's profits. Each lawyer who begins at a firm knows that he might not reach partner status, but each is willing to give up some income today for the chance to make much more tomorrow. The term "tournament" applies to the multiyear process of deciding who wins the coveted partnership prizes.[120]

If no associates were promoted to partner, the argument runs, a firm could not attract the quality associates that it needs. Thus some new partners must be made each year. But each time a partner is created, the firm needs more associates to generate revenue needed to pay the new partner a generous share of the profits without reducing the shares earned by the rest. Although they did not say so, in effect, the authors of this account, Professors Marc Galanter and Thomas

---

Koppel, *Partnership is No Longer a Tenured Position*, WALL ST. J., July 6, 2007, at B1; Alexia Garamfalvi, *Firms Grow Tiery-Eyed*, LEGAL TIMES, May 7, 2007, at 34. One study suggests that single-tier partnerships are more profitable than firms that have aggressively tried to reduce the number of equity partners, William D. Henderson, *An Empirical Study of Single-Tier Versus Two-Tier Partnerships in the Am Law 200*, 84 N.C. L. REV. 1691 (2006), but even that study concedes that the single-tier firms studied were more prestigious quite apart from how they distributed profits. Similarly, another study shows that firms with a lockstep compensation system, on average, make more money than those who pay based on an "eat what you kill" basis. Again, however, it appears that may be because of other characteristics of those firms, and that conversion to lockstep compensation would not itself increase revenues. S.S. Samuelson and L.J. Jaffe, *A Statistical Analysis of Law Firm Profitability*, 70 B.U. L. REV. 185 (1990). In any event, some of the firms that have demoted or de-equitized senior lawyers have been sued for discrimination. *E.g.*, Anthony Lin, *EEOC Sues Sidley for Age Discrimination*, LEGAL TIMES, Jan. 17, 2005, at 1. The EEOC was held to have authority to obtain financial damages on behalf of the senior lawyers in *EEOC v. Sidley & Austin, LLP*, 437 F.3d 695 (7th Cir. 2006).

120. *See* MARC GALANTER & THOMAS PALAY, TOURNAMENT OF LAWYERS: THE TRANSFORMATION OF THE BIG LAW FIRM (1991). The authors published the thesis earlier in Marc Galanter & Thomas Palay, *Why the Big Get Bigger: The Promotion-to-Partner Tournament and the Growth of Large Law Firms*, 76 VA. L. REV. 747 (1990).

Palay, were likening law firms to a Ponzi scheme, i.e., an organization that has to keep growing to provide current returns and that is likely to collapse if the growth cannot be sustained.

In spite of its inherent logic and the data offered in support of the theory, it seems clear that tournament theory at most explains only part of the growth of modern law firms.[121] First, new associates have many reasons to work for a firm. Reaching partnership status may not even be attractive to many of them; they may know they plan to leave the firm in a few years—before a partnership decision is even a possibility. Indeed, one can argue that high salaries recently paid by large firms to beginning lawyers reveal that lawyers are increasingly unwilling to play in the tournament and to defer income to tomorrow instead of today.

Second, throughout their lives, lawyers and other successful people have engaged in lots of "tournaments" of the kind the theory describes. They fought to get the top marks in the first grade, struggled to win the spelling bee, and took pride in being the high school valedictorian. They competed to beat the grading curve in college and to get into a good law school. In law school, they competed to be on the law review, and in practice, they fought for the attention of clients. The tournament label can thus be applied to a process that takes multiple forms across a lawyer's life.

Third, firms no longer necessarily promote partners from within. They bring in lateral partners from other firms, or they merge with another firm and grow larger overnight. Indeed, to the extent

---

121. Two early, not entirely sympathetic reviews of the Galanter-Palay hypothesis were Frederick W. Lambert, *An Academic Visit to the Modern Law Firm: Considering a Theory of Promotion-Driven Growth*, 90 MICH. L. REV. 1719 (1991), and Vincent Robert Johnson, *On Shared Human Capital, Promotion Tournaments, and Exponential Law Firm Growth*, 70 TEX. L. REV. 537 (1991). The initial most impressive challenge to Galanter & Palay was offered in Kevin Kordana, *Law Firms and Associate Careers: Tournament Theory Versus the Production-Imperative Model*, 104 YALE L.J. 1907 (1995). The theory was criticized but given some credit by David B. Wilkins & G. Mitu Gulati, *Reconceiving the Tournament of Lawyers: Tracking, Seeding, and Information Control in the Internal Labor Markets of Elite Law Firms*, 84 VA. L. REV. 1581 (1998), but it was attacked again in George Rutherglen & Kevin Kordana, *A Farewell to Tournaments? The Need for an Alternative Explanation of Law Firm Structure and Growth*, 84 VA. L. REV. 1695 (1998).

tournament theory is helpful at all, the relevant tournament for many lawyers may be to become a partner at a firm that pays more than one's own.[122] The tournament metaphor struck a responsive chord because much of what lawyers do involves interpersonal competition, but tournament analysis can never explain more than part of the growth of modern firms.

F. TRANSFORMATION OF THE HEMISPHERES OF THE BAR

A perhaps less obvious but equally fundamental move in the character of American lawyering has been the change in the proportion of lawyers who primarily represent business corporations compared to those who primarily represent non-affluent individuals. In 1960, Jerome Carlin reported that in New York, business lawyers made up 45 percent of the bar, while individual-oriented work, such as personal injury, criminal, divorce, wills, and real estate, made up the other 55 percent.[123] Almost all lawyers in firms of fifteen or more did business or probate work, while a majority of solo practitioners or lawyers in firms of five or fewer met the needs of individual clients.[124] Lawyers tended "to have contact primarily with other lawyers in their own stratum," and "movement of lawyers among the various strata of the bar is highly selective."[125]

---

122. The move to a now-endless, multi-form tournament was stimulated by Stephen Brill's creation in the mid-1980s of American Lawyer Media, a diverse collection of national and local publications for lawyers. Probably its most anticipated reports each year are those ranking law firms based on their revenues and profitability. Being competitive people, even lawyers who are paid very well ask what would make them look even better in the *American Lawyer* and convince others they have become successful. Lawyers compete, not for places in heaven, but to achieve a high firm ranking in the *American Lawyer* profits-per-equity-partner tables.

123. JEROME E. CARLIN, LAWYERS' ETHICS: A SURVEY OF THE NEW YORK BAR 11–13 (1966). Carlin noted that even 95 percent of lawyers who represented individuals represented those with incomes above the median $5,000. *Id.* at 13–16.

124. *Id.* at 22–27.

125. *Id.* 34–35.

Just fifteen years later, John Heinz & Edward Laumann's exhaustive study of the Chicago Bar further documented the distinction between lawyers for what they called the corporate sector and the individual/small business sector. Calling these two parts of the bar "hemispheres," they showed that the lawyers who populated each differed in terms of social class, where they went to law school, how much money they made on average, their status as leaders of the bar, and the like.[126] Heinz & Laumann concluded that in 1975, 53 percent of lawyers focused on business issues, while 40 percent focused on individuals.[127]

After another two decades, in 1995, the hemispheres metaphor was still powerful. Although its authors recognized that it tended to oversimplify "the full complexity of the social structure of the profession,"[128] it is clear that lawyers are concentrating their practice in specialized areas, and the day of the generalist is largely over.[129] Ultimately, the authors concluded that the proportion of corporate lawyers had increased from 53 percent to 64 percent, while lawyers for individuals had fallen from 40 percent to 29 percent.[130] While growth in the absolute number of lawyers means that those available to serve individuals had increased over the period,[131] the more important conclusion is that

---

126. JOHN P. HEINZ & EDWARD O. LAUMANN, CHICAGO LAWYERS: THE SOCIAL STRUCTURE OF THE BAR 28–54, 92–175 (rev. ed. 1994). The number of solo practitioners fell from 61 percent of all lawyers in 1948 to 37 percent by 1970. *Id.* at xvii.

127. *Id.* at 23–26. Within the group focusing on individuals and small business, about half worked on personal financial issues (real estate, tax, and probate) while the other half worked on personal plight issues (personal injury, criminal, divorce).

128. *Id.* at 7. *See also* John P. Heinz, Edward O. Laumann, Robert L. Nelson & Ethan Michelson, *The Changing Character of Lawyers' Work: Chicago in 1975 and 1995*, 32 LAW & SOC'Y REV. 751 (1998); John P. Heinz, Robert L. Nelson & Edward O. Laumann, *The Scale of Justice: Observations on the Transformation of Urban Law Practice*, 27 ANN. REV. SOC. 337 (2001).

129. *Id.* at 51–54.

130. *Id.* at 43 (2005). In both samples, 7 percent of lawyers worked for government or were otherwise not capable of characterizing as in either broad grouping. See also, DONALD D. LANDON, COUNTRY LAWYERS: THE IMPACT OF CONTEXT ON PROFESSIONAL PRACTICE 19 (1990).

131. Heinz & Laumann make the plausible suggestion that demand for legal services by individuals may not be as elastic as demand by corporations,

almost two-thirds of the legal talent in this country is now focused largely on meeting the needs of corporate clients.[132]

That does not mean lawyers for individuals are unimportant. It does not even mean all such lawyers are poor. Successful plaintiffs' personal injury lawyers, for example, can earn incomes that make corporate lawyers jealous. Lawyers who preserve and help manage large pools of individual wealth can similarly charge high fees. What the trends do mean, however, is that a realistic look at the legal profession reveals that the number of attractive opportunities available to lawyers who do not want to do corporate work is getting smaller and at a faster rate than ever before.

G. TRANSFORMATION OF THE RELATIVE POWER OF IN-HOUSE AND OUTSIDE COUNSEL

The growth of law firms and the major shift of law practice toward corporate work pale by comparison to the rising power of in-house counsel. Thirty years ago, and in many cases much more recently, lawyers in private firms saw their role to be providing legal services to lay officers or employees of corporate clients. That is usually no longer true. The people many of today's lawyers have to please are other lawyers—this time, lawyers acting in the role of general counsel to corporations, government agencies, and other organizations. In short, private law firms advise—and market their services to—corporate

---

suggesting that the change in the proportion of lawyers serving each group might not be as significant as it might first appear. JOHN P. HEINZ & EDWARD O. LAUMANN, CHICAGO LAWYERS: THE SOCIAL STRUCTURE OF THE BAR xx (rev. ed. 1994). However, doubt is cast on that hypothesis in Roger C. Cramton, *Delivery of Legal Services to Ordinary Americans*, 44 CASE W. RES. L. REV. 531 (1994) (suggesting that pervasive problems remain before meeting the legal needs of poor and middle class Americans).

132. Donald Landon says, "The central finding of the Chicago study is that the bar is shaped ultimately by a variety of influences, most of which are external to the profession. . . . The emergence of the public corporation essentially generated a new species of law practice, the corporate law firm." DONALD D. LANDON, COUNTRY LAWYERS: THE IMPACT OF CONTEXT ON PROFESSIONAL PRACTICE 4 (1990).

lawyers who decide what outside services the corporate client requires and why.[133]

For many years, employment by a single client—as in the case of a company general counsel—was considered ethically suspect. Having only one client was said to expose the lawyer to client pressure to act improperly because the lawyer could not afford to lose her only job. Now, however, close to 25 percent of all lawyers act as employed counsel in government or other single-client situations. Of those, 40 percent—or 10 percent of all lawyers—act as inside corporate counsel.[134]

---

133. Carl Liggio, former general counsel of Arthur Young & Co., says that the "golden years" for in-house corporate counsel were the 1920s and 1930s. They were in eclipse from the 1940s to the mid-1970s, but then began the resurgence described here. *See* Carl D. Liggio, *The Changing Role of Corporate Counsel*, 46 EMORY L.J. 1201 (1997); *see also* Carl D. Liggio, Sr., *A Look at the Role of Corporate Counsel: Back to the Future—Or Is It the Past?*, 44 ARIZ. L. REV. 621, 621–24 (2002). The resurgence period is discussed in EVE SPANGLER, LAWYERS FOR HIRE: SALARIED PROFESSIONALS AT WORK (1986); Robert Eli Rosen, *The Inside Counsel Movement, Professional Judgment and Organizational Representation*, 64 IND. L.J. 479, 481–90 (1989) (calling this the "age of enlightenment" for in-house counsel). *See also* MILTON C. REGAN, JR., EAT WHAT YOU KILL: THE FALL OF A WALL STREET LAWYER 33 (2006). The phenomenon of salaried "professionals" is not limited to lawyers. "Increasingly, doctors find themselves salaried employees or beholden to large, third-party payers and provider organizations. Other professionals, such as engineers, accountants, lawyers, and academicians, have long since submitted to some institutional control over their practices as they massively work for large organizations and professional firms." WILLIAM F. MAY, BELEAGUERED RULERS: THE PUBLIC OBLIGATION OF THE PROFESSIONAL 3 (2001).

134. "Within a single generation the legal profession has been transformed. At mid-century, 87 percent of the bar was in private practice, 59 percent in solo practice. By 1980 only one-third were solo practitioners, and for each lawyer still practicing alone another now held a salaried position in industry, in government, or in a law firm." EVE SPANGLER, LAWYERS FOR HIRE: SALARIED PROFESSIONALS AT WORK 9 (1986). On the other hand, the proportion of the American bar serving as in-house counsel has remained about 10 percent for many years. Susan Hackett, *Inside Out: An Examination of Demographic Trends in the In-House Profession*, 44 ARIZ. L. REV. 609, 610 (2002). An Association of Corporate Counsel (ACC) study in 2006 found that one-third of in-house counsel are women, and 11 percent are minorities.

Thirty years ago, as well, a lawyer employed by a corporation was

> a relatively minor management figure, stereotypically, a lawyer from the corporation's principal outside law firm who had not quite made the grade as partner. The responsibilities of general (corporate) counsel were confined to corporate housekeeping and other routine matters and to acting as liaison (perhaps a euphemism for channeling business) to his former firm.[135]

Today, by contrast, it is in-house lawyers—not the partners in large law firms—who primarily counsel corporate management.[136] It is they who hire outside counsel and who sometimes pressure outside counsel to conform to management's demands.[137] Robert Nelson, for example found:

> Even if law firm counsel were inclined to act as the conscience of their clients, their opportunity to do so has diminished as a result of the rise

---

They worked an average of six years prior to becoming in-house counsel. *See also* Lisa H. Nicholson, *Making In-Roads to Corporate General Counsel Positions: It's Only a Matter of Time?*, 65 MD. L. REV. 625 (2006) (describing diversity efforts by corporate legal offices).

135. Abram Chayes & Antonia H. Chayes, *Corporate Counsel and the Elite Law Firm*, 37 STAN. L. REV. 277 (1985). At least that was true from about 1940 to 1980. One prominent writer recalls that the "golden age of corporate counsel lasted from the early part of the 20th century through the late 1930s" when "75% of the CEOs of the major companies were lawyers compared to less than 5% today." Carl D. Liggio, Sr., *A Look at the Role of Corporate Counsel: Back to the Future—Or Is It the Past?*, 44 ARIZ. L. REV. 621 (2002). *See* also, James W. Jones & Bayless Manning, *Getting at the Root of Core Values: A "Radical" Proposal to Extend the Model Rules to Changing Forms of Law Practice*, 84 MINN. L. REV. 1159, 1169–70 (2000).

136. Susan Hackett, *Inside Out: An Examination of Demographic Trends in the In-House Profession*, 44 ARIZ. L. REV. 609, 611 (2002) (over 61 percent of in-house general counsel who responded to a survey said that they report to the CEO of their organization, while another 15 percent report to the president). *See also* MARY ANN GLENDON, A NATION UNDER LAWYERS 34–36 (1994).

137. Abram Chayes & Antonia H. Chayes, *Corporate Counsel and the Elite Law Firm*, 37 STAN. L. REV. 277 (1985); Sarah Helene Duggin, *The Pivotal Role of the General Counsel in Promoting Corporate Integrity and Professional Responsibility*, 51 ST. LOUIS U. L.J. 989 (2007). ROBERT L. NELSON, PARTNERS WITH POWER: THE SOCIAL TRANSFORMATION OF THE LARGE LAW FIRM 56–62 (1988), was among the earliest to identify this trend.

of internal counsel within the corporation and the changing nature of relationships with corporate clients . . . . [T]hrough the process of advocating the interests of clients, large-firm attorneys come to strongly identify with them. It is highly unlikely, therefore, that lawyers in large law firms will act as an independent voice that checks the self-interest of clients.[138]

Recruiting in-house lawyers rather than depending exclusively on outside firms began as a way to permit clients to avoid high law firm billing rates[139] and as a form of vertical integration that reduced the cost of searching for lawyers to do recurring tasks.[140] It also was a

---

138. ROBERT L. NELSON, PARTNERS WITH POWER: THE SOCIAL TRANSFORMATION OF THE LARGE LAW FIRM 5 (1988). Nelson goes on: "The dominance of client interests in the practical activities of lawyers contradicts the view that large-firm lawyers serve a mediating function in the legal system." *Id.* at 232. *See also* Robert L. Nelson & Laura Beth Nielsen, *Cops, Counsel, and Entrepreneurs: Constructing the Role of Inside Counsel in Large Corporations,* 34 LAW & Soc. REV. 457, 477–78 (2000) (in-house counsel may try to "market" their services to non-lawyers within the corporation by making their advice more palatable). Furthermore, there is a potential problem when actions taken by managers advised by the corporate lawyer may be in tension with positions taken by the corporate board. *See* E. Norman Veasey & Christine T. Di Guglielmo, *The Tensions, Stresses, and Professional Responsibilities of the Lawyer for the Corporation,* 62 BUS. LAW. 1, 2–25 (2006); Sally R. Weaver, *Ethical Dilemmas of Corporate Counsel: A Structural and Contextual Analysis,* 46 EMORY L.J. 1023 (1997).

139. Michael Trotter traces part of the shift to use of inside counsel to the increased salaries paid law firm associates. "When starting salaries were raised to $60,000 a year in Atlanta in 1990 ($83,000 in New York), for the first time corporate clients could pay their in-house lawyers less than law firms paid and still attract a number of excellent attorneys . . . . [I]t was possible for companies to pay their in-house lawyers less than law firm lawyers earned but more than enough for their in-house lawyers to live very comfortably and pay off their student loans." MICHAEL H. TROTTER, PROFIT AND THE PRACTICE OF LAW: WHAT'S HAPPENED TO THE LEGAL PROFESSION 76 (1997). *See also* Mary C. Daly, *The Cultural, Ethical, and Legal Challenges in Lawyering for a Global Organization: The Role of the General Counsel,* 46 EMORY L.J. 1057, 1059-63 (1997); Carl D. Liggio, *The Changing Role of Corporate Counsel,* 46 EMORY L.J. 1201, 1204–06 (1997).

140. Robert Eli Rosen, *The Inside Counsel Movement, Professional Judgment and Organizational Representation,* 64 IND. L.J. 479, 503–25 (1989). Two American Bar Foundation researchers describe three corporate counsel

response to expanding government regulation and the consequent burden of continuing compliance and litigation.[141] But a strong internal lawyer staff also helps assure that legal service decisions are made by people who understand the client's business, know the type of legal work that is required, and are able to help managers think about the issues inherent in important business decisions.[142] A survey of CEOs for the Corporate Counsel Association (CCA), for example, said that 93 percent of senior executives believe inside counsel understand the company better, 60 percent say inside counsel are preferred because they are cheaper, and 37 percent even say they trust inside counsel more.[143]

---

roles—cops, counsel, and entrepreneurs. Robert L. Nelson & Laura Beth Nielsen, *Cops, Counsel, and Entrepreneurs: Constructing the Role of Inside Counsel in Large Corporations*, 34 LAW & SOC. REV. 457 (2000).

141. Carl D. Liggio, Sr., *A Look at the Role of Corporate Counsel: Back to the Future—Or Is It the Past?*, 44 ARIZ. L. REV. 621, 623–24 (2002). *See also* Richard S. Gruner, *General Counsel in an Era of Compliance Programs and Corporate Self-Policing*, 46 EMORY L.J. 1113 (1997).

142. Abram Chayes & Antonia H. Chayes, *Corporate Counsel and the Elite Law Firm*, 37 STAN. L. REV. 277, 280–89 (1985) (describing this as the "planning and prevention" function of corporate counsel). *See also* EVE SPANGLER, LAWYERS FOR HIRE: SALARIED PROFESSIONALS AT WORK 70–72 (1986). David Wilkins sees the position of influence in-house lawyers have as an opportunity for minority lawyers to make a positive contribution to social welfare, not just the welfare of their employer. David B. Wilkins, *From "Separate Is Inherently Unequal" to "Diversity is Good for Business": The Rise of Market-Based Diversity Arguments and the Fate of the Black Corporate Bar*, 117 HARV. L. REV. 1548, 1611–15 (2004).

143. *Measuring Stick*, AM. LAW., July 2001, at 20. *See also* Sally R. Weaver, *Ethical Dilemmas of Corporate Counsel" A Structural and Contextual Analysis*, 46 EMORY L.J. 1023, 1035–46 (1997) (inside counsel may be asked to sit on executive management committees or even the board of directors).

As inside counsel become more involved in management issues, they run the risk that they will be said to be giving business advice instead of legal advice and thus that their advice may not be shielded by the attorney-client privilege. Richard S. Gruner, *General Counsel in an Era of Compliance Programs and Corporate Self-Policing*, 46 EMORY L.J. 1113, 1115–16 (1997) (advocating that the discussions should be privileged). In the European Union, communications with inside counsel are not protected by privilege at all, no matter what the subject. *See* Australian Mining & Smelting Europe Ltd. (AM & S) v. Comm'n,

Corporate general counsel typically run independent offices within a corporation. They are paid well,[144] and they tend to view their job as one of facilitating their internal client's—i.e., the business person's— task.[145] Inside counsel often see issues through the lens their business clients do, i.e., as involving trade-offs and ambiguous facts. Some in-house counsel act as entrepreneurs, such as by managing inventories of intellectual property or by doing deals to sell off corporate assets.[146] Inside counsel with such instincts often move on to executive roles, including becoming CEO.[147]

Case 155/79, [1982] E.C.R. 1575, [1982] 2 C.M.L.R. 264; Akzo Nobel Chems. Ltd. v. Comm'n, Case T-125-03, Ct. First Ins., Sept. 17, 2007.

144. The 2007 compensation survey by Corporate Counsel magazine found that the average salary for the general counsel of Fortune 500 companies was over $550,000. Added to that, however, were bonuses that exceeded $1 million and stock awards that also averaged over $1 million. *See Bonus Round,* CORP. COUNS., Aug. 2007, at 77. *See also* Debra Cassens Weiss, *Top In-House Lawyers Make $645K, Survey Says, ABA Journal - Law News Now,* Feb. 26, 2008. One can, of course, question paying lawyers salaries tied to corporate performance when at least some legal advice might properly counsel against engaging in risky practices that may lead to apparently high short-run profits.

145. *See* Mary C. Daly, *The Cultural, Ethical, and Legal Challenges in Lawyering for a Global Organization: The Role of the General Counsel,* 46 EMORY L.J. 1057, 1068–73 (1997) (describing this as a "proactive" model of lawyering that requires "a detailed understanding of business, financial, and managerial concepts and a commitment to integrate this understanding into client counseling"). Professor Daly suggests that this model of lawyering is less familiar in other parts of the world. *Id.* at 1077–84. *See also* EVE SPANGLER, LAWYERS FOR HIRE: SALARIED PROFESSIONALS AT WORK 74–75 (1986).

146. Robert L. Nelson & Laura Beth Nielsen, *Cops, Counsel, and Entrepreneurs: Constructing the Role of Inside Counsel in Large Corporations,* 34 LAW & SOC. REV. 457, 466–68 (2000). Some entrepreneurial outside counsel are described in JERRY VAN HOY, FRANCHISE LAW FIRMS AND THE TRANSFORMATION OF PERSONAL LEGAL SERVICES (1997).

147. A partial list of general counsel who became CEO of their companies includes Jeffrey Kindler at Pfizer, Charles Prince at Citigroup, Chris Kearney at SPX Corp., David Steiner at Waste Management, and Russ Strobel at Nicor. Sheri Qualters, *Corner Office Fits GC Style,* NAT'L L.J., Aug. 16, 2006, at 1.

Much of what both inside and outside counsel do consists of help-ing the organization comply with applicable regulatory standards.[148] Outside lawyers argue that they are better positioned to tell manage-ment when proposed conduct will cross the line of illegality because their promotion does not depend on management's good will.[149] In-house lawyers, by contrast, see their power flowing from the fact they understand the business and the fact that managers do not want to be on record as failing to follow counsel's advice.

In the current environment, companies hire outside counsel for more than half the client's legal needs, but they tend to see it as com-pany managers see any other make-or-buy decision the company faces. A company might choose to make spare parts itself, for exam-ple, or buy them on an as-needed basis from an outside firm. So too with outside legal help.[150] According to a survey of in-house counsel in 2001, about 60 percent of their budget is spent on in-house lawyers

---

148. *See, e.g.,* Richard S. Gruner, *General Counsel in an Era of Compliance Programs and Corporate Self-Policing*, 46 EMORY L.J. 1113 (1997); Abram Chayes & Antonia H. Chayes, *Corporate Counsel and the Elite Law Firm*, 37 STAN. L. REV. 277, 287 (1985) ("legal department bears primary, though not exclusive, responsibility for compliance efforts"). *See also* Robert L. Nelson & Laura Beth Nielsen, *Cops, Counsel, and Entrepreneurs: Constructing the Role of Inside Counsel in Large Corporations*, 34 LAW & SOC. REV. 457, 463–64 (2000) (calling this the "cop" role of corporate counsel); Hugh P. Gunz & Sally P. Gunz, *The Lawyer's Response to Organizational Professional Conflict: An Empirical Study of the Ethical Decision Making of In-House Counsel*, 39 AM. BUS. L.J. 241 (2002).

149. EVE SPANGLER, LAWYERS FOR HIRE: SALARIED PROFESSIONALS AT WORK 93–98 (1986); Robert Eli Rosen, *The Inside Counsel Movement, Professional Judgment and Organizational Representation*, 64 IND. L.J. 479, 525–31 (1989). The argument was found to have force in JOHN P. HEINZ & EDWARD O. LAUMANN, CHICAGO LAWYERS: THE SOCIAL STRUCTURE OF THE BAR (1982). *See also* Sarah Helene Duggin, *The Pivotal Role of the General Counsel in Promoting Corporate Integrity and Professional Responsibility*, 51 ST. LOUIS U. L.J. 989 (2007); Sung Hui Kim, *The Banality of Fraud: Re-situating the Inside Counsel as Gatekeeper*, 74 FORDHAM L. REV. 983 (2005).

150. Two excellent analyses of this process are LARRY SMITH, INSIDE/OUTSIDE: HOW BUSINESSES BUY LEGAL SERVICES (2001), and Steven L. Schwarcz, *To Make or to Buy: In-House Lawyering and Value Creation*, 13 J. CORP. L. 497 (2008).

and overhead, 22 percent on outside litigation counsel, and 18 percent on outside counsel for other matters.[151]

Law firms are familiar with the practice of hiring "contract lawyers," i.e., lawyers hired to do particular tasks when the firm is especially busy on a case or regulatory filing but whom the firm will not need in the long run. Today, private law firms can best be understood as inside counsel's version of contract lawyers. Sometimes they may be retained for commodity legal work that can be done inexpensively, such as by firms in India or elsewhere.[152] Or, private firms might be retained when it is more cost-effective to consult experienced outside counsel than to hire an expert internally.

But the reasons for going outside are often less clearly economic. Inside counsel may want someone else to take the heat or assume liability for a risky decision,[153] for example, or to make a record that inside counsel sought "the best" advice so as to avoid criticism if the advice leads to an unsuccessful result.[154] Inside counsel positions are

---

151. Susan Hackett, *Inside Out: An Examination of Demographic Trends in the In-House Profession*, 44 ARIZ. L. REV. 609, 613 (2002).

152. *See, e.g.*, Laura Lewis Owens, *With Legal Services, World is Flat*, NAT'L L.J., Jan. 15, 2007, at 15; Jennifer Fried, *Looking Abroad for Low-Cost Lawyers*, LEGAL TIMES, Jan. 19, 2004, at 21; Renee Deger, *Following DuPont's Model*, LEGAL TIMES, Dec. 15, 2003, at 24.

153. *See, e.g.*, EVE SPANGLER, LAWYERS FOR HIRE: SALARIED PROFESSIONALS AT WORK 104 (1986); Abram Chayes & Antonia H. Chayes, *Corporate Counsel and the Elite Law Firm*, 37 STAN. L. REV. 277, 294 (1985) (outside counsel "tend more to be 'hired guns' chosen for a particular job, and less and less members of an ongoing relationship with responsibility for the client's overall well-being").

154. *See, e.g.*, Tamara Loomis, *The Untouchables*, AM. LAWYER, Sept. 2006, at 81 (saying when a big issue is on the line, the same firms tend to get called again and again). Professor Hazard suggests that corporate counsel also have the benefit and burden of access to "water cooler" information, the informal rumors that run through a corporation and which might prevent inside counsel from being able to accept representations from corporate officials as wholly true. Use of outside counsel who lack such back-channel information might produce a legal opinion more consistent with a course of action management wants to pursue. Geoffrey C. Hazard, Jr., *Ethical Dilemmas of Corporate Counsel*, 46 EMORY L.J. 1011, 1019 (1997). *See also* Richard S. Gruner, *General Counsel in an Era of Compliance Programs and Corporate Self-Policing*, 46 EMORY L.J. 1113, 1142–46 (1997); Sally R. Weaver, *Ethical Dilemmas*

also often "the last preserve for generalists in sophisticated corporate practice,"[155] and specialized advice may be required to be sure that inside counsel is up to date.

The matters for which outside counsel are retained may indeed be important. The best of the outside firms develop specialties in "new forms of corporate finance, innovative applications of the tax code, and the creation and widespread use of new tactics for acquiring other corporations and blocking takeover attempts" and can "mobilize groups of legal experts on short notice for uncertain and unpredictable periods of time."[156] The goal of the best outside lawyers has been said to be

> like the work of a fine custom tailor: highly individualized and with exquisite fit to a particular situation. Custom tailoring may, indeed, be only a tiny percentage of the garment trade, but it is a highly lucrative niche for those who occupy it successfully. And so, while senior partners are concerned with efficiency and with cost containment, they are also concerned with developing a labor force skilled enough to supply custom-crafted services.[157]

Until somewhat recently, outside lawyers have been relatively sheltered from the pressure to control their fees, but that cannot last. Among the major costs corporate clients face are those associated with deals and disputes, costs represented in large part by outside lawyer fees. In general, companies spend twice as much for the services of outside counsel as they do on their in-house legal department, and in recent years, as compensation of outside counsel has increased, the trend toward moving things in-house has increased

---

of Corporate Counsel" A Structural and Contextual Analysis, 46 EMORY L.J. 1023, 1028 (1997).

155. Susan Hackett, Inside Out: An Examination of Demographic Trends in the In-House Profession, 44 ARIZ. L. REV. 609, 611 (2002) (noting that over 40 percent of inside counsel surveyed described themselves as "generalists," "general commercial lawyers," or as working on "general corporate transactions").

156. ROBERT L. NELSON, PARTNERS WITH POWER: THE SOCIAL TRANSFORMATION OF THE LARGE LAW FIRM 8 (1988).

157. EVE SPANGLER, LAWYERS FOR HIRE: SALARIED PROFESSIONALS AT WORK 50 (1986).

as well.[158] The days are over when a CEO would say with a half-smile, "Our general counsel's office is the only one with an unlimited budget—and it has already exceeded it!"[159]

One observer summarizes:

> [T]he trend toward establishing in-house law departments is fueled by more than considerations of cost containment. It is also a response to pronounced changes in the legal and economic environment of the corporation . . . . [Quoting the board chairman of IC Industries, law has become highly regulatory and] "most active companies now require–or are best served by–the constant availability of counsel who is informed on a day-to-day basis of the company's activities and directions." . . . The chairman of Bell and Howell adds that if a corporation wants lawyers who know their business, it also wants officers to know their lawyers . . . . [T]o the extent that corporations want lawyers who are both knowledgeable and known, they want an in-house law department."[160]

Further, "changes in the legal context of business are matched by changes in the economic organization of the corporation."[161] Much of today's corporate growth is through vertical organization, i.e., internal staffing. Outside counsel can talk about delivering high-quality service and try to judge their own quality by internal professional standards, but the ultimate test for the value of a lawyer's services is going to be whether clients find them worth what the lawyer wants to charge.[162] More and more in-house counsel are cutting the number of outside firms a company retains, requiring highly detailed case budgets, early assessments, regular updates, use of specific technology, and minimum experience levels for lawyers working on their

---

158. 2007 ACC/Serengeti Managing Outside Counsel Survey, reported in N.Y. LAWYER, October 31, 2007.

159. The statement, attributed to the Chairman of the Board of I.B.M. by a journalist in the 1970s, is *quoted in* THOMAS D. MORGAN AND RONALD D. ROTUNDA, PROBLEMS AND MATERIALS ON PROFESSIONAL RESPONSIBILITY 312 (10th ed. 2008).

160. EVE SPANGLER, LAWYERS FOR HIRE: SALARIED PROFESSIONALS AT WORK 71–72 (1986).

161. *Id.* at 71.

162. Derek Bok, in a work otherwise critical of legal fees, remarks that "the most promising remedy by far . . . is more aggressive bargaining by corporations over the fees they will pay their outside lawyers." DEREK BOK, THE COST OF TALENT 153 (1993).

cases (e.g., no first-year associates).[163] Other clients are issuing requests for proposals (RFPs), sometimes online, asking to enter into flat fee arrangements with outside firms.[164] Sometimes the request will be for a firm to handle multiple cases for a single fixed fee covering all of them. That gives outside firms an ability to spread across several cases the risk that one or more of them will prove unusually difficult and costly, and it allows the firms to keep profits they generate by efficient disposition of the rest.[165]

Inside general counsel is more likely to receive rewards for reining in outside firms, not for coddling them. Successful outside firms will be those who project a sense that they understand the new rules and are prepared to be as entrepreneurial as the business people.[166] The ultimate challenge for outside lawyers, in turn, will be to demonstrate the value added that their services bring to a given client's situation.[167]

---

163. 2008 ACC/Serengeti Managing Outside Counsel Survey, reported in a joint news release, Oct. 20, 2008, found at www.acc.com; Susan Hackett, *Viva La Revolution?*, CORP. COUNS., April 2007, at 63; Thomas Sager, *Not Going to Take it Anymore*, CORP. COUNS., Sept. 2007, at 67; Debra Cassens Weiss, *Wal-Mart Refuses Law Firm Fee Hikes, Cites High Associate Salaries*, A.B.A. J.-Law News Now, Nov. 9, 2007. *See also* LARRY SMITH, INSIDE/OUTSIDE: HOW BUSINESSES BUY LEGAL SERVICES 151–69 (2001); EVE SPANGLER, LAWYERS FOR HIRE: SALARIED PROFESSIONALS AT WORK 100 (1986).

164. *See, e.g.,* Sheri Qualters, *Small Firms Use Flat Fees to Gain Edge*, NAT'L L.J., Nov. 12, 2007, at 8 (reporting, however, that such arrangements represent only 5 percent of all contracts with outside firms); Jeffrey W. Carr & Daniel S. Hapke, Jr., *Retaining Outside Counsel Online at Market Price*, ACCA Docket 19, No. 9, at 76 (2001). One of the leading Web sites matching firms with clients is www.elawforum.com.

165. *See, e.g.,* Sheri Qualters, *Small Firms Use Flat Fees to Gain Edge*, NAT'L L.J., Nov. 12, 2007, at 8 (describing use of the technique by Whirlpool, Cisco, Pitney Bowes); *Panel: Saving Even More Budget Dollars By Aggregating Demand*, The eLawForum, METROPOLITAN CORP. COUNS., October 2002, at 38.

166. MARK STEVENS, POWER OF ATTORNEY: THE RISE OF THE GIANT LAW FIRMS, ch. 2 (1987).

167. *See* William C. Kelly, Jr., *Reflections on Lawyer Morale and Public Service in an Age of Diminishing Expectations, in* ROBERT A KATZMANN, ED., THE LAW FIRM AND THE PUBLIC GOOD (1995).

There is no escaping the reality that the practice of law has become more competitive, and lawyers are more personally insecure.[168] Although some client companies are said to be cutting down on their number of suppliers and stressing "partnering" or even "convergence" with relatively few outside firms,[169] many lawyer-client relationships are likely to remain less like marriages and more like one-night stands.

H. THE DIMINISHED SIGNIFICANCE OF LICENSING

The logical outcome of the growing significance of corporate counsel managing legal needs, and the worldwide availability of help with legal matters, is the declining significance of having an American law license before providing traditional legal services. Although it is misleading to speak of lawyers in universal terms, as we saw in Chapter 1, the legally significant meaning of the term "lawyer" in the United States is someone with a license from a state supreme court that allows the "practice of law" within that court's jurisdiction, i.e., a single state.[170]

---

168. MICHAEL H. TROTTER, PROFIT AND THE PRACTICE OF LAW: WHAT'S HAPPENED TO THE LEGAL PROFESSION, ch. 12 (1997).

169. *See, e.g.,* Susan Hackett, *Inside Out: An Examination of Demographic Trends in the In-House Profession,* 44 ARIZ. L. REV. 609, 614 (2002). Indeed, some inside counsel "partner" with outside firms in the sense of having outside counsel use the client's computer resources, for example, or requiring that inside counsel have access to the outside firm's computer files. Abram Chayes & Antonia H. Chayes, *Corporate Counsel and the Elite Law Firm,* 37 STAN. L. REV. 277, 291 (1985). *See also* LARRY SMITH, INSIDE/OUTSIDE: HOW BUSINESSES BUY LEGAL SERVICES 171–212 (2001).

170. This is not entirely accurate. Some federal courts now impose experience requirements before admitting lawyers to practice before them, and agencies such as the U.S. Patent & Trademark Office may impose significant requirements of technical training before granting a license to practice specialized fields such as patent law.

Further, the power to grant a law license implies the power to deny or revoke it. Thus, licensing authorities have also established systems for professional discipline. Regulation and discipline of lawyers used to be based on alleged violation of their oath, as opposed to violation of separate canons of ethics. The requirement of such an oath goes back to at least 1275 and was brought over and required of U.S. lawyers. ORIE L. PHILLIPS & PHILBRICK McCOY, CONDUCT OF JUDGES AND LAWYERS: A SURVEY OF PROFESSIONAL

Individuals may represent themselves pro se, but if they represent anyone else—including even their own one-owner or family corporation—they must have a license to do so.

As we also saw in Chapter 1, a useful working definition of the practice of law is that it consists of applying the general body of law to a specific client's question or problem.[171] One might think that concept makes the boundaries of law practice sufficiently clear that the idea of being a lawyer will remain constant. As we have seen, however, changes ranging from globalization to the way clients get information foreshadow similar changes in what it will mean to be a lawyer. Prohibitions of the unauthorized practice of law are likely to have very little effect in protecting American lawyers against these fundamental changes. An Executive Order signed by President Clinton,[172] for example, requires federal agencies to allow non-lawyers to counsel and represent clients in agency proceedings. Many agencies have opened their proceedings to non-lawyer advisors, and the effect has been both increased assistance available to claimants and a decline in the number of potential clients that must rely on lawyers.

Lawyers themselves are breaking down traditional unauthorized practice barriers as they assist their clients, not only in the state in which the lawyer is licensed to practice, but in other states or nations where the client has legal needs.[173] It was an open professional secret

---

ETHICS, DISCIPLINE AND DISBARMENT 8–10 (1952). In 1908, the A.B.A. adopted its Canons of Ethics. A committee to amend it was appointed in 1923, and the amendments were approved in 1928. Canons of Judicial Ethics were adopted in 1924. *Id.* All but four states adopted the A.B.A. Code or something close to it, although by 1950, in only eighteen of the states was the Code adopted by the state supreme court. In the rest of the states, it was adopted by the state bar association. Even where the Code was not adopted by the state supreme court, it was apparently looked to as a basis for discipline.

171. This definition was used in A.B.A. CODE OF PROF'L RESPONSIBILITY EC 3–5 (1970). A law professor does not practice law when teaching, for example, because she teaches the law as it relates to hypothetical, not real, clients. Similarly, one who writes a book about law is not thereby engaged in law practice.

172. Exec. Order No. 12988, 3 C.F.R. 157: Civil Justice Reform (Feb. 5, 1996).

173. *See, e.g.,* Demetrios Dimitriou, *Legal Ethics in the Future: What Relevance?, in* SEIZE THE FUTURE: FORECASTING AND INFLUENCING THE FUTURE OF THE LEGAL PROFESSION (Gary A. Munneke ed., 2000).

that many lawyers regularly violated unauthorized practice rules by taking depositions, negotiating contracts, and even giving legal advice in states where they were not licensed until the California Supreme Court struck terror into lawyers' hearts with its *Birbrower* decision[174] that denied lawyers the right to collect a fee for such work. California and other states have now responded with changes in their rules to approve at least "temporary" work in states where a lawyer is unlicensed, and law firms have long used paralegal and other support personnel nominally working under the lawyer supervision that ethical standards require.

In addition, corporations now use non-lawyers to help deliver a total package of services that they need done. Negotiating contracts, troubleshooting discrimination claims, even writing court documents can all be done by non-lawyers within an organization receiving a level of lawyer supervision and training to which unauthorized practice rules cannot effectively speak.[175] Non-lawyers can help lower costs, but more important, they can help the client get its whole problem solved, not just the legal elements.[176] Often, the non-lawyers will benefit from a degree of lawyer supervision, but particularly where a law firm opens an ancillary or law-related entity, the non-lawyers might be accountants or lobbyists, economists or nurses, statisticians or business specialists who are more than capable of acting on their own. Current legal ethics rules require a lawyer in a private law firm

---

174. Birbrower, Montalbano, Condon & Frank, P.C. v. Superior Court, 949 P.2d 1 (Cal. 1988).

175. Professor Kritzer calls such persons "law workers" and sees them as examples of the kinds of people with whom lawyers are likely to compete in the future. *See* Herbert M. Kritzer, *The Future Role of "Law Workers": Rethinking the Forms of Legal Practice and the Scope of Legal Education*, 44 ARIZ. L. REV. 917 (2002). *See also* HERBERT M. KRITZER, THE JUSTICE BROKER: LAWYERS & ORDINARY LITIGATION (1990); HERBERT M. KRITZER, LEGAL ADVOCACY: LAWYERS AND NONLAWYERS AT WORK (1998); Herbert M. Kritzer, *The Professions Are Dead, Long Live the Professions: Legal Practice in a Postprofessional World*, 33 LAW & SOC'Y REV. 3 (1999).

176. At one time, the fourth largest American law firm was named Arthur Andersen, and both Ernst and Young & KPMG/Peat Marwick were in the top fifteen. *See, e.g.,* David Rubenstein, *Accounting Firm Legal Practices Expand Rapidly: How the Big Six Firms are Practicing Law in Europe; Europe First, Then the World?*, CORP. LEGAL TIMES, November 1997, at 1.

to supervise and take responsibility for the non-lawyer's work, but that requirement is easily met, and within an organizational client, lawyer supervision need only be provided if it is cost-effective to do so.[177]

Looking at these kinds of developments, Judge Richard Posner observed:

> Something like the evolution of the textile industry from guild production to mass production, and the concomitant decline of artisanality, is occurring today in the market for legal services . . . .
>
> Technical and organizational innovations have increased the vigor of competition in the legal-services market, but they have also an independent significance for the transformation of the profession. The rise of the paralegal has demonstrated that much of the traditional work of lawyers can be done by non-lawyers. It has also made the production of legal services a less homogeneous activity.[178]

Even the A.B.A. has now recognized that law firms may find it helpful to offer non-legal services that are "ancillary" to their regular legal practice to help meet recurring client needs.[179] Whoever does particular work, however, efficient delivery of services will be essential and will put pressure on lawyer fees.[180] Private lawyers are likely

---

177. *See, e.g.*, Susan Hackett, *Inside Out: An Examination of Demographic Trends in the In-House Profession*, 44 ARIZ. L. REV. 609, 616 (2002) (compliance programs in areas such as environmental, human resources, tax, marketing/antitrust, health/safety, are often under the direction of non-lawyer compliance officers who have access to lawyers but do not necessarily report to them). *But see* Richard S. Gruner, *General Counsel in an Era of Compliance Programs and Corporate Self-Policing*, 46 EMORY L.J. 1113, 1163–75 (1997) (assuming a more proactive role for corporate counsel in developing compliance programs).

178. RICHARD A. POSNER, OVERCOMING LAW 47, 66 (1995). *See also* Jonathan Macey, *Occupation Code 541110: Lawyers, Self-Regulation, and the Idea of a Profession*, 74 FORDHAM L. REV. 1079 (2005).

179. See MODEL RULES OF PROF'L CONDUCT R 5.7.

180. SOL M. LINOWITZ WITH MARTIN MAYER, THE BETRAYED PROFESSION: LAWYERING AT THE END OF THE TWENTIETH CENTURY, ch. 8 (1994). There may be pressure for more use of ADR, although to the extent litigation is being employed to delay payment or impose other costs on an opponent, only one side is likely to want to reduce those costs. On the other hand, lawyers may have to change the methods by which law suits are financed. That will be likely to reduce lawyer control of litigation but put control in the hands of

to continue to feel overworked, more likely to feel undercompensated, and more likely to burn out more quickly than in earlier years.[181]

Thus, this chapter has looked at the increasing pressure on lawyers brought about by a dramatic increase in the number of lawyers, the impact of globalization, and the transforming effects of technology, changes in the clients lawyers serve, growth of law firms, increased power of corporate counsel, and the declining significance of licensure and protective regulatory standards. It is in the context of these developments that the vision of the lawyer the world once knew is vanishing.

Former Army Chief of Staff Eric Shinseki is quoted as saying, "If you don't like change, you're going to like irrelevance even less."[182] The statement is at least as important for lawyers as it was for the Pentagon. Lawyers now must understand themselves in terms of a world they did not create and whose changing dynamics they cannot ignore. The United States will not become a society with no persons specially trained to deal with legal issues, but the people we today call lawyers seem destined primarily to provide a form of consulting services rather than traditional legal advice and litigation.

The A.B.A. Committee on Research About the Future of the Legal Profession offered a similar insight when it cited management expert Peter Drucker as blaming the Penn Central bankruptcy on the railroad's acting, as if it had said, "We have a train. Would you like to get on?" instead of "We are in the transportation business. Where would you like to go?" The Committee continued, "And so it is for the legal profession and the organized bar. We must first get the question right. . . . Do we have a train that can only go where the tracks go, or

---

people who can control costs. *See* MACKLIN FLEMING, LAWYERS, MONEY, AND SUCCESS: THE CONSEQUENCES OF DOLLAR OBSESSION, ch. 18 (1997).

181. MICHAEL H. TROTTER, PROFIT AND THE PRACTICE OF LAW: WHAT'S HAPPENED TO THE LEGAL PROFESSION, chs. 5–7 (1997). *See also* Marc Galanter & Thomas Palay, *Implications of Evolving Firm Size and Structure, in* THE LAW FIRM AND THE PUBLIC GOOD (Robert A. Katzmann ed., 1995).

182. TOM PETERS, REIMAGINE!: BUSINESS EXCELLENCE IN A DISRUPTIVE AGE 17 (2003).

do we provide a form of transportation with the destination to be determined by our passengers?"[183]

We talk more about the future of lawyers and law firms in the next chapter. The point of this chapter has simply been that lawyers who do not take the new, inescapable realities seriously are going to find themselves irrelevant to their clients, and thus irrelevant to those who matter to them most.

Not too many years ago, one of the most secure jobs available was that of a toll booth operator on a bridge or highway. The bridge and road were there to stay, and cars on both had to stop at the booth and pay a toll. Lawyers were in much the same position; one could not safely write a contract or seek legal relief without passing the issues by a lawyer. Now, toll booths are largely empty as an electronic EZ Pass collects the tolls while cars pass by at highway speed. Lawyers have no choice but to try to avoid a similar fate.[184]

---

183. COMM. ON RESEARCH ABOUT THE FUTURE OF THE LEGAL PROFESSION ON THE CURRENT STATUS OF THE LEGAL PROFESSION, WORKING NOTES 4–5 (Aug. 31, 2001).

184. Lawyers would do well to heed what is said to be an American Indian proverb: "When the horse is dead—dismount." Remarks of Charles F. Robinson attributed to Dakota tribal wisdom, discussed in GARY A. MUNNEKE, CONFERENCE INSIGHTS: SEIZE THE FUTURE: FORECASTING AND INFLUENCING THE FUTURE OF THE LEGAL PROFESSION 25 (1999). Or, as management consultant Tom Peters bluntly reminds us: "Remember: *There's no opt-out button.*" TOM PETERS, REIMAGINE!: BUSINESS EXCELLENCE IN A DISRUPTIVE AGE 55 (2003).

4. HOW AMERICAN LAWYERS AND FIRMS SHOULD ADDRESS THE NEW REALITIES

This book has challenged the idea that each American lawyer is part of a profession that brings a common body of knowledge to bear on a similar range of problems. Lawyers have long known that they do not all concentrate their work in the same fields of practice, but the qualities and experience that united lawyers were once thought to be more significant than the differences in what they did from one day to the next. This book argues that, whatever past reality there may have been in a common professional identity, the future careers of people who share the fact they have had legal training will differ even more from each other than they do today.

Further, as seen in Chapter 3, today's purchasers of legal services require their services to be delivered promptly, at high quality, and potentially anywhere in the world. Clients looking for help have many service providers with different credentials from which to choose, and they can find and retain lawyers and non-lawyers as never before. The premise of this chapter, in turn, is that lawyers and law firms must have the imagination and flexibility to deliver legal services of the kind and in the manner clients are likely to require.

A. THE FUTURE COURSE OF AN INDIVIDUAL LAWYER'S CAREER

The future American lawyer is likely to spend his or her career in a perpetual tournament trying to stand out among a collection of diverse service providers, each offering to contribute more to a client than they charge the client for their service.[1] Even if some of the

---

1. Even one of the creators of the tournament rhetoric now adapts it to the kind of world described in this chapter. *See* Marc Galanter & William Henderson, *The Elastic Tournament: A Second Transformation of the Big Law Firm*, 60 STAN. L. REV. 1867 (2008). *See also* Andrew Bruck & Andrew Canter, *Supply, Demand, and the Changing Economics of Large Law Firms*, 60 STAN. L. REV. 2087 (2008).

providers still call themselves lawyers, such lawyers will likely have to focus their work in those fields where they can be known as among the best.

In principle, it still might be possible for someone with legal training and considerable free time to prepare hard enough in a new field to handle a case without committing malpractice, but the skills required to represent a client effectively will often be so multidimensional that few lawyers will likely stray far from the kinds of work they know how to perform extremely well. They might change fields of concentration as areas of need become obsolete or as others become attractive, but in a world where clients have technology available to find the specific kind of counselor they require, each legal service provider—whether a licensed lawyer or not—will want to become known as among the best at doing particular kinds of work that a reasonable number of clients need done.

1. Lawyers Offering Basic Services for Individual Clients

Many traditional lawyer services to individuals will tend to be delivered as commodities, that is, as standardized products sold primarily on the basis of price. Estate planning, real estate transactions, adoptions, and uncontested divorces, for example, can present unique negotiation and human relations problems, but the legal components of the cases tend to be highly predictable. Technological advances discussed in the last chapter will allow documents for many such cases to be sold as forms or tailored to individual needs using a few clicks of a computer mouse.[2] If a client needs face-to-face reassurance, needs help in locations to which it would be costly for the client to travel, or needs to take a matter to court, someone with legal training might become involved and provide valuable services. But for the kinds of work that many providers with modest training can do quite well, competition may drive fees and lawyer incomes to levels far lower than we see today.

---

2. One company selling such forms is called LegalZoom, whose spokesperson is Robert Shapiro, for a while a member of O.J. Simpson's "dream team." The company is found on the internet at www.legalzoom.com. Part of the company's Web site also provides written information about how to use each of the forms.

It will take a special kind of person to seek to build a career around doing work of such a routine kind. Professor Jerry Van Hoy, who has studied the rise of so-called "franchise law firms," describes lawyers' work there as "more clerical and sales-oriented" than "researching and solving legal problems."[3] He concludes that most lawyers who take such jobs do so because of a lack of other options. On the other hand, commodity work is work some clients need done, and people who enjoy developing ways to perform the work more efficiently for a high volume of clients may thrive in the new environment.[4] It may also be a kind of practice in which the principle of leverage will still work as lawyers use lower-paid staff to perform many of the basic tasks.

Other lawyers might try to handle packages of cases for small business clients. They might bid for the right to review contracts for the business or the right to collect its debts, for example.[5] Some matters may take the lawyer more time than others, but the lawyer will try to calculate a reliable average cost. What the lawyer will be selling is reduced uncertainty about the cost of legal service as the client decides how much legal service to use.

In finding a place in what is likely to be a mix of service providers for individual clients, American lawyers are likely to find themselves increasingly in competition with banks, insurance companies, investment advisors, and other organizations that employ legally trained, salaried personnel. In some states today, for example, insurance companies provide their defense of accident claims using lawyers employed by the insurance company, not lawyers in independent

3. See JERRY VAN HOY, FRANCHISE LAW FIRMS AND THE TRANSFORMATION OF PERSONAL LEGAL SERVICES 2 (1997).

4. The profitability of efficiency may also be an attraction. Managing attorneys in franchised law practices often share in the fees generated by the office. JERRY VAN HOY, FRANCHISE LAW FIRMS AND THE TRANSFORMATION OF PERSONAL LEGAL SERVICES 29–33 (1997). As discussed in Chapter 6, *infra*, development of efficient techniques for delivering services will be of particular importance in offices trying to deliver legal services to the poor.

5. Such alternative billing arrangements are explored in Herbert M. Kritzer, *The Commodification of Insurance Defense Practice*, 59 VAND. L. REV. 2051 (2006). *See also* Jennifer Vaculik, *Note, Bidding by the Bar: Online Auction Sites for Legal Services*, 82 TEX. L. REV. 445 (2003).

firms.[6] Lawyers, in turn, might themselves sell insurance and give investment advice, or they might hire others to do so and thereby provide more complete service to their clients.[7] Likewise, as long as companies may sell books of legal forms, it will be hard to continue preventing company employees from explaining to buyers how to fill in the blanks.[8] Common prohibitions of the "corporate practice of law" have slowed such institutional delivery of legal services, but that barrier seems likely to weaken as it becomes apparent that the barrier protects lawyers' interests much more than the interests of clients.[9]

Finally, handling basic matters for individual clients may provide some lawyers with a sense of personal satisfaction that transcends the lower income from such a practice. Lawyers who have acted as leaders in small communities over the years seem primarily to have come from this kind of practice, often supplemented by interests in real estate or other local business.[10] The number of lawyers who will enter that kind of practice in the future is uncertain, but there is no reason to expect the role to disappear entirely.

---

6. *See, e.g., In re* Allstate Ins. Co., 722 S.W.2d 947 (Mo. 1987) (en banc); Charles Silver, *Flat Fees and Staff Attorneys: Unnecessary Casualties in the Continuing Battle Over the Law Governing Insurance Defense Lawyers*, 4 CONN. INS. L.J. 205 (1997).

7. Under current law, a lawyer doing so must comply with the standards of Model Rule 1.8(a) that require that the transaction be fair and fully explained to the client and that the client consent after an opportunity to seek independent advice about dealing with the lawyer in this way. One law firm, for example, provides investment services using partners licensed as both securities dealers and investment advisers, as well as lawyers.

8. The leading case on writing books is *New York County Lawyers' Association v. Dacey*, 283 N.Y.S.2d 984 (N.Y. App. Div.), *rev'd*, 234 N.E.2d 459 (N.Y. 1967). *But see* Matter of Estate of Margow, 390 A.2d 591 (N.J. 1978) (unlawful for legal secretary to help elderly friend rewrite her will using the old will as a form).

9. A century ago, corporations did provide this kind of legal service for their customers. For insight into the politics behind the current prohibition, *see* Bruce A. Green, *The Disciplinary Restrictions on Multidisciplinary Practice: Their Derivation, Their Development, and Some Implications for the Core Values Debate*, 84 MINN. L. REV. 1115 (2000). *See also* LAWRENCE M. FRIEDMAN, A HISTORY OF AMERICAN LAW 641 (2d ed. 1985).

10. DONALD D. LANDON, COUNTRY LAWYERS: THE IMPACT OF CONTEXT ON PROFESSIONAL PRACTICE 19 (1990), describes the non-corporate lawyers he

2. Contested Disputes Requiring Resolution

It is a mistake to think of all cases for individuals as routine. Some individuals are injured and demand compensation from persons or organizations. Others find themselves charged with crime, have their immigration status challenged, or get an assessment for back taxes, fines, and penalties. Such situations are frightening and often serious, and clients—whether individuals or corporations—are likely to continue to entrust their future to legally trained providers.

The challenge for clients, of course, will be to find ways to meet the cost of litigation. To some extent, court rules may encourage mediation, simplify discovery, and reduce the cost of trial preparation.[11] In the field of personal injury cases, the traditional way of paying lawyers has been a contingency fee that requires payment only from sums the lawyer recovers for the client. As noted in Chapter 3, however, such fees often bear little relation to the work done by the lawyer or to the value added for the client.

In cases where the client gets no dollar recovery, such as those where the challenge is getting the government to drop a case or persuading a private plaintiff not to sue, the problem of payment will continue to be hard for both client and lawyer. Liability insurance often pays for a legal defense in cases seeking money damages, but it

---

studied in Missouri

> The country lawyer . . . is typically a male in his early 40s who was born and raised in the county where he is currently practicing. He is Caucasian, Protestant, and thinks of himself as a Democrat. His father is as likely to have been a blue-collar worker or farmer as he is to have been a lawyer. . . . or other professional. . . . He will do work for 350 or more clients a year, which he considers too many. He will work 48 hours a week or more. . . . The majority of his income will derive from practice in three areas: estate, domestic relations, and negligence (plaintiff). Besides his law practice he will be involved in one or more additional entrepreneurial activities . . . ranging from farming, real estate development, and construction to cable TV, newspaper publishing, and traveling carnival management.

11. Professor Hadfield reminds, however, that lawyers and even courts often have little incentive to reduce the cost of litigation. Gillian K. Hadfield, *The Price of Law: How the Market for Lawyers Distorts the Justice System*, 98 MICH. L. REV. 953, 992–1006 (2000).

is hard to buy insurance to defend against criminal charges or a deportation order.[12]

Even some litigation documents can involve use of standardized templates to be sure issues are addressed completely, but the costs of litigation are likely to remain high, and some litigators are likely to earn high incomes. The issue of fee payment will have a direct impact on the number of people available to serve such clients, an issue to which we return in Chapter 6. But suffice it to say here that many of those today called trial lawyers will find their services in demand in the years ahead. Negotiation and litigation of contested matters is likely to remain one of the last places from which American lawyers will vanish.

3. Lawyers for Corporate and Other Organizational Clients

The trend of American lawyers toward disproportionately serving organizational clients is likely to continue if only because business firms are likely to offer the most money for legal services.[13] Here, however, the issue for tomorrow's lawyers is likely to be that they will find themselves competing for attention against a wide range of foreign lawyers and non-lawyer consultants.[14]

Lawyers are likely to find that fewer issues will be seen as distinctively "legal" in character. Lawyers might be retained among a mix of advisors as a company formulates an environmental compliance

---

12. Sometimes indemnification may be available if a client's employer, for example, agrees to pay for defense against charges that an officer, director, or employee has violated the law while serving the employer's interest. If it turns out that the employee violated the law doing something the employer had prohibited or not authorized, however, indemnification may often be refused.

13. One of the best analyses of this phenomenon is Gillian K. Hadfield, *The Price of Law: How the Market for Lawyers Distorts the Justice System*, 98 Mich. L. Rev. 953 (2000).

14. *See, e.g.*, Laurel S. Terry, *The Future Regulation of the Legal Profession: The Impact of Treating the Legal Profession as "Service Providers,"* 2008 J. Prof. Law. 189; Tanina Rostain, *The Emergence of "Law Consultants,"* 75 Fordham L. Rev. 1397 (2006); Robert Eli Rosen, *"We're All Consultants Now": How Changes in Client Organizational Strategies Influences Change in the Organization of Corporate Legal Services*, 44 Ariz. L. Rev. 637 (2002).

program, for example, but the company is likely to give equal or even greater weight to the views of biologists, chemists, and ecologists. Legal training may add weight to a lawyer's opinion, but lawyers who cannot provide non-legal insights as well may find their phone rings less often.

A practitioner's value to clients, in short, will have two dimensions—what she knows about a particular body of law and what she knows about a client's industry or substantive concerns. A lawyer who tries back injury cases will need to know almost as much about backs, for example, as about tort law and trial practice. A securities lawyer will need to know as much about the economics of financial instruments as about SEC regulations. A trade lawyer will need to know the culture of the countries in which her clients do business, and all lawyers will benefit from knowledge of some of the languages in which their clients—or the clients' suppliers and customers—work.

Some lawyers have resisted developing such non-legal expertise and even assert that professional rules urge them not to intrude into a client's substantive decisions.[15] Good lawyers also know better than to become directors of their clients or otherwise go into business with them.[16] The issue is not about making or profiting from a client's decisions; it is about having enough training and experience to understand and advise about those decisions.

Patent lawyers, for example, long have been required to be trained in a scientific or technical discipline so that they can prepare patent applications and evaluate and negotiate patent disputes. They are not expected to be inventors, but they would be less helpful to their scientist and inventor clients without the ability to speak and understand the technical language that both the clients and the patent

---

15. MODEL RULES OF PROF'L CONDUCT R. 1.13, cmt. 3 provides: "When constituents of the organization make decisions for it, the decisions ordinarily must be accepted by the lawyer even if their utility or prudence is doubtful. Decisions concerning policy and operations, including ones entailing serious risk, are not as such in the lawyer's province."

16. Lawyers are traditionally discouraged from having such relationships, in part because they reduce the lawyer's independence and ability to say "no," but in part because they increase the likelihood the lawyers will be charged as co-conspirators with their clients in instances of wrongdoing.

examiners understand. Likewise, corporate mergers are increasingly driven by issues of accounting and finance at least as much as by corporate and antitrust law.

Lawyers like to think they are good at a lot of things, but experts in finance and accounting are equally likely to think they can look up the law themselves or hire less expensive lawyers to do it for them. Lawyers will continue to be called upon to be problem-solvers, but they will be working in competition with a million fellow lawyers—as well as several million other consultants—to try to advise in-house lawyers who themselves have training relevant to a client's needs.[17] Non-lawyer providers will make it a point to learn enough about the law relevant to their own activity that lawyers will not be able simply to bluff them away by asserting an exclusive right to explain legal issues.

The lawyers who prosper will be those who can make themselves the best available go-to person in a combined law-and-substantive field and who market themselves accordingly. Blogging and use of networking sites[18] are increasingly attractive to lawyers who want to make themselves known to potential clients.[19] To the extent someone else offers services of more value, clients will turn elsewhere.[20] In any

---

17. *See, e.g.,* HERBERT M. KRITZER, LEGAL ADVOCACY: LAWYERS AND NONLAWYERS AT WORK (1998); Robert Eli Rosen, *"We're All Consultants Now": How Change in Client Organizational Strategies Influences Change in the Organization of Corporate Legal Services,* 44 ARIZ. L. REV. 637 (2002); Tanina Rostain, *The Emergence of "Law Consultants,"* 75 FORDHAM L. REV. 1397 (2006).

18. Among the networking sites, *see* http://www.martindale.com/connected.

19. *See, e.g.,* Diana Rubin, *Time to Build Your Profile Online,* LEGAL TIMES, Nov. 3, 2008, at 26; *see also* The Blawg 100 – A.B.A. Journal – Law News Now, at http://www.abajournal.com/magazine/blawg_100_2008.

20. In considering the nature of his or her practice, the lawyer's focus will have to be client service. As one lawyer explained, "We only exist because of the client. Without the client there's no need to have a lawyer! And we exist to solve people's problems. So if you're the type of person who doesn't want to solve somebody else's problem, you should not be practicing law." CARROLL SERON, THE BUSINESS OF PRACTICING LAW: THE WORK LIVES OF SOLO AND SMALL FIRM ATTORNEYS 106 (1996). Another attempt to describe the evolving world in which lawyers work is John P. Heinz, Robert L. Nelson,

event, many client needs will have little or no relation to the subjects such as real property and wills that are traditionally tested on lawyers' bar examinations.

For lawyers trained to think they are good at dealing with a wide range of legal issues, the prospect of becoming a mere consultant in a narrow specialty or mode of practice delivery may not initially be attractive. There is no inherent reason that a practitioner could not try to become competent in more than one field, but those who will be in greatest demand are likely to be practitioners who have specific, recognizable skills and who can work well with a team of lawyers and complimentary professionals to meet a client's needs.

It seems to follow, then, that rather than living in an era like the golden age with a motto "nobody starves," future Americans with legal training are likely to face a world in which they will compete to be among the relatively few visible stars in the practice sky.[21] Star lawyers will have big personal reputations and the demonstrated ability to manage teams of other lawyers and non-lawyers. There will obviously be dimmer stars, or local stars, but many other practitioners—whatever their training—are likely to find themselves serving on stars' teams or as consultants to the stars, as they all the while seek to brighten their own star prospects. One effect of all this on people now in law school—or considering going to law school— is likely to be that many fewer will see the financial rewards top graduates have come to expect as their due.

4. Lives Individual Lawyers Are Likely to Lead

The image of straining for the spotlight and fighting for pieces of a shrinking pie may seem grim to lawyers—especially those now in the last twenty years or so of their careers. This was the time life was supposed to get easier and during which these now-senior lawyers could live off the work of their juniors.

Some of today's younger lawyers, on the other hand, may see opportunity where others see despair. Current law students are likely

---

and Edward O. Laumann, *The Scale of Justice: Observations on the Transformation of Urban Law Practice*, 27 ANN. REV. OF SOCIOLOGY 337 (2001).

21. It is obviously risky to try to offer specific figures as to the number of "star" lawyers there might be, but I believe the number will be fewer than 10,000, i.e., fewer than 1 percent of all practicing lawyers.

to practice in a world in which potential clients can readily find expertise on the Internet. Rising lawyers will be able to let their light shine—and even become moderately bright stars—relying less than do today's lawyers on whom they know, where they went to school, and even where they live.

Younger lawyers are likely to find themselves facing more competition from both lawyers and non-lawyers, but for many of them, the challenge of competition is nothing new. All around them, young lawyers have seen that—in a heartbeat—their parent's lifelong employer could be sold or their friends' work outsourced. As a result, many in the rising generations have already tended to focus more on developing transportable skills than on the size of today's paycheck.[22]

Many of us can remember sports teams whose players spent an entire career in a single organization. But just as free agency has transformed professional sports by paying individual stars to change loyalties overnight, many in the rising generations of lawyers are likely to be familiar with that approach to life. While members of any generation are never entirely of one mind, earlier generations' objective of "making partner" may increasingly be viewed as not worth attaining. As one young lawyer is said to have put it, "becoming a partner is like a pie eating contest where the first prize is more pie."[23] Few of today's young lawyers want to starve, but, unless persuaded, they are likely to have less loyalty to the institutional setting in which they work.[24] The challenge for law firms will be to provide practice settings and other incentives sufficient to make them stay.

---

22. CAROLYN A. MARTIN & BRUCE TULGAN, MANAGING THE GENERATION MIX: FROM URGENCY TO OPPORTUNITY, at xiii (2006).

23. This widely-quoted expression has an obscure origin. One discussion of that origin is on The Volokh Conspiracy blog, in response to a question by Professor Orin Kerr, Jan. 16, 2005, found at http://volokh.com/2005/01/page/5/.

24. As one pair of authors describes the attitude, "Jobs may come and jobs may go but my career belongs to me." CAROLYN A. MARTIN & BRUCE TULGAN, MANAGING THE GENERATION MIX: FROM URGENCY TO OPPORTUNITY, at xii (2006). Alvin Toffler predicted this development and called it the "coming ad-hocracy." He predicted that lawyers would be particularly adaptable to this approach to work and career. ALVIN TOFFLER, FUTURE SHOCK 131–35 (1970). *See also* Bryant G. Garth & Joyce Sterling, *Exploring Inequality in the Corporate*

People with a law degree will find that they can use their training in a wide variety of ways. Others may seek some legal training—but less than today's three-year law degree—as they see how an understanding of law can help them even if they never want to practice. Indeed, law may become the new liberal arts education—helping to develop people who are tough-minded but determined to use their education in ways their predecessors never considered. Rather than being over a million examples of the same kind of professional personality, however, people we today call lawyers are likely to wind up using their education in closer to a million different ways.

B. PRIVATE FIRMS ARE LIKELY TO BE AS IMPORTANT AS EVER

On the surface, the image of today's American lawyer becoming even more an individual specialist who markets his or her talent on the Internet might seem seems the antithesis of being part of a worldwide law firm. It does not follow, however, that if individual lawyers become more narrowly focused, law firms must become small. Specialized lawyers seem likely to continue to practice in groups that resemble today's law firms, just as business consultants now practice in multispecialty organizations. The organization and growth of modern law firms has been the subject of substantial analysis.[25] Whether as managers of offices producing high-volume commodity services, or as high-skill, go-to sources of high-value work, there are

---

Law Firm Apprenticeship: Doing the Time, Finding the Love, 22 GEO. J. LEGAL ETHICS (forthcoming 2009) (viewing time at a law firm as a way to gain experience and attain status).

25. *See* JAY W. LORSCH & THOMAS J. TIERNEY, ALIGNING THE STARS: HOW TO SUCCEED WHEN PROFESSIONALS DRIVE RESULTS (2002); DAVID H. MAISTER, MANAGING THE PROFESSIONAL SERVICE FIRM (1993); Randall S. Thomas, Stewart J. Schwab & Robert G. Hansen, *Megafirms*, 80 N.C. L. REV. 115 (2001). An alternative model sees individuals forming ad hoc coalitions of talent to deal with particular projects. Thus, wherever a given professional sees as his or her office, teams of people from multiple offices might work together on a given activity. *See, e.g.*, DON TAPSCOTT & ANTHONY D. WILLIAMS, WIKINOMICS: HOW MASS COLLABORATION CHANGES EVERYTHING 259–66 (2006).

at least three reasons that law firms will continue and that many are likely to thrive.

1. Firms Help Lawyers Diversify Risk

Over twenty years ago, Professors Gilson and Mnookin suggested that law firms are organized in significant part to diversify the economic risk lawyers face at different stages of a business cycle.[26] As just discussed, lawyers now and in the future will face the chronic problem that only the very best are likely to prosper. Any individual lawyer can expect to have to develop a specialized skill or field of expertise in which he can stand out. So long as that lawyer's expertise is widely needed, the lawyer may do well, but if clients' needs change, even able lawyers in a declining field will face problems.

A booming economy may keep experienced corporate and commercial lawyers busy, for example, as clients seek to expand or go public. Bankruptcy lawyers, on the other hand, get busier when the economy turns down.[27] The ability to form firms allows lawyers to diversify their personal risk by diversifying the firm's offerings with different specialties that support each other through good times and bad. Deal lawyers keep the revenue flowing in good times, and to

---

26. Ronald J. Gilson & Robert H. Mnookin, *Sharing Among the Human Capitalists: An Economic Inquiry into the Corporate Law Firm and How Partners Split Profits*, 37 STAN. L. REV. 313, 322–29 (1985). The authors concluded that objectives such as economies of scale, the ability to support specialists, and the ability to offer a range of services could be achieved by firms significantly smaller than the firms then seen, much less the large firms found today. *Id.* at 317. Professor Fred McChesney had earlier suggested that firms split profits as a way to provide incentives for marketing. Fred S. McChesney, *Team Production, Monitoring, and Profit Sharing in Law Firms: An Alternative Hypothesis*, 11 J. LEGAL STUD. 379 (1982).

27. Robert Nelson suggests an alternative analysis of the same point— firms can provide a base of general service to some clients that helps pay the bills during the times between successful periods for the specialty practices of the firm. ROBERT L. NELSON, PARTNERS WITH POWER: THE SOCIAL TRANSFORMATION OF THE LARGE LAW FIRM 50–56 (1988). For another view of the growth of law firms, *see* the discussion in Chapter 3, *supra*, of MARC GALANTER & THOMAS PALAY, TOURNAMENT OF LAWYERS: THE TRANSFORMATION OF THE BIG LAW FIRM (1991).

some extent pay the bankruptcy lawyers more than they deserve. Bankruptcy lawyers are expected to return the favor later.

It is a plausible account of what keeps firms together, and as individual lawyer skills become narrower, and adaptation to new conditions more complex, lawyers are likely to need this kind of protection even more. Anyone who has followed the decline in loyalty to firms, however, and the seemingly endless moves some lawyers make from firm to firm, can see that this is not the whole story. Some lawyers try to avoid working as hard as their partners but expect to receive a full share of the profits anyway, a phenomenon called "shirking." Or, they may accept full support from their partners in their own low-demand times but move to a different firm just as their skill becomes more valuable ("leaving'). And, when leaving, they may try to take good clients with them ("grabbing").[28]

To try to counter these tendencies, firms have tried to encourage clients to see themselves as clients of the firm rather than clients of any particular lawyer. It is harder for a lawyer to get a new firm to attract her away if the lawyer cannot successfully persuade important clients to follow her to the new firm. But given the unpredictability of retaining clients in such situations, many firms have moved toward paying lawyers more nearly in proportion to their current profitability. That system, euphemistically called "eat what you kill," moves firms away from the risk-sharing model and in the direction of making the lawyers self-insurers who must save in the good years and consume savings when times are slow.

Firms reason that it is less likely some other firm will offer their lawyers a better deal if the current firm routinely pays the lawyers

---

28. The father of these labels is Professor Robert Hillman. Regulation of the practices is described in ROBERT W. HILLMAN, HILLMAN ON LAWYER MOBILITY: THE LAW AND ETHICS OF PARTNER WITHDRAWALS AND LAW FIRM BREAKUPS (2d ed. 1998); Robert W. Hillman, *Law Firms and Their Partners: The Law and Ethics of Grabbing and Leaving*, 67 TEX. L. REV. 1 (1988); Robert W. Hillman, *The Law Firm as Jurassic Park: Comments on Howard v. Babcock*, 27 U.C. DAVIS L. REV. 533 (1994); Robert W. Hillman, *The Property Wars of Law Firms: Of Client Lists, Trade Secrets and the Fiduciary Duties of Law Partners*, 30 FLA. ST. U. L. REV. 767 (2003). *See also* Milton C. Regan, Jr., *Law Firms, Competition Penalties, and the Values of Professionalism*, 13 GEO. J. LEGAL ETHICS 1 (1999); Laurel S. Terry, *Ethical Pitfalls and Malpractice Consequences of Law Firm Breakups*, 61 TEMPLE L. REV. 1055 (1988).

what they contribute to the firm's bottom line.[29] That, of course, tends to undercut the risk-sharing justification for having a firm in the first place. Indeed, under an "eat what you kill" system, firms also have to worry about integrity control, i.e., preventing lawyers from cheating their clients through inefficient work or cheating the firm by taking on dishonest clients who produce high legal fees in the short run but expose the firm to significant liability in the future.[30] Once again, the challenge for firms will be to overcome these tendencies.

2. Firms Help Achieve Economies of Scope, i.e., the Ability to Work on "Projects"

Next, assembling lawyers into firms will also often be useful to provide the sheer number of people that a large client may require for the kind of work the client needs done. A firm can provide the numbers of people necessary to do the legal work required to close a major business deal, for example, or to try a major lawsuit. This so-called "project" work would overwhelm a solo practitioner or an in-house legal department, and while it would often be possible for a client to assemble ad hoc teams of unrelated people for each new project, having groups already available from a single supplier may be significantly more convenient.[31]

Similarly, members of a firm can make arrangements to serve clients whose problems might arise at any hour of the day or night.

---

29. Ronald J. Gilson & Robert H. Mnookin, *Sharing Among the Human Capitalists: An Economic Inquiry into the Corporate Law Firm and How Partners Split Profits*, 37 STAN. L. REV. 313, 341–71 (1985). The authors followed up this line of thinking in Ronald J. Gilson & Robert H. Mnookin, *Coming of Age in a Corporate Law Firm: The Economics of Associate Career Patterns*, 41 STAN. L. REV. 567 (1989).

30. The negative consequences of such a policy are developed well in MILTON C. REGAN, JR., EAT WHAT YOU KILL: THE FALL OF A WALL STREET LAWYER (2006).

31. George P. Baker & Rachel Parkin, *The Changing Structure of the Legal Services Industry and the Careers of Lawyers*, 84 N.C. L. REV. 1635, 1656–59 (2006); Randall S. Thomas, Stewart J. Schwab & Robert G. Hansen, *Megafirms*, 80 N.C. L. REV. 115 (2001). Other mid-size firms will thrive because of special expertise, e.g., Finnegan Henderson in intellectual property and Wiley Rein in communications law. *See, e.g.*, Alison Frankel, *A First Look at the Second Hundred Firms*, AM. LAW, Aug. 1999, at 59.

Just as obstetricians form group practices so that no one of them always has to make early-morning deliveries, a law firm can spread the globalized world's need for 24/7 coverage, whether by having lawyers on call after regular office hours or by having offices all over the world, some of which are open in time zones where lawyers will be available when lawyers at other offices are not.

Finally, a firm allows lawyers to diversify the services they can provide for clients. This is another side of the risk-sharing advantage we saw earlier. Because individual firm members will tend to limit their practices and position themselves so as to be at the top of relatively small fields, it will take groups of lawyers with different areas of expertise to provide clients with the range of legal services any given matter might require. A single firm that can provide what is sometimes called "one-stop-shopping" promises to be attractive to clients who want to retain a firm that is immediately ready to go.

On the other hand, it is not clear that, even in this environment, all law firms should try to grow or that only large law firms will survive. Even today, corporate clients often employ several firms, each of which handles part of the client's work. Clients understandably do not want to become dependent on a single source for their legal work. While the number of firms a client uses may increase or decrease at given points in time, in the future, clients seem likely to continue to create teams of practitioners and firms who together will provide the client's needed range of services.

Small to mid-size firms have proved to be remarkably successful, for example, in today's difficult economic environment. To be taken seriously by major clients, the firms must make up for what they lack in total size with human scale and a prestige that attracts and retains excellent lawyers.[32] They must also offer competitive rates.[33]

---

32. See, e.g., Cynthia Cotts, *Wall Street Lawyers Dumped for Lower-Priced Boutiques*, Apr. 6, 2009, at http://www.bloomberg.com/apps/news?pid=20670001&sid=aPaoB9uRSvQk; Lynne Marek, *Big-Firm Partners Go Small*, Nat'l L.J., Mar. 16, 2009, at 1; Zach Lowe, *The Mid-Sized Strike Back: Regional Firms Could be Winners in Current Mess*, N.Y. Lawyer, Feb. 5, 2009, at http://www.nylawyer.com/display.php/file=/news/09/02/020509n.

33. See, e.g., George P. Baker & Rachel Parkin, *The Changing Structure of the Legal Services Industry and the Careers of Lawyers*, 84 N.C. L. Rev. 1635, 1657 (2006). The authors' data show that while large firms are getting larger,

An important option for such mid-size firms may be participation in "networks" of firms like themselves[34] that provide services for member firms around the country and the world. At one extreme, virtual law firms such as AXIOM[35] and CPA Global[36] have grown up to provide individual lawyers to law firms or corporate counsel as needed for particular projects. Other firms provide outsourcing or "contract lawyer" services, particularly where talent is needed for short-term projects. Syndicates of people and firms formed to address clients' needs are already employed by other kinds of professional service firms, and the approach may spread to lawyers.[37]

3. Firms Can Develop Reputations and Brand Names—The Matter of Marketing

Longstanding American lawyer tradition once held that when a lawyer first moved to a community, he had to wait quietly by the telephone for clients to call. That attitude came from the days when English barristers were thought to come from a social class that was independently wealthy. Even the world of barristers changed long ago, but the rule against lawyers' "self-laudatory" marketing lasted a long time.

In the 1970s, however, when John Bates and Van O'Steen opened what they called a "legal clinic" to offer fixed-price legal services to middle-income clients, they advertised their services in the newspaper, and in a landmark decision, the U.S. Supreme Court held that

---

mid-size firms do not seem to be getting fewer. *Id.* at 1657–62. Of the *American Lawyer's* second 100 firms, some struggle each year, but others do very well.

34. One of the best known is called Lex Mundi; *see* http://www.lexmundi.com.

35. *See* http://www.axiomlegal.com/.

36. *See* http://www.cpaglobal.com/about_cpa. *See also* Erin Coe, *Virtual Law Firms May Rise Out of Tougher Times* (Nov. 4, 2008), at http://www.competiton.law360.com/print_article/75201.

37. *See, e.g.*, LARRY SMITH, INSIDE/OUTSIDE: HOW BUSINESSES BUY LEGAL SERVICES 85–109 (2001); Randall S. Thomas, Stewart J. Schwab & Robert G. Hansen, *Megafirms*, 80 N.C. L. REV. 115, 118–27 (2001). *See also* MARC GALANTER & THOMAS PALAY, TOURNAMENT OF LAWYERS: THE TRANSFORMATION OF THE BIG LAW FIRM 129–35 (1991) (predicting that large firms with under-utilized personnel will increasingly subcontract with smaller firms to help them when numbers of lawyers are required).

lawyer advertising constitutes constitutionally protected speech. A complete ban on lawyer advertising is unconstitutional, the Court said, if it goes beyond regulating messages that are "false or misleading."[38]

Many lawyers do not like the prospect of advertising on late-night television. An Internet Web site may seem more respectable, but by far the best way for a lawyer to get instant recognition, respectability, and the kind of credibility that becomes even more important as clients have many professionals from whom to choose is likely to be to join a well-regarded law firm.[39]

The challenge for many clients—even those with inside counsel—is knowing which lawyers they can count on to provide good service.[40] In an earlier era, consumers knew their service providers personally and could make their own assessment of trustworthiness and quality. Today, when dealings are distant and often under time constraints, it is often brand-names that provide the level of confidence and trust necessary to let transactions proceed.[41]

---

38. Bates v. State Bar of Ariz., 433 U.S. 350 (1977).

39. Lawyers can profit from a reputation for good performance. *See, e.g.,* Deborah Rhode, *Profits and Professionalism,* 33 FORDHAM URBAN L.J. 49 (2005); Bryant G. Garth & Joyce Sterling, *Exploring Inequality in the Corporate Law Firm Apprenticeship: Doing the Time, Finding the Love,* 22 GEO. J. LEGAL ETHICS (forthcoming 2009).

40. Professor Larry Ribstein has emphasized the value of firm reputation in explaining the growth of law firms. Larry E. Ribstein, *Ethical Rules, Agency Costs, and Law Firm Structure,* 84 VA. L. REV. 1707 (1998). Ribstein's argument that firms should thus grow even larger is challenged in Ted Schneyer, *Reputational Bonding, Ethics Rules, and Law Firm Structure: The Economist as Storyteller,* 84 VA. L. REV. 1777 (1998).

41. *See, e.g.,* Benjamin Klein, *Brand Names, in The Concise Encyclopedia of Economics* (2002), at http://www.econlib.org/library/ENC/BrandNames.html, and Christian Sarkar, *The Speed of Trust: Trust, Branding & Competitive Advantage: An Interview with Stephen M.R. Covey* (2004), at http://www.zibs. com/covey.shtml. German researchers report that MRI images of the brains of people exposed to brand-names show activity in brain areas involved with positive emotions, while exposure to lesser known brand-names produced a generally negative emotional response. Siri Nilsson, *Shoppers' Brains Under Brand-Name Control* (Nov. 28, 2006), at http://abcnews.go.com/Health/ print?id=2682341. Familiar brand-names may also serve to give people a sense

For many years, law firms did not acknowledge the importance of branding. A law firm's name could contain only the names of lawyers who were with or had practiced with the firm. After it became common for firms to use only the names of *deceased* lawyers, however, law firm brand-names were a reality, and the rules of professional conduct now permit brand names so long as they are not misleading, such as by suggesting an affiliation with a government agency.[42] Now, most national firms have no more than one or two words in their firm name, and efforts to bring that name to the attention of business travelers in airports, on television, and in other commercial settings are ubiquitous. Lawyers realize that, when a client faces a significant question, it wants its advice to come from someone with instant credibility. It is hard to generalize about how significant brand-names will be in clients' choice of counsel, but the growth of modern American law firms in part reflects a belief that potential clients all over the world will find brand-names important.[43]

C. THE CHALLENGE OF MEETING DIVERSE CLIENT NEEDS ANYWHERE IN THE WORLD

However attractive the law firm model that we saw in Chapter 3 has been up to now, it seems unlikely that an hourly-fee, high-leverage form of organization can survive the challenges facing American firms. Each firm of whatever size will have to determine the changes it needs to make, but clients' and potential clients' demands will primarily determine what each must do to survive. All firms, however,

---

of continuity in an otherwise rapidly changing world. ALVIN TOFFLER, FUTURE SHOCK 64 (1970).

42. MODEL RULES PROF'L CONDUCT R. 7.5(a).

43. ROBERT L. NELSON, PARTNERS WITH POWER: THE SOCIAL TRANSFORMATION OF THE LARGE LAW FIRM 66–69 (1988) stresses that the significance of a law firm's brand is not the same as that of a consumer good. A law firm brand-name conveys a sense of status based on its historic quality and its continuing to recruit the best students at the best schools. That practice, of course, may also drive the high salaries commanded by students who have those qualities.

are likely to find that meeting client needs will present at least three kinds of challenges.

1. The Need to Serve Clients that Have National and Worldwide Activities

The potentially global range of client activities will inevitably create a need for most lawyers—personally or institutionally—to see that those clients can get legal help wherever in the world they need those services. It is always daytime somewhere in the world, and firms seeking to help meet legal needs will have to be prepared to be responsive around the clock.[44]

The most aggressive efforts to provide such services have been those of the global law firms that have a single name and structure, and a mission to deliver services all over the world with the depth and flexibility to meet a client's needs wherever they arise. Several firms have made large investments to try to achieve the scale necessary for such a presence. Baker & McKenzie, DLA Piper, and Clifford Chance each has over 3,500 lawyers, and others are not far behind.[45]

It will not be in the interest of most firms to try to be all things to all potential clients. If nothing else, the revenue stream required to operate firms large enough to do that run into millions of dollars each and every business day.[46] If a firm has a very secure client base, it may be possible to have a sufficiently reliable revenue stream to cover those costs, but for firms competing for clients in the market

---

44. Norman K. Clark & Ward Bower, *Globalization of Legal Services: What Will It Mean?*, an Altman & Weil White Paper (1999).

45. *See, e.g.,* Jens Drolshammer, *The Future Legal Structure of International Law Firms—Is the Experience of the Big Five in Structuring, Auditing and Consulting Organizations Relevant?*, in THE INTERNATIONALIZATION OF THE PRACTICE OF LAW 449 (Jens Drolshammer & Michael Pfeifer eds., 2001). *See also By the Numbers*, AM. LAWYER, May 2009, at 118 (introducing data on the Am Law 100, American law firms generating the largest gross revenue in 2008; Latham & Watkins, Jones Day, and White & Case are each shown as each having over 2,000 lawyers).

46. Baker & McKenzie, for example, is reported to bill and collect in excess of $9 million per business day, based on a year of 260 such days. AM. LAWYER, May 2009, at 145. It is impossible to know the break-even point for such a firm, but if revenues and thus per-partner income were to start to fall precipitously, any firm would find it hard to survive.

generally, the risk will be too great. Just as individual lawyers will compete to be stars, law firms will stress one or more fields in which they stand out. Not all firms will be small boutiques, but clients will tend to look for firms that are among the very best at what they do.

Further, the amount of local knowledge required and legal barriers to cross-border delivery of legal services will make it hard for most firms to see themselves operating all over the world.[47] But even lawyers in local firms are likely to at least have to be the resource to which their clients turn for the name of a lawyer in a place where the client needs help. If a lawyer cannot provide at least that much information, there will be a risk that clients will turn to someone who can. The critical task for any local lawyer, then, will be to know what services the lawyer's clients may need nationally and globally and to be prepared to help the client meet those needs in particular locations, using people who understand the local culture as well as the law.[48]

Use of law firm networks seems the most promising way for most American firms to develop national and worldwide contacts. Firms should not enter a network casually, and they should not be seen as a panacea. Clients will expect the same level of service in each area of the world, and not all network members may be of equal quality. But if one of the key services clients are likely to expect from their own lawyers and firms is an ability to find others to meet their needs, law firm networks can be a useful way to start.[49] Informal networks

---

47. *See, e.g.,* WTO Secretariat, eds., Guide to the GATS: An Overview of Issues for Further Liberalization of Trade in Services (2000); Richard L. Abel, *Transnational Law Practice,* 44 Case W. Res. L. Rev. 737 (1994); Ronald A. Brand, *Professional Responsibility in a Transnational Transactions Practice,* 17 J.L. & Com. 301 (1998); Laurel S. Terry, *But What Will the WTO Disciplines Apply To?: Distinguishing Among Market Access, National Treatment and Article VI:4 Measures When Applying the GATS to Legal Services,* Prof'l Law. 83 (2003 Symposium Issue); Detlev F. Vagts, *Professional Responsibility in Transborder Practice: Conflict and Resolution,* 13 Geo. J. Legal Ethics 677 (2000); *Symposium: Paris Forum on Transnational Practice for the Legal Profession,* 18 Dickinson J. Int'l L. 1 (1999).

48. *See, e.g.,* Alan Hodgart, *Globalization and the Future of International Law Firms—The Perspective of a Management Consultant,* in The Internationalization of the Practice of Law 173 (Jens Drolshammer & Michael Pfeifer eds., 2001).

49. *See, e.g.,* Julian Gresser, *Strategic Alliance Mediation—Creating Value from Difference and Discord in Global Business,* in The Internationalization

based on personal relationships and experience are likely then to follow.

2. Developing Practice Teams with Diverse Skills

Few clients need only one kind of service even when they face particular legal issues. As individual lawyers become more focused in what they do, they will have to integrate their own services with those of others. While some clients will choose to retain only one or a limited number of a firm's members, one of the reasons for having a firm will be to make it possible to make available several of the services a client needs. Any firm will have to remember that the cost of replacing a current client who must turn elsewhere to get needed services will only get higher as the world the firm faces becomes more competitive.

And not all the services a firm will be asked to provide will be those of lawyers.[50] Using non-lawyers to help deliver legal services is, of course, already part of the DNA of American law firms.[51] "Paralegals" get paid a salary rather than sharing in firm profits, but their time is often billed as a lawyer's is. These non-lawyers may handle particular parts of the legal task, or they may be people such as economists who have complementary skills.

Further, several law firms already run non-law businesses that are "ancillary" to their law practice precisely because they see that solving many legal problems requires addressing non-law issues. Law firms are expanding their range of services by adding law-related services

---

OF THE PRACTICE OF LAW 227 (Jens Drolshammer & Michael Pfeifer eds., 2001).

50. *See* Robert Eli Rosen, *"We're All Consultants Now": How Change in Client Organizational Strategies Influences Change in the Organization of Corporate Legal Services*, 44 ARIZ. L. REV. 637 (2002). The converse of this development is the rise of non-lawyers (including some legally trained persons who have resigned from the bar) who are giving advice about legal issues. *See* Tanina Rostain, *The Emergence of "Law Consultants,"* 75 FORDHAM L. REV. 1397 (2006). For a cautionary note, *see* Alexis Anderson, Lynn Barenberg & Paul R. Tremblay, *Professional Ethics in Interdisciplinary Collaboratives: Zeal, Paternalism and Mandated Reporting*, 13 CLINICAL L. REV. 659 (2007).

51. On the relationship between lawyers and paralegals, *see* MODEL RULES OF PROF'L CONDUCT R. 5.3.

such as economic consulting or private investigation or financial management. Sometimes the services have been provided from within the firm; at other times, separate, stand-alone or side-by-side entities have been created.[52] In other cases, mutual referral networks among lawyers and non-lawyers might be used.[53] Australia and England have now both approved lawyers being part of such multidisciplinary or multiservice firms.[54]

Not all clients will be drawn to such multiservice firms, but the challenge for today's lawyers will be to make the transition to a new reality in which many clients will find such firms attractive.[55]

---

52. *See* GARY A. MUNNEKE & ANN L. MACNAUGHTON, EDS., MULTIDISCIPLINARY PRACTICE: STAYING COMPETITIVE AND ADAPTING TO CHANGE (2001); James W. Jones & Bayless Manning, *Getting at the Root of Core Values: A "Radical" Proposal to Extend the Model Rules to Changing Forms of Law Practice*, 84 MINN. L. REV. 1159, 1176–79 (2000). One lawyer's response has been to create a referral network of lawyers who act as part-time general counsel for small companies, handle single small matters for others, and take referrals from law firms. It is called i>path (www.ipath.com). Bruce Balestier, *Network Solution*, LEGAL TIMES, Mar. 26, 2001, at 48.

53. Referral relationships with non-lawyers are governed by MODEL RULES OF PROF'L CONDUCT R. 7.2(b)(4), which requires only that referral relationships be non-exclusive and that the client be "informed of the existence and nature of the agreement."

54. Adding non-lawyers to a law firm is not the only, or even the best, way to operate. Before the demise of Arthur Andersen, the model it used in the U.K. was to form an independent law firm (Garrett & Co.) that operated in close cooperation with the accounting firm, paying a fee for space, equipment, and staff and being advertised as part of the Andersen "global network." Ward Bower, *The Impact of MDPs on Law Firms*, an Altman & Weil White Paper (1999).

55. *See, e.g.,* Mary C. Daly, *Monopolist, Aristocrat or Entrepreneur?: A Comparative Perspective on the Future of Multidisciplinary Partnerships in the United States, France, Germany, and the United Kingdom After the Disintegration of Andersen Legal*, 80 WASH. U. L. REV. 589 (2002). *See also* Daniel R. Fischel, *Multidisciplinary Practice*, 55 BUS. LAW. 951 (2000); Lawrence J. Fox, *Dan's World: A Free Enterprise Dream; An Ethics Nightmare*, 55 BUS. LAW. 1533 (2000); Bryant G. Garth & Carole Silver, *The MDP Challenge in the Context of Globalization*, 52 CASE W. RES. L. REV. 861 (2002); Robert R. Keatinge, *Multidimensional Practice in a World of Invincible Ignorance: MDP, MJP, and Ancillary Business After Enron*, 44 ARIZ. L. REV. 717 (2002).

Through personal education and association with people of differing skills, today's lawyers will need to develop an ability to deliver sophisticated solutions to concrete problems that will be affected by law, but only parts of which will present traditional legal questions. An estate planner, for example, might transform herself into a wealth planner and give investment advice in addition to drafting wills and trusts. Real estate lawyers will have to become skilled in real estate finance, workouts when borrowers are close to foreclosure, and managing a high volume production of financing documents. Corporate lawyers will have to understand complex new financial instruments about which they have heretofore relied—sometimes to their detriment— on the explanations of others.[56]

The problem for American law firms trying to make such a transition today is that A.B.A. Model Rule 5.4(a) provides that a "lawyer or law firm shall not share legal fees with a nonlawyer,"[57] while Rule 5.4(b) prohibits a lawyer from forming "a partnership with a nonlawyer if any of the activities of the partnership consist of the practice of law."[58] Both provisions stand in the way of formation of multiservice practice organizations that would let firms provide clients with a wide range of integrated services.

A decade ago, the report of the A.B.A.'s Multidisciplinary Practice Commission[59] called for revisions to Rule 5.4, but the proposal was soundly defeated.[60] The proposal was considered by the A.B.A. around

---

56. Possibly serious problems arising from such reliance can be seen in, e.g., *In re Enron Corp. Securities, Derivative & ERISA Litigation*, 235 F. Supp. 2d 549 (S.D. Tex. 2002).

57. MODEL RULES OF PROF'L CONDUCT R 5.4(a).

58. MODEL RULES OF PROF'L CONDUCT R 5.4(b).

59. American Bar Association Commission on Multidisciplinary Practice, Report to the House of Delegates, August 1999.

60. Ultimate defeat of the proposals came in August 2000 when the A.B.A. House of Delegates adopted a proposal to develop rules making cooperation even more difficult. For an excellent discussion of the issues surrounding multidisciplinary partnerships, *see, e.g.,* Laurel S. Terry, *A Primer on MDPs: Should the "No" Rule Become a New Rule?*, 72 TEMPLE L. REV. 869 (1999); John S. Dzienkowski & Robert J. Peroni, *Multidisciplinary Practice and the American Legal Profession: A Market Approach to Regulating the Delivery of Legal Services in the Twenty-First Century*, 69 FORDHAM L. REV. 83 (2000); Mary C. Daly, *Choosing Wise Men Wisely: The Risks and Rewards of Purchasing*

the time of the Enron scandal, and the concern most often expressed was that association with non-lawyers would undermine lawyer independence. The time is right to re-examine that decision. Multiservice practice organizations are not only of interest to corporate clients. Social service agencies that want to provide legal services as part of a comprehensive package of services to the poor have an equal stake in changing the present rules. As discussed earlier, Great Britain and Australia have both recently paved the way for such practice organizations, and the District of Columbia has permitted them for many years with no loss of lawyer independence.[61]

The American Bar Association has acted as though lawyers still operate in a world in which communication and travel are difficult. Clients know better. Regulatory requirements might properly continue to require competent service, protection of privileged information, and avoiding conflicts of interest not waived by clients of the firm.[62] Blanket prohibition of multiservice firms, however, should no longer be the rule.

Legal Services From Lawyers in a Multidisciplinary Partnership, 13 GEO. J. LEGAL ETHICS 217 (2000).

61. The D.C. Rule is 5.4(b). Under the D.C. rule, the non-lawyer must undertake to abide by ethical standards applicable to lawyers in the firm.

62. The most comprehensive analysis of the multiple sources of lawyer regulation is David B. Wilkins, *Who Should Regulate Lawyers*, 105 HARV. L. REV. 799 (1992). The perceived tension between sources of regulatory authority is analyzed in an article published almost contemporaneously with Wilkins' article. Susan P. Koniak, *The Law Between the Bar and the State*, 70 N.C. L. REV. 1389 (1992). For a more recent discussion of examples of external regulation of lawyers, *see* Ted Schneyer, *An Interpretation of Recent Developments in the Regulation of Law Practice*, 30 OKLA. CITY U. L. REV. 559 (2005); James M. Fischer, *External Control Over the American Bar*, 19 GEO. J. LEGAL ETHICS 59 (2006); Andrew M. Perlman, *Toward a Unified Theory of Professional Regulation*, 55 FLA. L. REV. 977 (2003). Today, many more entities and institutions contribute to what is now called the law governing lawyers. Federal agencies such as the SEC, the IRS, and the Patent and Trademark Office, for example, have adopted practice standards and impose significant disciplinary sanctions on lawyers who practice before them. Federal criminal statutes, such as those prohibiting money laundering, mail fraud, and income tax evasion, apply to lawyers. And, as many lawyers have found to their dismay, lawyers can be prosecuted as part of conspiracies involving their clients. As lawyer practice becomes more interstate and international, we may

3. Making Racial and Gender Diversity a Part of the Firm's Reality

In the context of delivering diverse services worldwide, achieving racial and gender diversity will continue to be among the most challenging issues facing law firms. Candor requires most white Americans to acknowledge that they have seen most efforts at diversity as *noblesse oblige*. Affirmative action has sometimes been acknowledged as a moral obligation owed to persons or groups left behind at an earlier point in history, but diversity has too rarely been understood as a reality that characterizes all of American society.[63]

From 1900 to almost 1950, about 85 percent of Americans were Caucasian and 15 percent were African-American. Today, Caucasians have dropped to about 65 percent of U.S. society. African-Americans have fallen to about 12 percent; about 16 percent of Americans are Hispanic; Asians represent about 5 percent; and the remainder are Native Americans and other ethnic groups.[64] Census Bureau projections suggest that in 2050, Caucasians will be down to 46 percent of

---

expect increased pressure for federal regulation of lawyers and federal standards governing them. In addition, negotiations conducted under the umbrella of the General Agreement on Trade in Services may break down barriers to practice that national and state boundaries now create. *See, e.g.,* Laurel S. Terry, *GATS' Applicability to Transnational Lawyering and its Potential Impact on U.S. State Regulation of Lawyers,* 34 VAND. J. TRANSNAT'L L. 989 (2001).

63. It remains to be seen whether the election of President Obama will change this understanding in any way. Thoughtful insights about these questions are provided in PETER H. SCHUCK, DIVERSITY IN AMERICA: KEEPING GOVERNMENT AT A SAFE DISTANCE (2003). Schuck observes that the United States is perhaps the only country that sees diversity as a value in itself; in most other parts of the world, one or more groups have achieved dominance or are fighting to achieve it. *Id.* at 14, 60–61.

64. Of course, these particular groupings are not the only dimensions of diversity. Differences within racial or ethnic groups may be as important as the larger groupings. PETER H. SCHUCK, DIVERSITY IN AMERICA: KEEPING GOVERNMENT AT A SAFE DISTANCE 28–29 (2003). There are at least 35 million foreign-born people in the United States, and immigration accounts for almost 40 percent of our annual population growth. Immigrants and their U.S.-born children made up 55 percent of the last 100 million-person growth in the U.S. population. *The United States: 300 Million and Growing,* WALL ST. J., Oct. 21–22, 2006, at A7. Further, the United States birth rate is high: 14 per 1,000 people per year, and our death rate is low: 8 per 1,000 per year.

the population, African-Americans will be 12 percent, Asians will grow to 8 percent, and Hispanics will likely be 30 percent of the U.S. population.[65] The point of such numbers is that addressing issues of diversity is no longer a choice for American society and its lawyers; it is an inescapable necessity.[66] Many of the ways social issues are addressed will involve lawyers, and lawyers will be among those helping diverse individuals work their way through the regulatory and assistance systems that run through our economy.

The pressure for diversity among both law school students and faculty has grown and is likely to increase.[67] The number of women in law school has grown to about 50 percent of an entering class, and members of minority groups are about 25 percent of the class at many schools. Fewer than 18 percent of partners in large U.S. law firms are women, however, and non-whites are fewer than 4 percent.[68]

One effect of this is that the number of both older and younger Americans is rising.

65. Any projections of this kind are subject to error. The cited figures are from U.S. Bureau of Census, U.S. Population Projections, found at http://www.census.gov/population/www/projections/summarytables.html. See also PETER H. SCHUCK, DIVERSITY IN AMERICA: KEEPING GOVERNMENT AT A SAFE DISTANCE 53 (2003), and The United States: 300 Million and Growing, WALL ST. J., Oct. 21, 2006, at A7, which both offer somewhat higher projections of the Caucasian population in 2050.

66. See generally Robert L. Nelson, The Futures of American Lawyers: A Demographic Profile of a Changing Profession in a Changing Society, 44 CASE W. RES. L. REV. 345 (1994); David B. Wilkins, Why Global Law Firms Should Care About Diversity: Five Lessons from the American Experience, in THE INTERNATIONALIZATION OF THE PRACTICE OF LAW 43 (Jens Drolshammer & Michael Pfeifer eds., 2001).

67. See, e.g., A.B.A. PRESIDENTIAL ADVISORY COUNCIL ON DIVERSITY IN THE PROFESSION & LAW SCHOOL ADMISSION COUNCIL, COLLABORATING TO EXPAND THE PIPELINE (LET'S GET REAL): EMBRACING THE OPPORTUNITIES FOR INCREASING DIVERSITY INTO THE LEGAL PROFESSION (2005).

68. See, e.g., A.B.A. COMM'N ON WOMEN IN THE PROFESSION, CHARTING OUR PROGRESS: THE STATUS OF WOMEN IN THE PROFESSION TODAY (2006); DEBORAH L. RHODE, THE UNFINISHED AGENDA: WOMEN AND THE LEGAL PROFESSION (2001); Cynthia Fuchs Epstein, et al., Glass Ceilings and Open Doors: Women's Advancement in the Legal Profession, 64 FORDHAM L. REV. 306 (1995); Carrie Menkel-Meadow, Feminization of the Legal Profession: The Comparative Sociology of Women Lawyers, in LAWYERS IN SOC'Y, VOL. 3,

In 2004, there were "thirty-three minority general counsel of Fortune 500 corporations, including such heavyweights as Coca-Cola, Merck, and Sears."[69] Some of them, and many other corporate counsel, are increasingly making the diversity of a firm's lawyers an important factor in deciding which firms to retain.[70] Overt discrimination could be one explanation for the lack of diversity in law firms, of course, but few believe that firms are foolish enough not to be concerned about the problem. Whatever the reasons in the past,[71] however, firms acting in their own interest have little choice but to improve the reality of their diversity—probably particularly their Hispanic diversity—in the future.[72]

COMPARATIVE THEORIES (Richard L. Abel & Philip S.C. Lewis eds., 1988); Steve French, *Of Problems, Pitfalls and Possibilities: A Comprehensive Look at Female Attorneys and Law Firm Partnership*, 21 WOMEN'S RTS. L. REP. 189 (2000).

69. David B. Wilkins, *From "Separate Is Inherently Unequal" to "Diversity is Good for Business": The Rise of Market-Based Diversity Arguments and the Fate of the Black Corporate Bar*, 117 HARV. L. REV. 1548, 1557 (2004).

70. *See, e.g.*, David B. Wilkins & G. Mitu Gulati, *Why Are There So Few Black Lawyers in Corporate Law Firms? An Institutional Analysis*, 84 CAL. L. REV. 493 (1996). *See also* Lisa Stansky, *Pressuring Law Firms: Corporate Counsel Push for Diversity*, NAT'L L.J., Apr. 14, 2003, at A-14 (citing BellSouth and Sara Lee); Meredith Hobbs, *Wal-Mart's Outside Legal Team Sees More Diversity*, NAT'L L.J., Oct. 31, 2005, at 13; Nathan Koppel, *Courting Shell*, AM. LAWYER, June 2004, at 98; Bronwyn Eyre, *The Demands of Diversity*, EUR. LAW., Sept. 2005, at 20.

71. A controversial explanation of the reason for low retention of non-white lawyers is Professor Sander's assertion that when law firms engage in affirmative action to recruit minority lawyers, they set the lawyers up to fail in any promotion to partner tournament the law firm might create. Richard H. Sander, *The Racial Paradox of the Corporate Law Firm*, 84 N.C. L. REV. 1755 (2006). *But see* James E. Coleman, Jr. & Mitu Gulati, *A Response to Professor Sander: Is It Really All About the Grades?*, 84 N.C. L. REV. 1823 (2006). *See also* Elizabeth Chambliss, *Organizational Determinants of Law Firm Integration*, 46 AM. U. L. REV. 669 (1997).

72. Professor Wilkins properly decries focusing on the fact that diversity is good for a firm's business because it seems to diminish the sense that moral issues of human equality should animate diversity concerns. David B. Wilkins, *From "Separate Is Inherently Unequal" to "Diversity is Good for Business": The Rise of Market-Based Diversity Arguments and the Fate of the Black Corporate Bar*, 117 HARV. L. REV. 1548 (2004); David B. Wilkins, *"If You Can't Join 'Em, Beat 'Em!": The Rise and Fall of the Black Corporate Law Firm*,

D. DEVELOPING INSTITUTIONAL STRENGTH IN A WORLD OF INDIVIDUAL STARS

There is an important tension imbedded in what we have discussed so far. Clients are likely to require extensive, diverse services that will require multiple providers working together. At the same time, individual lawyers are likely to be under pressure to try to stand out as stars in their specialized fields. Accommodating the tension created by those two realities is likely to be the greatest single challenge facing law firms in the future.

1. Seeing Firms as Shopping Centers Rather than Department Stores

For many years, the top law firms have competed to hire the brightest people possible, pay them top dollar, and employ them more or less as generalists to be used to handle matters in which the firm had a need for help at the time they arrived or thereafter. There is good reason to doubt that such a strategy will work as well in the future.[73]

While rarely articulated as such, law firms have, in effect, traditionally seen themselves as "department stores," providing a cornucopia of products and services through a single entity. Clients who seek out particular lawyers become clients of the firm as a whole. Each lawyer in the firm owes each firm client—even clients the lawyer has never met—the same duties owed by any other lawyer in the firm. Further, just as a Macy's salesperson will try to get a clothing customer to patronize Macy's for jewelry needs as well, today's lawyers

---

60 STAN. L. REV. 1733 (2008). On the other hand, as Professor Wilkins notes, corporations and their lawyers are now advocating for equality and even affirmative action as never before. 117 HARV. L. REV. at 1555. It seems that arguments based on economic benefits may lead to desirable results more quickly than calls based on morality alone, but the risk of tokenism in minority hiring remains real. See, e.g., J. Cunyon Gordon, Painting By Numbers: "And, Um, Let's Have a Black Lawyer Sit at Our Table, 71 FORDHAM L. REV. 1257 (2003).

73. See, e.g., William D. Henderson, Are We Selling Results or Resumes?: The Underexplored Linkage Between Human Resource Strategies and Firm-Specific Capital (2008), found at http://ssrn.com/abstract=1121238 (predicting that firms will find it profitable to hire students with somewhat lower grade point averages and from somewhat lower-ranked schools rather than paying top dollar to hire top graduates of elite schools).

try to "cross sell," i.e., get the clients they serve to use the services of other lawyers in the firm for any other legal needs they may have.

In the future, clients are more likely to see professional service firms—including law firms—more as shopping malls in which providers share a common location and overall name, but in which multiple providers often independently supply their own services. In lieu of the traditional pyramid model of a law firm, in which lawyers try to attain a place at the narrow top, the dominant model for American law firms is likely to be a mountain range or island chain, consisting of practice groups built around peaks represented by its star lawyers.[74] Members of a practice group will be selected based more on their specialized skills than their law school grades alone. Lawyers with the right training and experience may be able to identify niches where they can prosper, while their counterparts with only a prestigious degree suffer by comparison.[75]

Lawyers and their teams will make their presence known by advertising, networking, writing articles and blogs, and in all other ways they can make themselves stand out. While firms will prefer to have clients employ several of its practice groups at once to deal with a matter, firms are likely to find themselves offering partial or "unbundled" services as an alternative to traditional legal representation. A firm might do only the tax analysis of a transaction, for example, but not negotiate the transaction itself. Or, a star trial lawyer might try a case after the client has assigned most of the discovery work to a less expensive firm or even outsourced parts of it to India.[76]

---

74. Although they express the point differently, the new version of "tournament" theory found in Marc Galanter & William Henderson, *The Elastic Tournament: A Second Transformation of the Big Law Firm*, 60 STAN. L. REV. 1867 (2008), seems consistent with this view.

75. *See, e.g.,* Tom Ginsburg & Jeffrey A. Wolf, *The Market for Elite Law Firm Associates*, 31 FLA. ST. U. L. REV. 909 (2004); William D. Henderson, *Are We Selling Results or Resumes?: The Underexplored Linkage Between Human Resource Strategies and Firm-Specific Capital*, found at http://ssrn.com/abstract=1121238 (2008); James J. Sandman, *The High Price of Escalating Associate Salaries, Washington Lawyers*, March 2007, found at http://www.dcbar.org/for_lawyers/resoources/publications/washington_lawyer/march_2007/president.cfm.

76. *See, e.g.,* Julie Triedman, *Temporary Solution*, AM. LAWYER, Sept. 2006, at 97; Bethany Broida, *The Unseen Legal Team*, LEGAL TIMES, Oct. 18, 2004, at

Unbundling is likely to seem unsettling to lawyers who formerly did a job from start to finish, but unbundled services will take maximum advantage of the lawyer specialization that seems likely to be inevitable.[77] Looked at as we did in Chapter 3, law firms and their members will be under pressure to think of themselves in relation to corporate counsel offices as contract lawyers are in relation to law firms. In each case, they will be hired to meet particular—sometimes short-term—needs. Firms will tend not to like this analogy. Firms tend to look down on contract lawyers, considering them a necessary

---

46; Bill Detamore, *Saving Money in Document Review*, Legal Times, Apr. 16, 2007, at 36 (describing client hiring temporary lawyers directly and cutting out law firm). There is an increasing scholarly literature on outsourcing legal work. *See, e.g.,* Jayanth K. Krishnan, *Outsourcing and the Globalizing Legal Profession*, 48 Wm. & Mary L. Rev. 2189 (2007); Mary Daly & Carole Silver, *Flattening the World of Legal Services? The Ethical and Liability Minefields of Offshoring Legal and Law-Related Services*, 38 Geo. J. Inter. L. 619 (2007); Laura D'Allaird, *"The Indian Lawyer": Legal Education in India and Protecting the Duty of Confidentiality while Outsourcing*, 18 Prof'l Law. 1 (No. 3, 2007); Richard Parnham, *In the Footsteps of Pioneers*, Eur. Law. 25 (Oct. 2004); Geanne Rosenberg, *"Offshore" Legal Work Makes Gains*, Nat'l L.J., Mar. 29, 2004 (predicting an increase from an $80 million annual market to a $4 billion market). The A.B.A. Standing Committee on Ethics and Professional Responsibility upheld outsourcing as ethical in its Formal Opinion 08-451 (Aug. 5, 2008), so long as the U.S. lawyer exercises reasonable judgment in selecting the Indian firm and exercises reasonable supervision of the firm. *See also* Ass'n Bar City of N.Y., Opinion 2006-3 (Aug. 2006).

77. *See* Robert L. Nelson, Partners With Power: The Social Transformation of the Large Law Firm 8 (1988) (the reputation of a firm or individual partner for a specific service is replacing general relationships between a firm and a corporate client). According to Nelson, "The trend toward specialty representation is a general phenomenon that is transforming the client base of even the most established general service firm." *Id*, at 273–74. There is already evidence of these development. In recent years, for example, law firm expansion has often been by acquisition of practice groups theretofore operating independently or as part of competing firms. Such specialized practice groups join large, multi-city organizations in part because of the credibility and reputation for quality control the firms enjoy. Unfortunately for the firm that they join, however, the footloose practice group is likely to stay at a firm only until a better offer comes along, and at that point they may again leave as a group.

evil but not up to the law firm's usual standards,[78] but American firms are likely to learn in the future how it feels to be hired help.

A difference between law firms and contract lawyers, of course, will be that some firm members will be acknowledged to have skills superior to those available in-house at the client company.[79] Firms may also be seen as a place to get a second opinion or to do an internal investigation as to which the general counsel's office might appear to have a conflict of interest. Firms equally might, however, be retained to provide bodies to help handle a lawsuit that will end and at the conclusion of which the corporate counsel does not want to have lawyers with personnel rights. Like make-or-buy decisions faced by companies throughout all their operations, lawyers in private practice are likely to be under pressure to agree to meet only particular needs at particular times.[80] Those who fail to do so are likely to suffer in the legal services marketplace.

On the other hand, the risks of law firms becoming "shopping centers" are substantial, and will present particular problems for law firm managers. Under such a decentralized model, lawyers in a firm will be even more likely than today to "eat what they kill," to try to operate independent of central firm authority, and to take on cases presenting greater risks than the firm might otherwise find acceptable. Traditionally, every partner in a law firm is liable for the malpractice of every other lawyer in the firm.[81] That principle has been modified by limited liability statutes in many states, but effectiveness

---

78. See, e.g., Vincent R. Johnson & Virginia Coyle, *On the Transformation of the Legal Profession: The Advent of Temporary Lawyering*, 66 NOTRE DAME L. REV. 359 (1990); Julie Kay, *Cheaper By the Hour*, NAT'L L.J., Jan. 12, 2009, at 1.

79. Among firms standing by to provide lawyers to perform relatively sophisticated services today are Axiom, a virtual firm whose individual lawyers work from home or at the offices of clients to whom they are assigned, and CPA Global, a firm that supplies lawyers teams to support litigation, review documents, and manage intellectual property. See www.axiomlegal. com and www.cpaglobal.com.

80. See, e.g., LARRY SMITH, INSIDE, OUTSIDE: HOW BUSINESSES BUY LEGAL SERVICES (2001).

81. RESTATEMENT (THIRD) OF THE LAW GOVERNING LAWYERS § 58 (2000); see also Anthony V. Alfieri, *The Fall of Legal Ethics and the Rise of Risk Management*, 94 GEO. L.J. 1909 (2006).

of the statutes is a matter of doubt.[82] When law firm members offer unbundled services and do not have control over an entire matter, it may be hard later to demonstrate which provider's acts caused a client's loss. The firm and each of its members may be at risk, then, for conduct over which they had little control.

Even more unsettling, when a lawyer knows that she will get paid for work she brings in—but that others will share the liability if the client turns out to be dishonest or the work is done poorly—the "moral hazard" risk to the firm can be enormous. Firms will try to exercise some control over decisions regarding what risks to assume, but unlike mountains or islands in nature that are largely fixed in place, current rules of lawyer conduct prohibit restricting a lawyer's ability to leave a firm with little or no notice.[83] Law firm peaks or islands are free to join different "ranges" or "chains," i.e., other firms, as their personal interests warrant. Among the things managers will have to do to keep firms together is to foster developing a firm reputation from which each lawyer sees that he or she benefits.

In such a world, it should be in the interest of clients as well as lawyers to have lawyer professional standards support efforts by law firms to establish a culture of ethical conduct by each of its lawyers and non-lawyers.[84] Firm culture can make a difference. Young lawyers learn quickly that their future in the firm depends on how well

---

82. The problem is that, while the statutes make a lawyer liable only for his or her personal misconduct, other lawyers can be charged with failure to supervise such a lawyer, thus rendering many more unsuspecting people subject to potential liability. *See, e.g.*, Susan Saab Fortney, *Seeking Shelter in the Minefield of Unintended Consequences—The Traps of Limited Liability Law Firms*, 54 WASH. & LEE L. REV. 717 (1997).

83. MODEL RULES OF PROF'L CONDUCT R. 5.6(a).

84. MODEL RULES OF PROF'L CONDUCT R. 7.1–7.3. Furthermore, today, the process of lawyer discipline is no longer exclusively in the hands of designated enforcement officials. Suits for malpractice, breach of contract, and other forms of civil liability have put every client—and every new lawyer those clients might consult—in a position to rectify lawyer carelessness or dishonesty. As a result, lawyer malpractice insurers have become the toughest enforcement agents of all, seeking to limit the kinds of lawyer misconduct that might require the insurer to pay a claim. *See, e.g.*, Anthony E. Davis, *Professional Liability Insurers as Regulators of Law Practice*, 65 FORDHAM L. REV. 209 (1996); David Barnhizer, *Profession Deleted: Using Market and*

they please their elders.[85] Clients as well as lawyers have a stake in firms having the ability to preserve their reputations. Reputation and firm culture are firm-wide assets.[86] The challenge for managers—and for those regulating lawyers and their firms[87]—will be to hold firms together and try to preserve those assets at a time many lawyers find it in their personal interest to leave and let others concern themselves with the law firm as an institution.[88]

2. Making Firms Attractive Places in Which to Build a Career

Young lawyers used to complain about the hours they were forced to work at many firms. Firms responded that the long hours were necessary to justify the high salaries that beginning lawyers were often paid. Even when the current economic emergency concludes,

---

Liability Forces to Regulate the Very Ordinary Business of Law Practice for Profit, 17 GEO. J. LEGAL ETHICS 203 (2004).

85. *See* Kimberly Kirkland, *Ethics in Large Law Firms: The Principle of Pragmatism*, 35 U. MEM. L. REV. 631 (2005).

86. The point is made well in Richard Painter, *The Moral Interdependence of Corporate Lawyers and Their Clients*, 67 S. CAL. L. REV. 507 (1994). A similar point is made in Larry E. Ribstein, *Ethical Rules, Agency Costs, and Law Firm Structure*, 84 VA. L. REV. 1707 (1998). But doubt about the reputation thesis is expressed in Ted Schneyer, *Reputational Bonding, Ethical Rules, and Law Firm Structure: The Economist as Storyteller*, 84 VA. L. REV. 1777 (1998).

87. As law is increasingly practiced in institutions, we might expect professional discipline to be imposed on law firms instead of only the lawyers who practice within them. The leading article making this proposal is Ted Schneyer, *Professional Discipline for Law Firms*, 77 CORNELL L. REV. 1 (1991). The article has led to several responses, *e.g.*, Julie Rose O'Sullivan, *Professional Discipline for Law Firms? A Response to Professor Schneyer's Proposal*, 16 GEO. J. LEGAL ETHICS 1 (2002); Elizabeth Chambliss, *The Nirvana Fallacy in Law Firm Regulation Debates*, 33 FORDHAM URBAN L.J. 119 (2005).

88. *See generally, e.g.*, Milton C. Regan, Jr., *Moral Intuitions and Organizational Culture*, 51 ST. LOUIS U. L. REV. 941 (2007); Ted Schneyer, *A Tale of Four Systems: Reflections on How Law Influences the "Ethical Infrastructure" of Law Firms*, 39 S. TEX. L. REV. 245 (1998). See also Elizabeth Chambliss & David B. Wilkins, *The Emerging Role of Ethics Advisors, General Counsel, and Other Compliance Specialists in Large Law Firms*, 44 ARIZ. L. REV. 559 (2002); Elizabeth Chambliss, *The Professionalization of Law Firm In-House Counsel*, 84 N.C. L. REV. 1515 (2006); Timothy L. Fort, *Getting that Culture Thing*, NAT'L L.J., Feb. 5, 2007, at 22.

however, the prior law firm business model likely will not be restored. Even firms that pride themselves on hiring the best available talent cannot continue to pay large salaries to lawyers who are free and likely to leave the firm in two or three years.

In general, it has cost law firms anywhere from $200,000 to $500,000 to bring a recent law graduate into the firm as an associate. The sum includes recruiting costs associated with a pre-graduation summer employment program, the tuition for a bar exam preparation course, often a salary while the recent graduates study for the bar examination, and the inevitable costs associated with writing off time spent on assignments the new lawyer did not fully understand. Nevertheless, at many firms, at least 40 percent of new hires have voluntarily resigned by the end of their third year in practice, hardly having made back their cost to the firm.[89]

Some lawyers stay beyond the initial period, of course, and the system worked well enough for several years that leverage produced huge profits for partners at many firms. But the economic realities do not bode well for the future. Several jumps in entry level salaries paid to young lawyers were justified by the sense that investment banks and other financial institutions were pursuing many of the same people, and the belief that law firms had to match their offers. Now, offers from investment firms are likely to fall significantly, and law firms will have to recognize that high salaries will not be enough to make the firms attractive places to work.[90]

---

89. Deborah Rhode, *Profits and Professionalism*, 33 FORDHAM URBAN L.J. 49, 66 (2005). *See also* DEBORAH RHODE, BALANCED LIVES: CHANGING THE CULTURE OF LEGAL PRACTICE, A.B.A. COMM'N ON WOMEN IN THE PROFESSION (2002). Robert Nelson observed, however, that even in 1988, the turnover was one-third to one-half by the end of three years. ROBERT L. NELSON, PARTNERS WITH POWER: THE SOCIAL TRANSFORMATION OF THE LARGE LAW FIRM 143 (1988). For an interesting study of what students and clients expect from law firms, *see* Andrew Bruck & Andrew Canter, *Supply, Demand, and the Changing Economics of Large Law Firms*, 60 STAN. L. REV. 2087 (2008).

90. Who gets hurt by the present system? PAUL M. BARRETT, THE GOOD BLACK: A TRUE STORY OF RACE IN AMERICA (1999), is an important account of Lawrence Mungin, a lawyer chewed up by the present system, and of the depersonalization of modern practice from the perspective of a young lawyer. Mungin had been at two other firms but then joined a third to work for a rainmaker, i.e., a partner expected to attract clients to the firm. The clients the

Even now, firms are finding that government offices, corporate legal departments, and law schools pay less but attract lawyers who have paid off of their student loans and are seeking ways better to balance the demands of work, family, and community.[91] Firms are likely to have to take other steps to help young lawyers see that they have a future at the firm that will be attractive over a multiyear career.[92] Helping young lawyers work out arrangements that will cause them to stay is likely to improve everyone's bottom line.[93]

A significant problem for many young lawyers has been that they cannot see themselves growing in their practice. At most large firms

---

rainmaker anticipated never appeared, and the firm was unsuccessful in working Mungin into another field.

91. On the problem of work-life balance, *see generally* GEORGE W. KAUFMAN, THE LAWYER'S GUIDE TO BALANCING LIFE & WORK (2d ed. 2006); Carrie Menkel-Meadow, *Culture Clash in the Quality of Life in the Law: Changes in the Economics, Diversification and Organization of Lawyering*, 44 CASE W. RES. L. REV. 621 (1994).

92. One should not expect a return to the days of lifetime tenure at a single employer. In an environment of rapid change, the "free agent" mentality that sees organizations as simply places at which one employs his or her individual skills seems likely inevitably to prevail. ALVIN TOFFLER, FUTURE SHOCK 131–35 (1970). Toffler saw the willingness to change jobs as inevitable in a world where conditions are constantly changing. He said all of us need to learn to deal with "the economics of impermanence." *Id.* at 52–53 (1970).

93. Joan Williams & Cynthia Thomas Calvert, *Don't Go! We Can Change*, LEGAL TIMES, Feb. 5, 2001, at 20. *See also* Terry Carter, *Your Time or Your Money*, A.B.A. J., Feb. 2001, at 26. Further, because retention of associates is such a big issue for firms, more and more are letting associates review their supervising partners. It is cheaper to keep current associates happy than to hire new ones. Cameron Stracher, *Making Nicey*, AM. LAW., July 2000, at 47. Additional studies of the part-time phenomenon include CYNTHIA FUCHS EPSTEIN, CARROLL SERON, BONNIE OGLENSKY, AND ROBERT SAUTE, THE PART-TIME PARADOX: TIME NORMS, PROFESSIONAL LIVES, FAMILY, AND GENDER (1999); JOAN WILLIAMS & CYNTHIA THOMAS CALVERT, BALANCED HOURS: EFFECTIVE PART TIME POLICIES FOR WASHINGTON LAW FIRMS: THE PROJECT FOR ATTORNEY RETENTION, FINAL REPORT (3d ed. 2002); REPORT OF THE BOSTON BAR ASSOCIATION TASK FORCE ON PROFESSIONAL CHALLENGES AND FAMILY NEEDS, FACING THE GRAIL: CONFRONTING THE COST OF WORK-FAMILY IMBALANCE (2007).

in recent years, young lawyers have been expected to be productive from their first day on the job. The days of learning from senior lawyers and maturing within a supportive environment have been gone. Recently, Howrey and a few other firms have announced an "apprenticeship" model under which recent law graduates will be paid a reduced salary in exchange for more personalized training and involvement with clients.[94]

The model is promising. Actual work under the direction of more experienced lawyers is certainly among the most effective ways to make the transition from student to practitioner. It remains to be seen, however, just how popular such an option will prove to be. Under the existing regime of three years of very expensive legal education before starting the apprenticeship, the reduced initial salary may present problems for the transitioning new lawyer. Likewise, under the existing regime under which a firm may impose no sanction or penalty on a young lawyer who takes the training and leaves the firm immediately, it is not entirely clear that firms will have the incentive to provide the training they promise. The challenge of making this model work is real, but the importance of giving it a chance cannot be overstated.

And while positive efforts to build lawyer loyalty to firms are best, a regulatory change to increase the institutional strength of law firms should be considered as well. In the name of not restricting lawyer mobility, A.B.A. Model Rule 5.6(a) now prohibits any "agreement that restricts the right of a lawyer to practice after termination of the relationship" between the law firm and one of its lawyers.[95] It seems that Model Rule 5.6(a) should be amended to permit a law firm to negotiate contracts with its lawyers that impose reasonable restrictions on the lawyers' changing firms.

---

94. *E.g.*, Jeff Jeffrey, *For Some Firms, An Extra Step For the Newest Recruits*, NAT'L L.J., June 29, 2009, at 1 (Howrey). Drinker Biddle & Reath is another large firm that has announced this kind of program. The amount of the salary such "apprentices" would earn is said to be $100,000 per year, or about one year's law school tuition less than the $145,000 that seems to be 2009's most-announced starting rate at traditional firms.

95. MODEL RULES OF PROF'L CONDUCT R 5.6(a): "Restrictions on Right to Practice." The only exception is when the restriction is a condition to receiving retirement benefits.

The traditional argument in favor of prohibiting restrictions on departure has been that they would violate a lawyer's status as an independent professional. One can certainly understand that a lawyer who is ordered by a law firm superior to violate the law must have the right to refuse the order and, if necessary, to leave the firm. Today, however, there is no such narrow application of the rule.

Today, this limitation permits a lawyer to start looking for a new job the day he arrives at a firm, and then with little or no notice to the firm to try to persuade clients to follow the lawyer to a new practice organization. The Rule has long been interpreted to prohibit most kinds of financial penalties that firms might try to use to discourage such "dark of night" departures.[96] The current rule almost certainly gives too much latitude to the departing lawyer. Rule 5.6(a) may have made sense in a world in which most lawyers practiced alone. Today, however, a majority work within some kind of firm or other organization and the financial viability of such firms and organizations depends on a reasonably stable number of contributing lawyers.

One need not argue that lawyers must be yoked to the same firm for long periods to recognize that reasonable limits on departure can allow firms the financial security and flexibility to maintain and develop an institutional identity. Law firms that agree to train associates in their early years of practice and otherwise make a long-term investment in those lawyers will have little incentive to do so unless the associates can make an enforceable promise to stay around for a reasonable period—say up to three years—after receiving the training.[97] Indeed, with such protection, the firm might even be willing to pay lawyers more during the training period.

In employment cases generally, the law will not enforce restrictive covenants that are excessive in breadth or duration, but there seems

---

96. There is a great deal of case law on the issues of lawyers' departure from their firms. *See, e.g.,* Adler, Barish, Daniels, Levin & Creskoff v. Epstein, 382 A.2d 1226 (Pa. Super. 1977), *rev'd*, 393 A.2d 1175 (Pa. 1979); Cohen v. Lord, Day & Lord, 550 N.E.2d 410 (N.Y. 1989); Dowd & Dowd, Ltd. v. Gleason, 693 N.E.2d 358 (Ill. 1998). *See generally* ROBERT W. HILLMAN, HILLMAN ON LAWYER MOBILITY: THE LAW AND ETHICS OF PARTNER WITHDRAWALS AND LAW FIRM BREAKUPS (2d ed. 1998).

97. *See generally* Milton C. Regan, Jr., *Law Firms, Competition Penalties, and the Values of Professionalism*, 13 GEO. J. LEGAL ETHICS 1 (1999).

no good reason to subject law firm covenants to greater restriction. Some courts have implicitly acknowledged this view, recognizing that persons who make up a law firm should be capable of reaching arrangements appropriate to their situations.[98] Conforming the rules to the decisions should help firm managers deal with the pressure toward "free agency" that is otherwise likely only to get worse.

3. The Challenge of Financing Firm Operations and Growth

Professional service firm consultant Edward Wesemann describes what he calls the principal challenge facing any firm: "creating dominance." In any given field, he says, only a limited number of firms will be viewed as the best. Building upon the work of Peter Drucker, he suggests that in most fields of practice, one firm will tend to have about 40 percent of the market, one 20 percent, and one 10 percent. Everyone else in the industry will fight over the remaining 30 percent of the work.[99] Lawyers' conflict of interest rules make those market shares less than easily transferable to law firms, but the overall idea is sound. The task for each firm will be to find the field or fields in which it can achieve something like dominant status. Trying simply to be pretty good is likely to be a recipe for law firm failure.[100]

---

98. *E.g.*, Howard v. Babcock, 863 P.2d 150 (Cal. 1993) (firm may impose restriction on right to receive profits for work left before completed); Shuttleworth, Ruloff & Giordano, P.C. v. Nutter, 493 S.E.2d 364 (Va. 1997) (firm may require departed partner to continue to pay share of rent on space rented believing he would stay). *But see* Cohen v. Lord, Day & Lord, 550 N.E.2d 410 (N.Y. 1989) (may not limit lawyer's right to uncollected fees).

99. H. EDWARD WESEMANN, CREATING DOMINANCE: WINNING STRATEGIES FOR LAW FIRMS (2005).

100. W. Edwards Deming's analysis of how organizations deliver high quality services also applies to law firms. Deming's first principle is that clients define quality; what lawyers think constitutes outstanding service does not count for much if clients disagree. "Benchmarking" requires testing how a firm is doing against acknowledged leaders in an industry, and Deming urged firms to empower employees by giving them authority and responsibility and demanding that they be responsible for results. David G. Oedel, *Deming, TQM and the Emerging Managerial Critique of Law Practice*, 37 ARIZ. L. REV. 1209 (1995); Frederick L. Trilling, *The Strategic Application of Business Methods to the Practice of Law*, 38 WASHBURN L.J. 13 (1998).

As we saw in Chapter 3, the challenge of serving clients in diverse fields and in locations all over the globe has led some law firms to grow rapidly, and others may face pressure to grow. Growth can be expensive. New lawyers require office space, technological and administrative support, and time for transition into their new situation. Law firms traditionally have financed themselves using partners' initial contributions, plus a portion of the firm's earnings retained and reinvested each year. Internal financing of that kind has been attractive to lawyers. It has allowed the firm's lawyers to retain all the economic value of the firm, and it is typically the lowest cost form of financing that a firm can use.

Another way to finance growth at a relatively modest cost has been through law firm mergers that allow each firm to expand its size and scope immediately. Indeed, mergers have become almost a routine form of expansion in recent years. A merger of two weak firms will not make one strong one, and mergers may not be as low cost as they appear. Participants can often only estimate in retrospect whether the merged firm has attracted the new clients the merger sought to serve and whether both the new and existing clients are satisfied with what the new firm can deliver.

A third form of law firm financing has been the use of lines of credit[101] and other leveraged financing. Such financing involves relatively high risk, however, and an inability to meet debt obligations has led in part to the demise of several firms.[102] It is almost certain that firms that rely heavily on leverage to finance significant growth will face problems as managers must ask firm lawyers to pay increasing amounts of debt service in order to keep the firm alive. We have already seen that American lawyers are largely free to leave their firms at any time,[103] and defections of that kind can be devastating to a firm's future.

A logical fourth approach to law firm finance, then, would be the selling of equity shares in a law firm to non-lawyer investors.[104]

---

101. Otis Bilodeau, *On Borrowed Time*, AM. LAWYER, Sept. 2001, at 32.

102. *See, e.g.*, Danilo DiPietro, *The Brobeck Syndrome*, AM. LAWYER, July 2005, at 63.

103. MODEL RULES OF PROF'L CONDUCT R 5.6(a) forbids a law firm's placing restrictions on a lawyer's right to leave a firm.

104. Edward S. Adams & John H. Matheson, *Law Firms on the Big Board?: A Proposal for Nonlawyer Investment in Law Firms*, 86 CALIF. L. REV. 1 (1998).

Both Great Britain and Australia have recently allowed such financing flexibility, and as we saw in Chapter 3, an Australian firm, Slater and Gordon, sold an Initial Public Offering of $35 million in shares in 2007.[105]

The possible conversion to corporate status will be anathema to many lawyers, but it should not be. While the partnership form of organization has long been preeminent for law firms, it may not be well suited to the world facing future practice organizations.[106] Many situations require quick responses that are inconsistent with partners' rights to debate decisions. Even today, many law firms are delegating considerable decision-making authority to firm management as might be true if law firms adopted a corporate style of management.[107]

As part of an informal "conversation" published by Georgetown, writer "Adam Smith, Esq." proposed that the law firm sell derivative instruments granting no actual rights of ownership so as to try to avoid the technical Rule 5.4 problem.

105. The object was said to be to raise capital with which to finance personal injury cases that often take time to resolve. *See, e.g.*, Peter Lattman, *Slater & Gordon: The World's First Publicly Traded Law Firm*, WALL ST. J., May 22, 2007, found at http://blogs.wsj.com/law/2007/05/22/slater-gordon-the-worlds-first-publicly-traded-law-firm/; Jason Krause, Selling Law on an Open Market: The World's First Publicly Traded Law Firm Ignites Debate, A.B.A. J., July 2007, at 34; Richard Lloyd, *British Firms Watch Australia's Law Firm IPOs With Interest*, AM. LAWYER, June 6, 2007, found at http://www.law.com/jsp/law/LawArticleFriendly.jsp?id=1181034331105.

106. ROBERT L. NELSON, PARTNERS WITH POWER: THE SOCIAL TRANSFORMATION OF THE LARGE LAW FIRM 16–17, 23 (1988) explores the evolving organization of law firms that used to run on a principle of consensus and increasingly are managed more bureaucratically. *See also* Gunter Muller Stewens & Jens Drolshammer, *Managing the International Law Firm: Nuisance or Necessity, in* JENS DROLSHAMMER & MICHAEL PFEIFER, EDS., THE INTERNATIONALIZATION OF THE PRACTICE OF LAW 203 (2001).

107. There is beginning to be a literature on the organization of professional services firms, including law firms. *See, e.g.*, DAVID H. MAISTER, MANAGING THE PROFESSIONAL SERVICE FIRM (1993); MANAGING THE MODERN LAW FIRM: NEW CHALLENGES, NEW PERSPECTIVES (Laura Empson ed., 2007); PROFESSIONAL SERVICE FIRMS (Royston Greenwood & Roy Suddaby eds., 2006); Elizabeth Chambliss, *New Sources of Managerial Authority in Large Law Firms*, 22 GEO. J. LEGAL ETHICS 63 (2009); Robert W. Hillman, *Law, Culture, and the Lore of Partnership: Of Entrepreneurs, Accountability, and the Evolving Status of Partners*, 40 WAKE FOREST L. REV.

The more important issue is that, under current A.B.A. Model Rule 5.4, firms may not allow non-lawyers either to invest in the firm or to share in allocation of legal fees earned by the firm's lawyers.[108] One might fairly ask why lawyers would want to recruit outside investors if they know their firm can afford to finance itself internally and thereby avoid paying investors a risk premium. One answer might be that the need to raise large amounts of expansion capital today is simply a different problem than law firms previously have faced.

But a better answer might be that sales of stock to non-lawyers may create institutions that can give its current and future lawyers an incentive to stay focused on the firm's success as an integral part of their own future. Presumably, not all the stock in a law firm would be sold to outsiders. The stock might be locked up, i.e., issued but not available to the shareholder-lawyer if the lawyer leaves within, say, three years. Or, lawyers might simply prefer having a liquid market in which to value their interest so that they can sell the shares—hopefully at a higher value—when they decide to retire.[109]

An actual market in shares of a law firm would give lawyers an incentive to build value and reduce the moral hazard inherent in decisions about whether to take, or how to handle, a case. Lawyers have been granted traditional corporate protection of limited malpractice liability for partners organized as an LLC, so it is hard to see why the law should forbid a firm's adopting the corporate form altogether[110]

---

793 (2005); S. S. Samuelson, *The Organizational Structure of Law Firms: Lessons From Management Theory*, 51 OHIO ST. L.J. 645 (1990).

108. MODEL RULES OF PROF'L CONDUCT, R 5.4(d). "A lawyer shall not practice with or in the form of a professional corporation or association authorized to practice law for a profit if: (1) a nonlawyer owns any interest therein... , (2) a nonlawyer is a corporate director or officer thereof . . . , or (3) a nonlawyer has the right to direct or control the professional judgment of a lawyer."

109. Today, what a lawyer can realize on retirement from practice is by a sale to other lawyers under narrow, legally prescribed terms. *See, e.g.,* MODEL RULES OF PROF'L CONDUCT R 1.17.

110. Law firm operations have become so much like those of their corporate clients that the Harvard Business School has created a case study based on the Philadelphia-based Duane Morris firm's growth from 242 to over 600 lawyers. The study is Boris Groysberg & Robin Abrahams, Duane Morris: Balancing Growth and Culture at a Law Firm, Harvard Business

and raising capital as any corporation might. Many law firms generate significant income streams, and allowing lawyers to sell their firms to outside investors would permit lawyers to realize something of the economic value they have created.[111] Indeed, a desire to attract and retain outside investors may tend to impose financial and behavioral discipline on law firms whose members have not experienced serious pressure to exercise it.

Further, if one accepts the first proposal to permit multiservice partnerships, the sale of stock in a law firm is but a short logical step. Non-lawyer participation in firm operation and management will itself involve recognition of non-lawyers' investing time and sharing the benefits of a law firm's potential success. Permitting firms to raise capital and establish liquidity for its members' investments should not be a shocking prospect. The incentives created by this change to Rule 5.4(d) should benefit firms, the firms' clients, and the public.

E. FINDING NEW WAYS FOR CLIENTS TO PAY FOR LEGAL SERVICES

Finding a new model for billing legal services has been an almost endless quest in recent years,[112] but the goal of finding a perfect methodology is likely to prove elusive. Almost everyone agrees in theory

---

School #9-407-025, Rev: Aug. 17, 2006. It is described in Terry Carter, *A Heck of a Good Story*, A.B.A. J., Dec. 2006, at 28–30. Other firms have been rushing to register their names as trademarks. *See* Ashby Jones & Michael Ravnitzky, *Counselor At Law*, AM. LAWYER, January 2001, at 47.

111. The evidence is ambiguous as to how many firms would take advantage of the opportunity to sell stock. Many firms have long financed expansion internally or with borrowing alone. Indeed, management consulting firm Booz Allen went public in 1970, but six years later it bought back its stock and returned to being a partnership. *See* Christopher J. Whelan, *The Paradox of Professionalism: Global Law Practice Means Business*, 27 PENN ST. INT'L L. REV. 465, 484 (2008).

112. *See, e.g.*, REPORT OF THE A.B.A. COMM'N ON BILLABLE HOURS (2001–2002); A.B.A. SECTION OF LAW PRACTICE MANAGEMENT, TASK FORCE ON ALTERNATIVE BILLING METHODS, WIN-WIN BILLING STRATEGIES: ALTERNATIVES THAT SATISFY YOUR CLIENTS AND YOU (1992); Herbert M.

that each of the traditional methods of setting legal fees is flawed. Lawyers paid a fixed fee might deliver too little service, and lawyers paid a contingent fee might receive more than their services contributed to the result. Hourly-rate billing, in turn, often leads to reliance on inexperienced lawyers, excessive research, and lawyer burnout.[113] Often, clients simply ask for lower hourly rates or a rate no higher than the firm's other comparable clients,[114] but others are sensitive to the leveraging phenomenon and have been forcing firms to staff cases with fewer first- and second-year lawyers and more of the experienced partners that attracted the clients to the firm in the first place.[115] Ultimately, then, it may be clients who drive firms to the lower-paid apprenticeship model for young lawyers that we saw earlier.

The challenge will become to find a blend of bases for billing that comes closest to paying the lawyer the value of his or her services to a particular client. The fee approach appropriate for any particular case will almost certainly vary with the type of client and type of service provided. For example, a living trust for a client with a small estate will likely be billed at a modest fixed fee set by competitive realities. On the other hand, a "bet the company" lawsuit, for which only the best possible lawyer would be acceptable, might be compensated at a high fixed rate with bonuses for identified success and an hourly-rate supplement for work on unanticipated issues.[116]

Kritzer, *Lawyers' Fees and the Holy Grail: Where Should Clients Search for Value*, 77 JUDICATURE 187 (1994).

113. MICHAEL H. TROTTER, PROFIT AND THE PRACTICE OF LAW: WHAT'S HAPPENED TO THE LEGAL PROFESSION, Chap. 5–7 (1997); George B. Shepherd & Morgan Cloud, *Time and Money: Discovery Leads to Hourly Billing*, 1999 U. ILL. L. REV. 91 (1999).

114. *See, e.g.,* Derek Bedlow, A Revolution in the House, The European Lawyer, Apr. 2009, at 18; Leigh Jones, *Law Firm Fees Defy Gravity*, NAT'L L.J., Dec. 8, 2008, at S-1.

115. MICHAEL H. TROTTER, PROFIT AND THE PRACTICE OF LAW: WHAT'S HAPPENED TO THE LEGAL PROFESSION, ch. 9 (1997). *Cf.* SOL LINOWITZ WITH MARTIN MAYER, THE BETRAYED PROFESSION: LAWYERING AT THE END OF THE TWENTIETH CENTURY, ch. 8 (1994).

116. There is a substantial literature on new kinds of billing strategies, *e.g.,* A.B.A. COMM'N ON BILLABLE HOURS, REPORT (2002); A.B.A. SEC. LAW PRACTICE MANAGEMENT TASK FORCE ON ALTERNATIVE BILLING METHODS,

Some clients are now requiring other new ways of calculating fees altogether, and some lawyers see the methods as a way to reward productivity. Clients are setting up case budgets, for example, with the lawyer sharing in any savings and the client paying only part of any overrun.[117] Over thirty years ago, Skadden Arps pioneered the premium "performance fee," i.e., a bonus of several times hourly rates if a takeover goes through or a takeover defense is successful.[118] Bills for "success" are the kinds that are relatively easy for clients to accept, and services that lead to success are correctly seen as those on which providers can make the most money.[119] Such a success model—having some similarities to a contingent fee but without the all-or-nothing quality—might make even today's dissatisfied lawyers willing to devote the hours needed to do work they see as interesting and important.[120]

Nor are traditional fees likely to be the only way firms will try to charge for services. Investments in clients are a way some firms have tried to increase lawyer returns, although there is legal regulation of that conduct,[121] and if the client's business fails, the law firm may

---

WIN-WIN BILLING STRATEGIES: ALTERNATIVES THAT SATISFY YOUR CLIENT AND YOU (1992); *Comm. on Lawyer Business Ethics, A.B.A. Sec. Business Law, Business and Ethics Implications of Alternative Billing Practices: Report on Alternative Billing Arrangements*, 54 BUS. LAW. 175 (1998); Ronald D. Rotunda, *Moving from Billable Hours to Fixed Fees: Task-Based Fees and Legal Ethics*, 47 U. KAN. L. REV. 819 (1999); Harold See, *An Alternative to the Contingent Fee*, 1984 UTAH L. REV. 485 (1984).

117. *See, e.g.*, Lynne Marek, *Kirkland Expands Use of Special Fee Structures*, NAT'L L.J., Jun. 15, 2009, at 8; Julie Kay, *Billing Gets Creative in Souring Economy*, NAT'L L.J., Nov. 10, 2008, at 1.

118. LINCOLN CAPLAN, SKADDEN: POWER, MONEY, AND THE RISE OF A LEGAL EMPIRE 102–04 (1993).

119. TOM PETERS, REIMAGINE!: BUSINESS EXCELLENCE IN A DISRUPTIVE AGE 83 (2003). Peters tells the story of Louis Gerstner, who, as CEO of IBM, moved the company largely out of computer manufacture and into the service of creating computer systems for individual purchasers. Peters quotes Gerstner, "You are headed for commodity hell if you don't have services." *Id.* at 88.

120. TOM PETERS, REIMAGINE!: BUSINESS EXCELLENCE IN A DISRUPTIVE AGE 197 (2003). *But see* Rees Morrison & Paul Morrison, *When Your Values Aren't Shared*, LEGAL TIMES, Nov. 17, 2008, at 24.

121. See MODEL RULES OF PROF'L CONDUCT R. 1.8(a): "Business Transaction With a Client."

deeply regret its choice.[122] Yet other firms are inventing Web-based services or may try to charge for visits to substantive parts of their Web site. Other firms are trying to patent tax avoidance and other methods they have created.[123] Likewise, copyright protection for a law firm's forms may yield royalties each time the forms are used by someone else.

F. WHY HAVEN'T WE SEEN A MORE RAPID RESPONSE TO THESE TRENDS?

If changes in law practice are as likely or inevitable as this book has suggested—and as they have seemed to many for a decade or more—one can reasonably ask why clients and firms have not responded in the predicted ways.[124] The fact is that several changes have occurred, but one should not be naive about the speed of market adaptation to the new realities. It takes a brave firm to admit that a new paradigm of practice is coming at them and an even braver manager to commit to the steps necessary to meet and prosper in it.

---

122. The Brobeck firm tried that and itself collapsed when the technology bubble, in which their clients had been leading participants, burst.

123. One might not think of tax avoidance as an "invention," but business method patents have increasingly been granted. *See, e.g.,* Dan L. Burk & Brett H. McDonnell, *Patents, Tax Shelters, and the Firm,* 26 VA. TAX. REV. 981 (2007); Leo J. Raskind, *The State Street Bank Decision: The Bad Business of Unlimited Patent Protection for Methods of Doing Business,* 10 FORDHAM INTELL. PROP. MEDIA & ENT. L.J. 61 (1999); John R. Thomas, *The Patenting of the Liberal Professions,* 40 B.C. L. REV. 1139 (1999). The availability of business method patents has recently been cast in doubt by the Court of Appeals for the Federal Circuit in *In re Bilski,* 545 F.3d 943 (Fed. Cir. 2008); the Supreme Court has granted certiorari and will decide the availability of such patents sometime in 2010.

124. *See, e.g.,* James W. Jones, *The Challenge of Change: The Practice of Law in the Year 2000,* 41 VAND. L. REV. 683 (1988); James F. Fitzpatrick, *Legal Future Shock: The Role of Large Law Firms by the End of the Century,* 64 IND. L.J. 461 (1989); RICHARD A. POSNER, OVERCOMING LAW (1995); COMMITTEE ON RESEARCH ABOUT THE FUTURE OF THE LEGAL PROFESSION ON THE CURRENT STATUS OF THE LEGAL PROFESSION, WORKING NOTES 4–5 (Aug. 31, 2001).

First, lawyers enjoy significant regulatory protection of their sphere of practice, and if the past is any indication, they will resist such changes until market forces compel them to react.[125] Ultimately, however, clients are likely to see they have more power and options than they have heretofore acknowledged. As American lawyers in private firms recognize that corporations can staff internally in ways that largely avoid the regulation most lawyers face, outside counsel will have to change if they are to survive at all.

Second, it may not always be in the interest of corporate counsel to change the present system as fast as they could. Independent law firms give corporate counsel entities to which to pass "hot potato" issues. When a significant corporate investigation must be conducted or a major piece of litigation prepared, corporate counsel often welcomes the ability to say that she has hired the best outside firm to handle it. The cost of outside help may be high, but corporate counsel may find her superiors willing to bear it. If anything goes wrong, then, corporate counsel can make it known that she was not to blame. Smaller law firms may be less expensive, and their insights may even be more valuable than better-known firms, but corporate counsel are human, and, until pushed by what other companies are doing, many may resist pushing their options as far as they might.

Third, the world is awash in lawyers, so there is less reason to hire non-lawyers to do work if lawyers will reduce their charges for services. We are already seeing this happen. While a narrow slice of top graduates still earn high entry-level salaries, the majority of graduates each year earn much less. Indeed, many lawyers are even now working for little more than paralegal pay,[126] and as long as the lawyers are capable of doing the non-legal aspects of a matter as well, there will

---

125. *See, e.g.*, David B. Wilkins, *Who Should Regulate Lawyers*, 105 HARV. L. REV. 799 (1992); Susan P. Koniak, *The Law Between the Bar and the State*, 70 N.C. L. REV. 1389 (1992); Ted Schneyer, *An Interpretation of Recent Developments in the Regulation of Law Practice*, 30 OKLA. CITY U. L. REV. 559 (2005); James M. Fischer, *External Control Over the American Bar*, 19 GEO. J. LEGAL ETHICS 59 (2006).

126. *See, e.g.*, Anthony Lin, *BigLaw Contract Attorneys Struggle With Their Identity as 'Lawyers,'* N.Y. LAWYER, Oct. 18, 2004, found at http://www.nylawyer,com/news/04/10/101804c.html (pay $30 per hour); Julie Triedman, *Temporary Solution*, AM. LAWYER, Sept. 2006, at 97 (pay $32 per hour).

be less pressure to diversify. Indeed, the attorney-client privilege protects client communications against disclosure if they are with persons who have law licenses. Discussions with non-lawyers acting as agents of lawyers are sometimes similarly protected, but there is less reason to test that issue if lawyers are available at a comparable cost.

Finally, there are many ways to integrate non-lawyers into matters today, such as by using affiliated businesses, engaging in mutual referral arrangements with other consulting firms, and hiring non-lawyers as paralegals. These alternatives may be less efficient than those this chapter has suggested the future may bring, but it may sometimes be easier to avoid creativity than to initiate it. What is unlikely, however, is that the issues facing lawyers and law firms will simply go away. Putting a date on client action on these issues is difficult, but it seems likely that many firms and clients who understand the issues and deal with them effectively will be able ultimately to profit from their insights.[127]

---

127. *See, e.g.,* James W. Jones and Bayless Manning, *Getting at the Root of Core Values: A "Radical" Proposal to Extend the Model Rules to Changing Forms of Legal Practice,* 84 MINN. L. REV. 1159 (2000).

5. THE IMPACT OF THE COMING CHANGES ON AMERICAN LEGAL EDUCATION

So far we have seen that lawyers have reason for concern. The professional label will not protect them from the changing world facing their clients and thus facing themselves. Indeed, unless changed, the rules created in part to protect lawyers from competition will tend to limit their ability to respond to the new reality.

The effect of these changes on the multibillion-dollar world of American legal education will be inescapable. In any given year, over 100,000 students spend up to $45,000 each[1] to take courses leading to the juris doctor degree, the one most states require before a person can take a bar examination and be licensed to practice law. The license to practice has long seemed the key to what many students see as a high-paying career. But if this book is correct that the license is losing its significance and that the demand for uniquely legal services as we think of them today is likely to decline, the impact on legal education will be inescapable.[2] Students are likely to want only those parts of a legal education that add sufficiently to their understanding and skill to justify the tuition they are required to pay.

A. WHAT STUDENTS LEARN IN LAW SCHOOL

At its best, legal education provides a time in a person's life when he or she can take law and legal process seriously. The best law schools traditionally are worlds uncluttered by the demands of clients or seemingly even questions about how a student's education will be used. Professors are rewarded for thinking with imagination more

---

1. In 2008–2009, tuition at major private law schools was approaching $40,000 per year. Room, board, and books take the cost well over $50,000 per year at those schools. The $45,000 figure is intended to describe slightly less expensive schools as well.

2. Parts of this chapter were originally published as Thomas D. Morgan, *Educating Lawyers for the Future Legal Profession*, 30 OKLA. CITY L. REV. 537 (2005).

than with practicality. Students, in turn, are pressed to think broadly, write intelligently, and critically evaluate the work of others.

That vision of a legal education is attractive to many and may still have some reality at American law schools, but the vision of most law students is more focused on getting a job, and in that enterprise, there is little coherent about a legal education. All that is legally required for a student to get a degree, take a bar examination, and receive a license to practice law in most states is defined in law school accreditation standards.[3] To become a lawyer, a student must receive as at least 58,000 minutes of instruction in classes at a law school accredited by the American Bar Association. Typically, that amounts to a total of about thirty one-semester courses. The training must be offered over a minimum of sixty-five weeks. Those sixty-five weeks, amounting to fifteen actual calendar months, are for most students spread out over thirty-two months, i.e., three academic years.[4]

Obviously, even a full three years of law school introduces students to only a relatively few areas of substantive law. At most law schools, less than half of a law student's courses are required, and there is normally no "major" or field of concentration. Most law students still elect courses in largely unrelated fields, often based on things no weightier than the time of day at which they are taught or the time final examinations will be given.

Technical requirements aside, however, in preparing students to become what have traditionally been called lawyers, law schools provide what can be grouped into four categories: (1) how to analyze legal issues and "think like a lawyer," (2) enough substantive law to be able to place later-acquired knowledge into context, (3) concrete skills to

---

3. Once again, the standards are the product of the American Bar Association. *See* STANDARDS FOR APPROVAL OF LAW SCHOOLS, updated annually.

4. The specific requirements are that law schools offer training in academic years of at least twenty-six weeks. That works out to two semesters of thirteen weeks each. No student may take more than 20 percent of his credits in a single semester, so while most students go to law school for six semesters, i.e., seventy-eight weeks spread over three academic years, technically, a student may attend law school for five semesters of thirteen weeks each, so long as graduation does not come until at least twenty-four months after the student enrolled. STANDARDS FOR APPROVAL OF LAW SCHOOLS, STANDARD 304.

use to improve a client's situation, and (4) non-legal understanding sufficient to see a problem from the client's point of view.

1. What it Means to Think Like a Lawyer

The first of these categories, learning to "think like a lawyer," is what most law students find life-changing. Lawyer-think involves at least five elements. First, it involves learning how to read carefully. A large part of a lawyer's initial training consists of studying relatively short judicial opinions, statutes, or other texts and asking what each paragraph, sentence, and word means within the larger whole.[5] Does it matter that the case is in a supreme court rather than a court of appeals? Is it important that the property was worth more than $1,000? Does it matter that the conduct is to be assessed against a standard of negligence rather than a standard of recklessness? Reading skills taught in most high schools and colleges do not demand such a detailed, fact-driven focus; law school does.

The discipline and ability to read carefully is learned by repetition, and its corollary—sensitivity to ambiguity—is essential to a lawyer's work. Lawyers' families may be frustrated when a budding lawyer seems not to take their statements at face value—and few can forget President Clinton's focus on "what the meaning of 'is' is"—but among the defining characteristics of a lawyer is a careful use of words and an intolerance of the ambiguity that words can create or mask.

Second, thinking like a lawyer involves learning to reason from a specific case to a general principle.[6] Most people probably think of lawyers as doing just the opposite, i.e., reasoning from general

---

5. The process is described extremely well and in much more detail in ELIZABETH MERTZ, THE LANGUAGE OF LAW SCHOOL: LEARNING TO THINK LIKE A LAWYER 43–83 (2007). *But see* Nancy B. Rapoport, *Is "Thinking Like a Lawyer" Really What We Want to Teach?*, 1 J. ASS'N LEGAL WRITING DIRECTORS 91 (2002).

6. *See, e.g.,* EDWARD H. LEVI, AN INTRODUCTION TO LEGAL REASONING (1949); KARL E. LLEWELLYN, THE BRAMBLE BUSH: ON OUR LAW AND ITS STUDY 44–50 (1960). *See also* MARY ANN GLENDON, A NATION UNDER LAWYERS 237–39 (1994) (describing reasoning she attributes to Edgar Bodenheimer and calls Aristotelian or "dialectical" in which the lawyer reasons from the specific to the general and back to the specific to develop a rule that is both practical and principled).

principles or statutory provisions back to the facts of particular cases. Lawyers do indeed often reason deductively, particularly when they try to apply constitutional provisions and statutes,[7] but it tends to be inductive reasoning from the conclusions in prior cases to the principles that govern all cases that constitutes the special art in which lawyers are trained. It is the ability to reason inductively—and by analogy between one set of facts and another, in turn—that allows lawyers to predict how a new case is likely to be decided.

Third, thinking like a lawyer involves seeing legal issues in a larger context of morality and social policy. One can use legal reasoning to justify all kinds of terrible results, but a lawyer who does so without realizing that few judges would decide a case to reach such a result would not serve a client well. Indeed, many would say that the difference between good law schools and great ones is most often measured by the extent to which graduates come away from their education capable of seeing the social implications of legal rules and the long-term viability of the principles.

Fourth, lawyers develop the ability to narrow the focus of their analysis on facts that are most immediately relevant to the matter at issue. Understanding what the actual facts are may be contested in any situation, of course, and in a quest for critical facts, lawyers sometimes tend to filter out human realities that many observers find important. In doing so, however, lawyers tend to be somewhat like doctors who are engaged in saving lives and who have learned to ignore the shock most people have at seeing blood. At their best, in the same way, lawyers clear away the facts that might attract others, so as to focus the parties'—and potentially a court's—attention on the facts on which a case is likely to turn.[8]

---

7. In many ways, deductive reasoning is increasingly difficult as a lawyer tries to reconcile statutory and constitutional provisions with cases that pre-existed or construed the statute. Probably the best treatment of such issues is GUIDO CALABRESI, A COMMON LAW FOR THE AGE OF STATUTES (1982).

8. Thoughtful critics recognize that the professional distance lawyers learn to develop can cut the lawyer off from some of the emotional realities facing clients and the social implications or consequences that may be inherent in what superficially appears to be a simple legal question. The consequence may be what some call a lawyer's assumption of a "moral void." *See, e.g.*, WALTER BENNETT, THE LAWYER'S MYTH 15–27, 91, 135 (2001).

Next, lawyers must think about the facts they know, other facts they would find useful to know, and how to find out facts they do not have before them. They also must recognize that, sometimes, facts their clients characterize subjectively and in particular ways are likely to be described quite differently by others. Thus, the ability to develop information and characterize facts as accurately and persuasively as possible is part of the work experience of a lawyer. The value of those instincts and skills will be as great in the future as it has ever been.

Finally, lawyers learn how to investigate legal issues they have not studied before and how to keep abreast of changes in the law over the years. Lawyers cannot assume that the experience they have gained will keep them ahead of people newly entering practice. In a world of many legally trained people and multiple sources of legal information, knowing "the law" alone will be insufficient to set a lawyer apart and to cause a client to seek out a particular lawyer's assistance.

The ability to employ each of these six analytic skills in varied situations helps explain why lawyers are valuable to clients and why the study and practice of law is satisfying to many lawyers. The important question for the future, however, will be what, beyond training in the lawyer's version of critical thinking, is required to produce individuals who can provide representation of the kind reserved to licensed lawyers today.

2. Adding Additional Substantive Legal Knowledge

Even in a world of specialized skills, the more a practitioner knows about related or analogous issues, the more he can bring to his own area of expertise. A person who assists corporations to enter into complex deals, for example, will benefit from knowing the tax implications of doing things one way rather than another. Knowing international and comparative aspects of otherwise local issues is another example of the benefits of a broad background in substantive law.

A corporate lawyer may not find it practical to learn all the nuances of taxation and international law, and a specialist in each of those issues may be brought into a transaction before it closes; but tunnel vision does not help a specialist, and often even seemingly "impractical" law school courses will prove useful to a graduate in the long run. Thus, it is not all wasted effort when students take a somewhat random mix of courses during their legal education, but a more systematic effort may be preferable, and it would be desirable not to make all those course choices in ignorance of what the student later hopes to do in practice.

3. Learning Practical Skills to Meet Client Needs

A third element of a legal education is an introduction to skills that help a lawyer get things done on a client's behalf. Sometimes, skills are practiced by simulating an appellate argument or other lawyer task. Sometimes, they are learned by working with a clinical instructor on the case of an actual client. Either way, one of the defining characteristics of a successful lawyer is the recognition that a theoretical understanding of the law is rarely the goal. A client's bottom-line objective is typically getting help to change a real-life situation for the better. The practical art of getting things done, in turn, takes at least four forms.

First, getting things done requires knowing what institutions, if any, are available from which to obtain an authoritative statement of a client's rights. Lawyers call these legal principles jurisdiction, civil procedure, and evidence. Understanding the relevant institutions to which the client might turn also helps the lawyer estimate the cost and time that might be involved in reaching a result the client will find to be in his or her interest.

Second, lawyers think in terms of processes more broadly. A trial is often neither the only nor the best alternative. When a client describes a problem with her supervisor, for example, the lawyer's first question is likely to be whether the client has talked to the supervisor about the problem. If so, the next step might be to talk with the supervisor's boss or the office's human resources department. It might then be necessary to take the matter to an administrative agency before going to a court. The example is arbitrary, but the point is that lawyers at their best see problems in a context of possible routes to resolution. Some routes are simply possible, while some are legally required before later steps can be pursued; but getting results for a client without going to court is part of the thought process of any successful lawyer.[9]

---

9. In each of these results-driven types of conduct, lawyers focus much of their attention on procedure, that is, on how to put contested facts or issues before parties for negotiation or before an impartial third person for decision. It may seem as though a focus on procedure must be at the expense of substance.

Third, lawyers get things done using techniques such as negotiation to deal directly with another person or another lawyer to seek common ground and to accommodate differences. Too often, we think of lawyers primarily as combatants. In reality, it is in their role of avoiding disputes and calming emotions where lawyers often can make their greatest contributions. We may think of some people as natural negotiators, but negotiation is also a skill that can be taught, and law schools are among the places to teach it.[10]

Fourth, lawyers get things done through their ability to organize facts in ways that tell a persuasive story, and lawyers must develop the skill of fact-finding in particular settings. All law schools teach classes in legal writing, and two law schools have recently announced that they have appointed journalists to their faculties.[11] Lawyer fact-finding techniques are not exactly like those used in journalism, but journalists might be useful teachers of systematic ways of ascertaining the "who, what, when, where, and why" facts in lawyers' cases. Lawyers must resist a temptation to be novelists,[12] but ideally, lawyers will be part poet and will have the ability to tell stories that develop in ways that provide information but leave little doubt about what reasonable people should conclude will be the just resolution of a matter.

A thoughtful reader may well have concluded that these categories of lawyer skills—the ability to read carefully, reason systematically, negotiate effectively, and organize relevant facts to solve concrete problems—are not unique to lawyers. Successful people in many areas of life are well served by such skills, and that may be why lawyers

---

At its best, however, it is the lawyer's procedural sense that can make it possible to address the substance of an issue at all.

10. *See, e.g.,* CHARLES B. CRAVER, EFFECTIVE LEGAL NEGOTIATION AND SETTLEMENT (2005).

11. Yale Law School hired Linda Greenhouse when she recently retired from the New York Times, and the University of California Law School at Irvine has hired Henry Weinstein from the Los Angeles Times. Clearly, their roles at those schools will be much broader than those suggested in this paragraph.

12. Obvious exceptions are lawyers such as Louis Auchincloss and Scott Turow, who have maintained careers as lawyers while simultaneously being successful novelists. More common are former lawyers, such as John Grisham, who have found the world of fictional lawyers more interesting than their own practice.

often move easily into leadership positions in business, public service, or other organizations. Indeed, this chapter will suggest that today's law schools could, and increasingly may, find themselves teaching these skills to people who never plan to complete law school and become a lawyer.

4. Understanding a Client's Substantive Problem

The final broad category of skills a lawyer needs consists of the ability to understand the non-legal reality facing a client. Lawyers are not always prepared for this aspect of their work, even upon graduation from law school. There are no substantive prerequisites for entry into most law schools. Unlike medical schools that require extensive scientific study during the undergraduate years, a college degree in basketball theory or music performance is sufficient for entry into most law schools, so long as the student's undergraduate grade point average and standardized Law School Admission Test score are sufficiently high.

The lawyer best able to help a client will typically be one who has the best understanding of the business or other subject matter in which the client works. Professor Karl Llewellyn made the point directly almost a half-century ago.

> [I]t should be clear even to the blind that the work of business counsel is impossible unless the lawyer who attempts it knows not only the rules of the law . . . but knows, in addition, the life of the community, the needs and practices of his client—knows, in a word, the *working situation* which he is called upon to shape *as well as* the law with reference to which he is called upon to shape it.[13]

Most law schools do not make development of that non-legal understanding a part of their curriculum; indeed, for a law school to do so within its own walls would require replicating much of the rest of the university. Indeed, many lawyers like to brag about their ability to learn things "just in time"—just when and what they need to know to complete a narrow task. If a trial lawyer has a case about a dangerous chemical, for example, he will have to learn as much as practical about the chemical. The lawyer often might not have learned such

---

13. KARL E. LLEWELLYN, THE BRAMBLE BUSH: ON OUR LAW AND ITS STUDY 16 (1960).

non-legal knowledge before the case, however, and getting educated efficiently and effectively often proves easier said than done.

The closest law schools typically come to recognizing this need is when they allow students to receive credit for courses taken in other parts of the university, sometimes as part of programs offering joint degrees in law and business, law and medicine, law and public health, and the like. These opportunities are important, and it may make sense for law students to devote more of their training to non-legal courses. But for many lawyers, how they use their undergraduate years will most fundamentally determine the context they have in which to situate the knowledge they need to use to help a client.[14]

B. HOW THE AMERICAN SYSTEM OF LEGAL EDUCATION DEVELOPED

The present system of legal education did not arise in a vacuum. As we saw earlier, people we now call "lawyers" were originally officers of the English king's court. Law practice in that early society was typically based on the king's grant of lawyer status, refined by the lawyer's own experience. Legal information was scanty. Later, as their role became less defined by a given king's wishes, barristers were oriented into the traditions of their role by living and working at the Inns of Court.[15] Some candidates for the bar could be assumed to

---

14. The most obvious example of this is the requirement of the U.S. Patent & Trademark Office that a lawyer have scientific or technical training in order to be able to become a patent lawyer, regardless of how much purely legal knowledge the lawyer may have about the patent field.

15. Dean Harno says that legal historian Sir William S. Holdsworth found reference to the teaching of law as early as the late thirteenth century. He found references to the Inns of Court in the fourteenth century; Sir John Fortescue, a major English political theorist, was a governor of Lincoln's Inn in the fifteenth century; and the great days of the Inns were during the sixteenth century. For a while, training in the Inns extended over seven or eight years; it was twelve years during the reign of Elizabeth I. ALBERT J. HARNO, LEGAL EDUCATION IN THE UNITED STATES 4–8 (1953).

have had a classical education, but they got none at the Inns where the training was almost exclusively practical.[16]

Systematic study of the substance of English law—as opposed to how law is practiced—began around 1628 with the publication of *Coke on Littleton*, the first English treatise that gave a comprehensive overview of both substantive law and procedure. Indeed, it was study of *Coke* and other texts that formed the basis for training many lawyers in the body of legal principles for at least two centuries.

Sir William Blackstone started teaching at Oxford in 1753 and became Vinerian professor in 1758. His four-volume *Commentaries* updated and corrected *Coke*. His work was also considered more readable, and it replaced *Coke* as the primary basis for personal study, support for lectures, or both.[17] Indeed, when we hear that Abraham Lincoln studied law at home by his fireside, it was books such as Blackstone's *Commentaries*, Chitty's *Pleadings*, Greenleaf's *Evidence*, and Story's *Equity* and *Equity Pleading* that made up the heart of that study.[18]

There was no American institution comparable to the Inns of Court, although several young eighteenth-century Americans went to England to study at the Inns.[19] Beyond reading law from

---

16. ALBERT J. HARNO, LEGAL EDUCATION IN THE UNITED STATES 4–8 (1953). *See also* David Maxwell-Fyfe, *The Inns of Court and the Impact on the Legal Profession in England*, 4 Sw. L. REV. 391 (1950). It seems highly unlikely that education in the Inns paid any significant attention to social criticism of law or the legal profession.

17. ALBERT J. HARNO, LEGAL EDUCATION IN THE UNITED STATES 8–15 (1953).

18. LAWRENCE M. FRIEDMAN, A HISTORY OF AMERICAN LAW 606 (2d ed. 1985) (quoting Jack Nortrup, *The Education of a Western Lawyer*, 12 AM. J. LEGAL HIST. 294 (1968), as saying Lincoln believed the best way to become a lawyer was to read those books, get a license, go into practice "and still keep reading").

19. ROSCOE POUND, THE LAWYER FROM ANTIQUITY TO MODERN TIMES 144–58 (1953). *See also* Richard B. Morris, *The Legal Profession in America on the Eve of the Revolution*, in POLITICAL SEPARATION AND LEGAL CONTINUITY 7–8, 11–12 (Harry W. Jones ed., 1976) (propertied class in America sought the safety and security that English legal principles provided for property).

available texts,[20] most American law students trained by personal apprenticeship to lawyers and paid the practitioners for the privilege.[21] Just as one became a wheelwright by sitting alongside someone who made wheels, a person became a lawyer by reading classic law books[22] and working in a lawyer's office for a period of time, typically five years. Some apprenticeships were undoubtedly more exploitive than educational; endless document copying seemed the order of the day for many trainees. The apprenticeship form of education was not necessarily inadequate, however, for someone whose ambition extended no farther than filing documents and trying cases at the county seat.

What apprenticeship education lacked was any organized legal understanding or chance for professional growth for the lawyer who hoped for more. Law schools began as simple institutions created by individual lawyers with good reputations for being able to expedite a young lawyer's understanding of the standard treatises. In addition, they provided training in the ins-and-outs of a non-specialized practice. Of these institutions, the most celebrated was the Litchfield Law School begun by Tapping Reeve in 1784.[23] Sometimes attendance at lectures reduced the required period of apprenticeship, but even when it did not, students came voluntarily and paid for the privilege

---

20. Among the other texts were those by Bracton, Britton, Burlamaqui, Fleta and Glanville, Grotius, and Pufendorf. ALBERT J. HARNO, LEGAL EDUCATION IN THE UNITED STATES 19–21 (1953).

21. ALBERT J. HARNO, LEGAL EDUCATION IN THE UNITED STATES 19 (1953). In these days before typewriters and copying machines, the apprenticeships often consisted of little more than hand-copying documents for their masters. See ROBERT STEVENS, LAW SCHOOL: LEGAL EDUCATION IN AMERICA FROM THE 1850S TO THE 1980S, at 3 (1983).

22. An American edition of Blackstone's *Commentaries* was published in 1771. Coke's *Institutes* and Hale's *History of the Common Law* were part of the usual reading. Richard B. Morris, *The Legal Profession in America on the Eve of the Revolution, in* POLITICAL SEPARATION AND LEGAL CONTINUITY 13–17 (Harry W. Jones ed., 1976).

23. Most of this history is based on ROBERT STEVENS, LAW SCHOOL: LEGAL EDUCATION IN AMERICA FROM THE 1850S TO THE 1980S (1983). *See also* LAWRENCE M. FRIEDMAN, A HISTORY OF AMERICAN LAW 97–99 (1985); ALBERT J. HARNO, LEGAL EDUCATION IN THE UNITED STATES 28–32 (1953).

because they recognized that lawyers required a broader perspective on the law than apprenticeship alone could provide.

In the late eighteenth century, law was also seen as an important part of the education of all citizens in the new republic. Professors of law were appointed to teach undergraduates at important universities. The influence of George Wythe on a young Thomas Jefferson, for example, is legendary.[24] Typically, schools had only a single chair in law, but the idea of law as a university-based discipline was thereby established.

Again, as mentioned in Chapter 2, the early nineteenth century was a turbulent time for legal education. David Hoffman tried but initially failed to create a seven-year program of legal study at the University of Maryland in 1812.[25] Harvard acquired the formerly proprietary Northampton Law School and made Chief Justice Issac Parker of the Supreme Judicial Court of Massachusetts the first Royall Professor of law at Harvard in 1815.[26] Yale absorbed a private law school in 1824[27] and appointed its owner, a local judge, as professor of law.[28] Thomas Jefferson provided for a law professor in the undergraduate program at his new University of Virginia in 1825.[29] But all these schools struggled, at least in part, because the political

---

24. Jefferson had been Wythe's apprentice. ROBERT STEVENS, LAW SCHOOL: LEGAL EDUCATION IN AMERICA FROM THE 1850S TO THE 1980S, at 3, n.5 (1983). Other important eighteenth-century American professors were James Kent at Columbia, Supreme Court Justice James Wilson at the College of Philadelphia, and St. George Tucker at William and Mary. ALBERT J. HARNO, LEGAL EDUCATION IN THE UNITED STATES 23–26 (1953). Legal training as an undergraduate function continues to be the model throughout most of Europe.

25. ROBERT STEVENS, LAW SCHOOL: LEGAL EDUCATION IN AMERICA FROM THE 1850S TO THE 1980S, at 4 (1983).

26. ALBERT J. HARNO, LEGAL EDUCATION IN THE UNITED STATES 35–39 (1953); ROBERT STEVENS, LAW SCHOOL: LEGAL EDUCATION IN AMERICA FROM THE 1850S TO THE 1980S, at 4 (1983).

27. An excellent description of such local schools is found in Steve Sheppard, *Casebooks, Commentaries, and Curmudgeons: An Introductory History of Law in the Lecture Hall*, 82 IOWA L. REV. 547 (1997).

28. ROBERT STEVENS, LAW SCHOOL: LEGAL EDUCATION IN AMERICA FROM THE 1850S TO THE 1980S, at 5 (1983).

29. ROBERT STEVENS, LAW SCHOOL: LEGAL EDUCATION IN AMERICA FROM THE 1850S TO THE 1980S, at 4 (1983); ALBERT J. HARNO, LEGAL EDUCATION IN THE UNITED STATES 35–39 (1953).

climate reflected in the era of Jacksonian democracy was hostile to educational or other preconditions to becoming a lawyer.[30] The de Tocqueville vision of lawyers as aristocrats was initially taken to heart, but Americans tended to be hostile to aristocrats, and educational barriers to bar admission tended to disappear.

Many might date the birth of the modern American law school as Joseph Story's appointment to the Dane chair at Harvard in 1829.[31] Simultaneously serving as a U.S. Supreme Court Justice while lecturing at Harvard, Story published eight legal treatises from 1832 to 1843. He stressed the idea that law was both an integral part of university academic study and a training in practical skills.[32] Even the best university-based law schools were not all of one type, however, and their rise did not make the system of apprenticeships disappear. By 1840,

---

30. ALBERT J. HARNO, LEGAL EDUCATION IN THE UNITED STATES 39–40 (1953); ROBERT STEVENS, LAW SCHOOL: LEGAL EDUCATION IN AMERICA FROM THE 1850S TO THE 1980S, at 6–8 (1983).

31. *See, e.g.*, ALBERT J. HARNO, LEGAL EDUCATION IN THE UNITED STATES 40–50 (1953).

32. *Id.* Robert Stevens, however, is much less impressed by Story, dismissing him as brought in "for prestige." Though Stevens acknowledges that Story's appointment "set that law school on its course toward becoming the preeminent law school in the United States," he says that while Story purported to want broadly educated students, what he built was "increasingly that of a trade school" whose students could not take courses at Harvard College. ROBERT STEVENS, LAW SCHOOL: LEGAL EDUCATION IN AMERICA FROM THE 1850S TO THE 1980S, at 13 n.25, 15 n.46 (1983). In any event, after Story's death in 1845, instruction at Harvard became the "textbook method" under which students were required largely to memorize and answer questions about portions of a text then explained by the instructor. LAWRENCE M. FRIEDMAN, A HISTORY OF AMERICAN LAW 610 (2d ed. 1985).

To lawyers today, the most important law teachers of the first three-quarters of the nineteenth century were David Hoffman and George Sharswood, both of whom conducted classes for prospective lawyers, and both of whom, as part of their instruction, articulated standards of ethical conduct to which they urged lawyers to adhere. *See* DAVID HOFFMAN, A COURSE OF LEGAL STUDY, ADDRESSED TO STUDENTS AND THE PROFESSION GENERALLY (2d ed. 1836), and GEORGE SHARSWOOD, A COMPEND OF LECTURES ON THE AIMS AND DUTIES OF THE PROFESSION OF THE LAW (1854). *See also* Maxwell Bloomfield, *David Hoffman and the Shaping of a Republican Legal Culture*, 38 MD. L. REV. 673 (1979); Norman W. Spaulding, *The Myth of Civil Republicanism: Interrogating the Ideology of Antebellum Legal Ethics*, 71 FORDHAM L. REV. 1397 (2003).

only eleven states still required an apprenticeship before admission to the bar, but all permitted it as a way to qualify for admission.[33]

By 1850, fifteen law schools had taken root in this country, among them the program at Hamilton College under the leadership of Theodore Dwight. He knew that many practitioners were skeptical of anything other than apprenticeship education, but Dwight stressed the idea of "principles before practice," and in 1858, he was hired to lead the School of Jurisprudence at Columbia.[34] Also a founder of the Association of the Bar of the City of New York, Dwight helped build the preeminent program training lawyers for New York firms advising large corporations.[35] His teaching method was the traditional lecture, although students typically spent part of each day working in a law office, and the debate over whether it was best to teach law from books or through an apprenticeship paralleled today's tension between classroom and clinical legal education.[36]

"In 1870, the total law student population in the country was 1,611. . . . Typically, no undergraduate work was required to get into law school."[37] Even by 1870, no school offered more than a two-year

---

33. That is not to say that all lawyers were created equal. The evidence suggests that at least half the lawyers in the mid-nineteenth century were from middle- or upper-class backgrounds and had been to college. LAWRENCE M. FRIEDMAN, A HISTORY OF AMERICAN LAW 305–06 (1985).

34. ROBERT STEVENS, LAW SCHOOL: LEGAL EDUCATION IN AMERICA FROM THE 1850S TO THE 1980S, at 23–25 (1983). Lawrence Friedman reports that Dwight's compensation arrangement was one that would raise eyebrows today. He collected student tuition of $100 each, paid expenses, gave himself a salary of $6,000 per year, and split whatever was left over 50/50 with the university. LAWRENCE M. FRIEDMAN, A HISTORY OF AMERICAN LAW 609 (2d ed. 1985).

35. ROBERT STEVENS, LAW SCHOOL: LEGAL EDUCATION IN AMERICA FROM THE 1850S TO THE 1980S, at 23 (1983). Stevens quotes the 1867 commencement speaker at Columbia, praising its restoration of de Tocqueville's lawyer-aristocrat and describing Columbia as the "very West Point" of the profession in its service of Wall Street. Id.

36. ROBERT STEVENS, LAW SCHOOL: LEGAL EDUCATION IN AMERICA FROM THE 1850S TO THE 1980S, at 23–25 (1983); see also ALFRED ZANTZINGER REED, TRAINING FOR THE PUBLIC PROFESSION OF LAW 55 (1921).

37. LAWRENCE M. FRIEDMAN, A HISTORY OF AMERICAN LAW 607–08 (2d ed. 1985). In 1870, the largest law school, with 308 students, was at the University of Michigan.

program of legal study, and twelve of the thirty-one schools had only a one-year program. Although some law students had taken some college work, law was normally not a graduate program.[38] Instruction was typically by lecture based on readings, and examinations were not always required.[39] Some states automatically admitted law school graduates to the bar under the "diploma privilege," a fact that helped preserve demand for formal education.[40] Movement to a written bar examination to determine which lawyers could be licensed reduced the incentive to go to law school at all, but it became part of the larger call to "raise standards" that ultimately served law school interests well.[41]

Important as this early period was, however, credit or blame for the modern method of legal instruction is properly attributed to Christopher Columbus Langdell, appointed Dane Professor of Law at Harvard in 1870.[42] President Eliot of Harvard was himself a revolutionary, throwing over the idea of universities as places to study the

---

38. LAWRENCE M. FRIEDMAN, A HISTORY OF AMERICAN LAW 608–09 (2d ed. 1985).

39. ALBERT J. HARNO, LEGAL EDUCATION IN THE UNITED STATES 51 (1953). Seventeen schools had a two-year program while the other two required a year and a half. In addition, bar examinations were often oral and casual. ROBERT STEVENS, LAW SCHOOL: LEGAL EDUCATION IN AMERICA FROM THE 1850S TO THE 1980S, at 25 (1983).

40. ROBERT STEVENS, LAW SCHOOL: LEGAL EDUCATION IN AMERICA FROM THE 1850S TO THE 1980S, at 26–27 (1983). See also ALFRED ZANTZINGER REED, TRAINING FOR THE PUBLIC PROFESSION OF LAW 79 (1921).

41. ROBERT STEVENS, LAW SCHOOL: LEGAL EDUCATION IN AMERICA FROM THE 1850S TO THE 1980S, at 26–27 (1983). In the view of Alfred Z. Reed, writing for the Carnegie Foundation, efforts to improve the bar sprung from the "militant political philosophy that sees in the administration of justice a primary function of the state, and demands that those who earn their livelihood in this particular way shall be regarded, not as private citizens, but as public servants of a democracy." ALFRED ZANTZINGER REED, TRAINING FOR THE PUBLIC PROFESSION OF LAW 43 (1921).

42. ALBERT J. HARNO, LEGAL EDUCATION IN THE UNITED STATES 53–62 (1953). Professor Pomeroy of New York University taught by the case method earlier, during the preceding decade, although Langdell was the first to build a whole school around the method. LAWRENCE M. FRIEDMAN, A HISTORY OF AMERICAN LAW 613, n.20 (2d ed. 1985).

classics and calling for study of all areas of life.[43] Eliot himself had been trained as a chemist, and he was sympathetic to Langdell's call for a "scientific" study of law in which decisions in appellate cases would be seen as data to be analyzed and assembled into propositions and theories. Central to this process was the idea that law was a self-contained discipline involving no interaction with history, economics, or other intellectual disciplines.[44] Robert Stevens thus credits Eliot, not Langdell, with turning legal education into the university-based discipline with professor-scholars that we know today.[45]

Whoever deserves the credit, Langdell increased Harvard's entrance requirements by requiring students without a college degree to pass a test of their knowledge of Latin or French, as well as Blackstone.[46] He divided the curriculum into courses, some basic and some advanced, and students had to pass the first-year courses before going on to the second year.[47] The Langdell method used case books that set forth whole cases chronologically. No statutes were included—even where they had changed the results of the case law— and there was none of the present-day note material prepared by the

---

43. ROBERT STEVENS, LAW SCHOOL: LEGAL EDUCATION IN AMERICA FROM THE 1850S TO THE 1980S, at 35 (1983). Stevens credits Eliot with stimulating the founding of private universities around the country and adoption of the Morrill Act that established land grant public universities after the Civil War. *Id.*

44. ALBERT J. HARNO, LEGAL EDUCATION IN THE UNITED STATES 57–60 (1953).

45. ROBERT STEVENS, LAW SCHOOL: LEGAL EDUCATION IN AMERICA FROM THE 1850S TO THE 1980S, at 36 (1983). Only thirty years after Langdell's appointment, the number of U.S. law schools had risen from 31 to 102. LAWRENCE M. FRIEDMAN, A HISTORY OF AMERICAN LAW 607 (2d ed. 1985).

46. LAWRENCE M. FRIEDMAN, A HISTORY OF AMERICAN LAW 612 (2d ed. 1985).

47. *Id.* Some of Langdell's own description and justification for what he was doing is collected in THE HISTORY OF LEGAL EDUCATION IN THE UNITED STATES: COMMENTARIES AND PRIMARY SOURCES, Vol. I, chs. 34 & 35 (Steve Sheppard ed., 1999). *See also* WILLIAM P. LAPIANA, LOGIC AND EXPERIENCE: THE ORIGIN OF MODERN AMERICAN LEGAL EDUCATION (1994); Paul D. Carrington, *Hail! Langdell!*, 20 LAW & SOC. INQUIRY 691 (1995); W. Burlette Carter, *Reconstructing Langdell*, 32 GA. L. REV. 1 (1997); Howard Schweber, *The "Science" of Legal Science, The Model of the Natural Sciences in Nineteenth-Century American Legal Education*, 17 LAW & HIST. REV. 421, 455–66 (1999).

collection's author.[48] Langdell's new methodology was apparently not even entirely popular at Harvard,[49] but Langdell seeded the faculty with young disciples such as James Barr Ames and William Keener—instead of with experienced judges and practitioners—and the experiment took root.[50]

Langdell's Harvard stressed the intellectual side of law study over the practical, and stressed study of legal principles in terms of how they fit into a network of legal principles, not whether they made sense in terms of the world outside the law. Thus, Langdell said, it was not necessary for a law professor to have engaged in law practice. Indeed, such experience might even tend to corrupt the purity of the professor's legal analysis. If the case method was seen as science, Lawrence Friedman says, "Langdell's science of law was a geology without rocks, an astronomy without stars."[51] But ultimately, Langdell's vision of legal science prevailed and spread around the country. William Keener took the vision to Columbia where he replaced Dwight. John Wigmore took the method to Northwestern, Joseph Beale took it to the new University of Chicago, and William Howard Taft adopted it at Cincinnati.[52]

To several in the generations of law professors that came after Langdell, however, his formalistic style of analysis was nonsense. Judges do not decide cases in terms of abstract theory, the "legal realists" argued. Nor should they do so. Judges grant relief to persons whom they believe merit relief, and the judgment about who merits

---

48. LAWRENCE M. FRIEDMAN, A HISTORY OF AMERICAN LAW 614 (2d ed. 1985).

49. *Id.* at 615. For an account of life at Harvard during the Langdell years, *see* Bruce A. Kimball, *Students' Choices and Experience During the Transition to Competitive Academic Achievement at Harvard Law School, 1876–1882,* 55 J. LEGAL EDUC. 163 (2005).

50. LAWRENCE M. FRIEDMAN, A HISTORY OF AMERICAN LAW 615 (2d ed. 1985).

51. *Id.* at 617.

52. *Id.* at 616. A contemporary of Langdell's, Thomas McIntyre Cooley of the University of Michigan had a different view of teaching and scholarship, described in Paul D. Carrington, *Law as "The Common Thoughts of Men": The Law-Teaching and Judging of Thomas McIntyre Cooley,* 49 STAN. L. REV. 495 (1997), and in Paul D. Carrington, *Legal Education for the People: Populism and Civic Virtue,* 43 U. KAN. L. REV. 1 (1994).

relief is a product of multiple aspects of the judge's personality and life history, as well as what the judge believes would be the effect of a decision on the parties and others. The dictates of legal doctrine might have to be worked into the judge's opinion, but they should rarely be controlling.[53] Today, modern versions of legal realists tend to predominate in most law school analysis of legal issues.

C. INTERACTION BETWEEN LEGAL EDUCATION AND PROFESSIONAL LICENSING

Insofar as legal education is solely a field of academic study, universities are largely free to define its shape and character. To the extent law school graduates want to practice law, however, bar admission authorities have a controlling influence on what law schools offer to and expect from their students.[54] An important way to cut the cost of legal education would be to reduce the amount of education required before taking a bar examination, for example, but the American

---

53. Among legal scholars holding this view were Herman Oliphant, Thurman Arnold, and William O. Douglas, and judges such as Learned Hand and Benjamin Cardozo were on their side. The Great Depression gave these arguments particular sway. It seemed to be a time when law could not ignore social reality. Law school teaching books began to have both cases and "materials" about their fields of law, and professors such as Arnold, Douglas, and Felix Frankfurter played prominent roles in the 1930s and thereafter. *See, e.g.,* Brainerd Currie, *The Materials of Law Study*, 3 J. LEGAL EDUC. 331 (1951) & 8 J. LEGAL EDUC. 1 (1955). Among the seminal articles in the realist period were Karl N. Llewellyn, *On What is Wrong with So-Called Legal Education*, 35 COLUM. L. REV. 651 (1935); Harold D. Lasswell & Myres S. McDougal, *Legal Education and Public Policy: Professional Training in the Public Interest*, 52 YALE L.J. 203 (1943). By contrast, *see* Roscoe Pound, *The Work of the American Law School*, 30 W. VA. L. Q. 1 (1923). Key articles about this period include Laura Kelman, *Professing Law: Elite Law School Professors in the Twentieth Century, in* LOOKING BACK AT LAW'S CENTURY (Austin Sarat, Bryant Garth & Robert A. Kagan eds., 2002); William W. Fisher, III, *Legal Theory and Legal Education, 1920–2000, in* THE CAMBRIDGE HISTORY OF LAW IN AMERICA, Vol. II, at 36, 57–67 (Michael Grossberg & Christopher Tomlins eds., 2007).

54. *See* ALFRED ZANTZINGER REED, TRAINING FOR THE PUBLIC PROFESSION OF LAW 38 (1921) (courts retained control of entry to the profession and kept America from having a self-determining bar like the one in England).

Bar Association has vigorously resisted regulatory efforts in that direction.

Although local bar associations had existed as social clubs since colonial times, the A.B.A. was not created until 1878. It considered the state of legal education in its early years,[55] and one of the first A.B.A. sections, created in 1893, was the Section on Legal Education.[56] The number of students in American law schools was up to 7,600 by that time, as compared to 1,611 a quarter-century earlier.[57]

While law professors initially participated in the A.B.A. Section of Legal Education, in 1900, the A.B.A. helped schools with the highest standards form the Association of American Law Schools (AALS).[58] To become an AALS member, a law school had to (1) admit only students who had completed high school, (2) offer a two-year program of law study (increased to three years after 1905), and (3) have or have access to a library with all its state's case reports and decisions of the U.S. Supreme Court.[59]

Until 1913, the AALS met together with the A.B.A. Section, and in 1914, the Section persuaded the Carnegie Foundation to support a survey of legal education.[60] Elihu Root became Chair of the A.B.A. Section in 1919, and he and Charles Taft became the chief advocates of the minimum standards for law schools that the A.B.A. adopted in 1923. The standards initially required schools to demand two years' pre-legal study and three years of law school work. Schools were required to have an adequate library and at least some full-time teachers.

---

55. ALBERT J. HARNO, LEGAL EDUCATION IN THE UNITED STATES 71–78 (1953).

56. Id. at 80–86. At the Section's first meeting in 1894, speakers included evidence expert John Wigmore and political scientist Woodrow Wilson. Id. at 81–82.

57. Remember that the figure today exceeds 100,000 students.

58. EDSON R. SUNDERLAND, HISTORY OF THE AMERICAN BAR ASSOCIATION AND ITS WORK 47 (1953). Thirty-five schools came to the initial meeting, and James B. Thayer of Harvard was elected the first president of the new Association of American Law Schools. Id. at 49.

59. ALBERT J. HARNO, LEGAL EDUCATION IN THE UNITED STATES 88–90 (1953).

60. The report was published as ALFRED ZANTZINGER REED, TRAINING FOR THE PUBLIC PROFESSION OF LAW (1921).

The list of approved law schools that met these requirements was prepared and made public.[61]

The result was the system of A.B.A. accreditation that we know today. Adopting accreditation standards was not without controversy; opponents argued that it would limit entry the profession to those sufficiently economically advantaged that they could afford the required legal and pre-legal education. But the proposal did pass, and by 1931, 77 of the 180 law schools operating in the United States had received A.B.A. approval.[62] By 1951, 124 of 164 schools were approved, and of those, 107 had also become members of the AALS.[63]

D. A ROAD NOT TAKEN

In the early 1970s, just at the time the number of law school applicants was rapidly increasing,[64] the Carnegie Commission again returned its focus to legal education.[65] This time, it made some startling proposals that could have had a dramatic effect on the study and practice of law as we know it today.

Adopting proposals made in an AALS report authored by Professor Paul Carrington, the Commission recommended making "legal education more functional, more individualized, more diversified, and

---

61. PHILIP C. JESSUP, ELIHU ROOT, Vol. 2, at 468–70.

62. ALBERT J. HARNO, LEGAL EDUCATION IN THE UNITED STATES 102–12 (1953). The standards were effective in changing the requirements for legal education. In 1930, thirty-two states required three years of law school; by 1935, the number was forty. In 1921, only one state had required two years of pre-law education; by 1936, the number was up to thirty-two. EDSON R. SUNDERLAND, HISTORY OF THE AMERICAN BAR ASSOCIATION AND ITS WORK 147 (1953).

63. Id. at 116–17. In 1950, the A.B.A. adopted a requirement that law schools could admit only students with at least three years' undergraduate study.

64. See Chapter 3, supra.

65. Two prior studies of pre-law education had been done during the Survey of the Legal Profession. Arthur T. Vanderbilt, A Report on Prelegal Education, 25 N.Y.U. L. REV. 199 (1950), and Albert P. Blaustein, College and Law School Education of the American Lawyer—A Preliminary Report, 3 J. LEGAL EDUC. 409 (1951).

more accessible."[66] It proposed having law schools adopt a "standard curriculum" that could be begun by students after three years of college. The curriculum could be finished in two academic years and would provide graduates with a grounding in core subjects and a chance for "intensive instruction" in professional skills. An "advanced curriculum" would be available to students who wanted a third year of law training, but that year could also be completed in noncontinuous units after leaving law school. An "open curriculum" would be available to nonprofessional students who simply wanted to learn more about law.

The proposal was imaginative and ambitious, and it thus met significant opposition when it was considered by the A.B.A. Most directly, it was opposed by law schools that foresaw a decline in tuition revenue if their program could be cut to two years.[67] Ultimately, the A.B.A. refused to recognize the two-year law school in its accreditation standards,[68] and because students studying in an unaccredited program could not be admitted to the bar in most states, no law school adopted the proposed program. If it is true that the world in which law students will practice will be different than that in which their professors practiced, it should not surprise us that legal educators may not be in the best position to help students deal with the new realities.

For at least the forty years since that report, law schools have been seeking ways to justify and give content to the third year of law school. Further, in the name of increasing law school quality, accreditation standards established by the A.B.A. have driven law schools toward homogeneity. Some schools are recognized to be better than others,

---

66. The AALS report was *Training for the Public Professions of the Law: 1971*. It may be found as an appendix to the Carnegie report, HERBERT L. PACKER & THOMAS EHRLICH, NEW DIRECTIONS IN LEGAL EDUCATION (1972).

67. *E.g.*, Robert A. Gorman, *Proposals for Reform of Legal Education*, 119 U. PA. L. REV. 845 (1971). *See also* Bayless Manning, *Law Schools and Lawyer Schools—Two-Tier Legal Education*, 26 J. LEGAL EDUC. 379 (1974) (proposing a two-year program of academic study, plus a one-year program run by the bar for trial lawyers and others who might want specialized training).

68. *See* Preble Stolz, *The Two-Year Law School: The Day the Music Died*, 25 J. LEGAL EDUC. 37 (1973).

but the model of legal education has been largely the same at all of them because the model is required.[69]

The message of this book is that the push toward homogeneity should end. The work of the A.B.A. Section on Legal Education and Admissions to the Bar has coerced state legislatures and university leaders to provide new buildings and to improve the quality of some law schools that in years past were not very good.[70] In the future, however, few law schools will be able to do everything well, and there is no reason most should even pretend to try. Large law schools may be able to be better in more fields than smaller schools can, but many law schools will be best advised to concentrate on being strong in a few fields and on training lawyers who seek those strengths.[71]

One current reality likely to delay such a development is law school applicants' focus on the annual ranking of law schools by *U.S. News & World Report*. Preoccupation with the "tier" into which their schools are placed—or their rank within the top tier—has already led law school administrators to engage in conduct of which they should be ashamed.[72] The fear of declining in rank is likely to discourage law

---

69. *See, e.g.*, E. Gordon Gee & Donald W. Jackson, Following the Leader? The Unexamined Consensus in Law School Curricula (1975).

70. Law school accreditation is not without controversy. One effect of complying with accreditation standards is to increase the cost of providing legal education, an effect that would traditionally raise antitrust issues. *See, e.g.*, George B. Shepherd & William G. Shepherd, *Scholarly Restraints? A.B.A. Accreditation and Legal Education*, 19 Cardozo L. Rev. 2091 (1998); Marina Lao, *Discrediting Accreditation: Antitrust and Legal Education*, 79 Wash. U. L. Rev. 1035 (2002). *But see* Massachusetts School of Law at Andover, Inc. v. Am. Bar Ass'n, 107 F.3d 1997 (3rd Cir. 1997) (rejecting antitrust claim on the ground that harm to the plaintiff arose from action of states that denied graduates the right to take the bar examination, not directly from A.B.A. denial of accreditation).

71. There is evidence that some law schools are taking this reality seriously and writing mission statements to guide their future developments. *See* Gordon T. Butler, *The Law School Mission Statement: A Survival Guide for the Twenty-First Century*, 50 J. Legal Educ. 240 (2000).

72. The New York Times reports, for example, that LexisNexis and Westlaw provide their electronic research services to law schools for flat rates ranging from $75,000 to $100,000 per year. Because the *U.S. News* ranks schools more highly if they "spend" more per student, however, the University of Illinois College of Law reported its "spending" for the services as

schools from admitting a student body as diverse as it could be or from introducing curricular innovations that might have rating consequences.[73] Ratings make sense only if one assumes that schools are trying to produce the same kind of graduate and thus are subject to the same standard of success. The diversity of student interests and the range of potential uses of a legal education are so great, however, that ultimately the ratings distort rather than measure reality. Meanwhile, however, the ratings game makes it hard to predict when law schools will recognize that they cannot afford not to change.[74]

$8.78 million per year, a sum it said was the "value" students receive from the services. Alex Wellen, *The $8.78 Million Maneuver*, N. Y. Times, July 31, 2005, Sec. 4A, at 18. Needless to say, if that school had been a publicly traded company, someone likely would have faced charges of securities fraud.

Another common law school practice was the creation or expansion of part-time programs, the grade point averages and LSAT scores of whose students were not considered by *U.S. News* in its calculation of a school's selectivity. Until this feature of the ratings was changed, several schools admitted students whose grades and test scores were lowest—up to as many as one-third of the entering class of some schools—only into the part-time category so as to avoid revealing the true composition of their class. *See, e.g.,* Bill Henderson & Jeff Lipshaw, *The Empirics and Ethics of USNWR Gaming*, at http://lawprofessors.typepad.com/legal_profession/2008/08/posted-by-jeff.html (Aug. 27, 2008).

73. There is good evidence, for example, that law schools regularly give admission preference to students with high undergraduate grades and high LSAT scores, which are considered in *U.S. News* rankings, at the expense of age, life experience, service to disadvantaged persons, intent to engage in public service practice, and the like. *See, e.g.,* William D. Henderson & Andrew P. Morriss, *Student Quality as Measured by LSAT Scores: Migration Patterns in the U.S. News Rankings Era*, 81 Ind. L.J. 163 (2006).

74. In the years since 1950, universities have tended to see law schools—with their high student-faculty ratios—as profit centers. Legal education requires specialized library materials, but it does not require expensive laboratories or small classes, and even colleges with no other graduate schools have founded law schools in an attempt to finance their undergraduate program. Then, once founded, the law schools have felt pressure to take more students to yield more and more profits for university reinvestment. Institutional budgets, in short, explain at least part of the rapid growth in the number of the nation's lawyers.

E. FAULTY MODELS DRIVING LEGAL EDUCATION TODAY

It would be a mistake to say that legal educators have not been interested in thinking about improving legal education. Both the A.B.A.'s MacCrate Task Force in 1992[75] and the Carnegie Commission in 2007[76] have urged that law schools move in new directions. Unfortunately, the changes they have urged point legal education in substantially the wrong directions and have seemingly ignored what is happening to the legal profession itself.

Originally set up to study a "gap" between law school and practice, the MacCrate Task Force report evolved into a study of an "educational continuum" seen as running over the course of a professional career. The Task Force's overarching presumption was that lawyers are more alike than different. It argued that, although the legal profession

> is larger and more diverse than ever before . . . the law has remained a single profession identified with a perceived common body of learning, skills and values . . . . [I]n virtually every practice setting the individual lawyer is compelled to concentrate in one or several areas of law, while clinging to the traditional image of being a "generalist."[77]

Noting that law schools had traditionally seen theirs as a role developing a student's analytic ability while other needed skills were to be learned in practice, the Task Force said law schools were capable of doing—and should do—more practical training before a student graduated.

---

75. Its report was A.B.A. SECTION OF LEGAL EDUCATION AND ADMISSION TO THE BAR, TASK FORCE ON LAW SCHOOLS AND THE PROFESSION: NARROWING THE GAP, LEGAL EDUCATION AND PROFESSIONAL DEVELOPMENT–AN EDUCATIONAL CONTINUUM (1992). The chair of the Task Force was distinguished lawyer Robert MacCrate of New York.

76. The report was published as WILLIAM M. SULLIVAN, ANNE COLBY, JUDITH WELCH WEGNER, LLOYD BOND AND LEE S. SHULMAN, EDUCATING LAWYERS: PREPARATION FOR THE PRACTICE OF LAW (2007).

77. A.B.A. SECTION OF LEGAL EDUCATION AND ADMISSION TO THE BAR, TASK FORCE ON LAW SCHOOLS AND THE PROFESSION: NARROWING THE GAP, LEGAL EDUCATION AND PROFESSIONAL DEVELOPMENT–AN EDUCATIONAL CONTINUUM II (1992). The Task Force's recommendations were based on the view that the primary task of a law school is to produce generalist graduates. *Id.* at 124.

The Task Force identified ten skills that every law student should develop—whatever he planned to do with a legal education.[78] The skills are (1) problem-solving, (2) legal analysis and reasoning, (3) legal research, (4) fact investigation, (5) communication, (6) counseling, (7) negotiation, (8) litigation and alternative dispute resolution procedures, (9) organization and management of legal work, and (10) recognizing and resolving ethical dilemmas. Further, no law student should graduate without absorbing four values: (1) personally providing competent representation, (2) personally striving to promote justice, fairness, and morality, (3) personally striving to improve the profession, and (4) personally seeking out his or her own professional self-development.[79]

The Task Force opined that those skills and values could be best enhanced by a student's active involvement in more law school clinical programs. Although its report eschewed any intention to affect law school accreditation standards or determine law school curricula, the clear direction on both fronts in the years following the report has been an expansion of the number of clinical professors and clinical offerings in U.S. law schools.[80]

---

78. A.B.A. Section of Legal Education and Admission to the Bar, Task Force on Law Schools and the Profession: Narrowing the Gap, Legal Education and Professional Development—An Educational Continuum 138–41 (1992).

79. Inevitably, not everyone thought the Task Force had comprehensively identified the relevant skills and values. *See, e.g.,* Carrie Menkel-Meadow, *Narrowing the Gap by Narrowing the Field: What's Missing From the MacCrate Report—Of Skills, Legal Science and Being a Human Being,* 69 Wash. L. Rev. 593 (1994); Russell G. Pearce, *MacCrate's Missed Opportunity: The MacCrate Report's Failure to Advance Professional Values,* 23 Pace L. Rev. 575 (2003).

80. A.B.A. Section of Legal Education and Admission to the Bar, Task Force on Law Schools and the Profession: Narrowing the Gap, Legal Education and Professional Development—An Educational Continuum 131–33 (1992). The A.B.A. requires that all law students receive "substantial instruction" in skills training, for example, including "substantial opportunities" to work with actual clients, A.B.A. Standards for Admission to the Bar, Standard 302(a)(4) & (b)(1), and the Clinical Legal Education Association has published "best practices" standards that the Association advocates all law schools should adopt. Roy Stuckey, et al., Best Practices for Legal Education: A Vision and a Road Map (2007).

More recently, in 2007, the always-hovering Carnegie Foundation weighed in once again on issues of law teaching.[81] No longer advocating a two-year law school, this time its premise was that legal education has suffered from the desire of universities to have their law students assume the "detached position of the theoretical observer" instead of "the stance of engaged practice."[82] A practice-oriented stance has equal intellectual integrity, the report's authors assert, and from that stance, students can be trained for the task of exercising "judgment in action."[83]

Citing what it said was new research about learning, the report calls for a return to the heretofore largely abandoned system of training lawyers by "apprenticeship," albeit this time in a university setting.[84] The authors posit that persons who are "experts" in a field based on their practice experience rather than academic study can be assumed to have worked out systematic ways to approach legal issues. The authors also assume everyone can be confident that these experts will know how to apply their practical skills in an academic context. Thus, the report concludes, law schools should focus on three kinds of "apprenticeship": "cognitive or intellectual" such as that provided in traditional law school classes; "expert practice" taught by practitioners to students in small groups; and professional "identity and purpose" apprenticeship taught by exposing students to the community of law practitioners more generally.[85]

---

81. WILLIAM M. SULLIVAN, ANNE COLBY, JUDITH WELCH WEGNER, LLOYD BOND AND LEE S. SHULMAN, EDUCATING LAWYERS: PREPARATION FOR THE PRACTICE OF LAW (2007).

82. *Id.* at 8.

83. *Id.* at 9.

84. *Id.* at 26.

85. *Id.* at 27–28. The call for professionalism training through apprentice-like experiences has been sounded by others as well. *See* James Moliterno, *Analysis of Ethics Teaching in Law Schools: Replacing Lost Benefits of the Apprenticeship System in the Academic Atmosphere*, 60 U. CIN. L. REV. 83 (1991); James Moliterno, *Legal Education, Experiential Education, and Professional Responsibility*, 38 WM. & MARY L. REV. 71 (1996); Patrick J. Schlitz, *Legal Ethics in Decline: The Elite Law Firm, the Elite Law School, and the Moral Formation of the Novice Attorney*, 82 MINN. L. REV. 705 (1998); Neil Hamilton & Lisa Montpetit Brabbit, *Fostering Professionalism Through Mentoring*, 57 J. LEGAL EDUC. 102 (2007).

The Carnegie report's authors acknowledge that their view is heavily based on their perception that law is a profession in the sociologists' sense we considered in Chapter 2. Indeed, some of the authors have made a similar call with respect to the professional training received by journalists and doctors.[86] Thus, in the view of this 2007 Carnegie report, a legal education would consist of some courses in legal analysis, but then be heavily supplemented with increased clinical training and experience working in public service jobs.[87]

A number of law schools are in the process of considering curricular revisions, at least in part in response to the Carnegie report. The most extreme response has been that of the law school at Washington & Lee, which has announced that its students will devote their entire third year in law school to "professional development through simulated and actual practice experiences."[88] Ironically, no one seems to have observed that students could get equal or better experience by working at real law firms and receiving a salary instead of being required to pay law school tuition in order to pretend to work on legal tasks.

Once again, the reason the MacCrate Task Force and the Carnegie Commissions can take the positions they have—and that fine schools can go far afield in trying to respond to their calls—is the underlying sense that legal education is engaged in production of credentialed persons who will each use a legal education in much the same way every other graduate will, and just as other members of the legal "profession" now do.[89] The proposals also presuppose that there is

---

86. Other groups, including engineers and academics, have claimed the title of professional, but it is not at all clear the same principles of hands-on instruction would appropriately apply to them. *See, e.g.*, ELLIOTT A. KRAUSE, DEATH OF THE GUILDS: PROFESSIONS, STATES, AND THE ADVANCE OF CAPITALISM, 1930 TO THE PRESENT 21 (1996).

87. WILLIAM M. SULLIVAN, ANNE COLBY, JUDITH WELCH WEGNER, LLOYD BOND AND LEE S. SHULMAN, EDUCATING LAWYERS: PREPARATION FOR THE PRACTICE OF LAW 29–45 (2007). The authors express admiration for CUNY Law School that was founded on a basis of training primarily in a clinical training, public service environment.

88. Message from Dean Rod Smolla, found on the Washington & Lee Web site at www.law.wlu.edu/thirdyear.

89. *See, e.g.*, FRANCES KAHN ZEMANS & VICTOR G. ROSENBLUM, THE MAKING OF A PUBLIC PROFESSION (1981).

something inevitable about training lawyers in a three-year, six-semester program, and that the only question is how to occupy students during those required years.

F. REDUCING THE COST OF LEGAL TRAINING

Law schools faced with more demand for seats than they could supply have felt free to act as though there is no need to find more efficient ways to provide a legal education. Another implication of, and reason for, the developments discussed in earlier chapters is that as students see the demand for three-year-trained lawyer-generalists tend to decline or disappear, schools are likely either to go out of business or face a need to reduce the cost of legal education considerably.

The cost of a year's study at several American law schools now exceeds $45,000, even before taking into account the income not earned as a result of being in school. Aggregate educational debt for many law graduates exceeds $100,000.[90] Those figures may seem tolerable for graduates who expect to start their legal career making over $150,000 per year, but such salaries are available only to a very few. The average lawyer makes only a little over $100,000 annually over the course of a career,[91] and many lawyers find themselves forever digging out of the financial hole that the cost of their education has created.[92]

---

90. *See, e.g.,* John A. Sebert, *The Cost and Financing of Legal Education*, 52 J. LEGAL EDUC. 516 (2002); June Knonholz, *More Students, Higher Prices, Tougher Competition,* WALL ST. J., Jan. 31, 2005, at. R4.

91. Average lawyer incomes are hard to determine. BUREAU OF LABOR STATISTICS, 2004 NATIONAL OCCUPATIONAL EMPLOYMENT AND WAGE ESTIMATES, at 211, reports the median earnings of all lawyers to be $108,790.

92. One particularly troubling dimension of legal education funding is the practice at some schools of providing scholarship aid to the students with the most promise out of the tuition dollars of those least likely to do well in law school. Such "merit" scholarships are typically designed to improve the school's ranking in the *U.S. News* survey discussed earlier, but the role they play in increasing the debt of less qualified students makes the practice extraordinarily hard to justify. On a more positive note, an important development in legal education was passage of the College Cost Reduction Act, Pub. L. 110-84 (2007) which provides for some forgiveness of student loans if a law

There are several reasons for the high cost of legal education. Law school faculty are among the best paid at a university, with salaries at many institutions exceeding $200,000 per year. Few faculty teach more than four courses each year, and at many schools, the figure is three courses or fewer. Some schools use adjunct faculty who are paid substantially less to teach some courses, but basically, the model of each student being taught each course by a faculty member whose primary occupation is scholarly research has driven the cost of legal education very high.[93]

Among the ways to reduce the cost of law study may be distance learning.[94] Such courses take two forms. Synchronous distance learning occurs when the law teacher and law students are in different places but talk over what is essentially a picture-phone. A class can take place in real time in which students in Buffalo, for example, can be taught by someone in Oxford or Tokyo. The professor can see, question, and answer questions just as if she were physically with the students. It is a form of distance learning that seems likely to enhance the legal education experience, and, while itself costly, it is possible that such a model might increase a given professor's contact with students each year, reduce the on-site staffing a school might need, or both.

Other distance learning uses CD-ROM or online technology to send lectures and recorded classes to individual students. There is no real-time communication between instructor and students at all. While probably not as good for the first-year "think-like-a-lawyer" phase of a legal education, such online instruction is an integral part

---

graduate goes into public interest work. *But cf.* Lewis A. Kornhauser & Richard L. Revesz, *Legal Education and Entry Into the Legal Profession: The Role of Race, Gender, and Educational Debt,* 70 N.Y.U. L. Rev. 829 (1995) (casting doubt on the importance of loan repayment assistance on getting students to choose public interest careers).

93. A similar insight was offered by Professor Bill Henderson in Law *School 4.0: Are Law Schools Relevant to the Future of Law?, Legal Profession Blog,* at http://lawprofessors.typepad.com/legal_profession/2009/07/ (July 2, 2009).

94. *See, e.g.,* Peter W. Martin, *Information Technology and U.S. Legal Education: Opportunities, Challenges and Threats,* 52 J. Legal Educ. 506 (2002); Linda C. Fentiman, *A Distance Education Primer: Lessons From My Life as a Dot.Edu Entrepreneur,* 6 N.C. J. Law & Tech. 41 (2004).

of lawyers' continuing education today. As one gets into detailed specialty training, at the very least, or into second- and third-year courses designed to add breadth to a student's education, such technology suggests a way to deliver information to students all over the country at a significantly reduced cost, perhaps supplemented by live classes using local instructors from time to time.[95]

Web-based instruction similarly has improved to a point that students can even do interactive drills with new material,[96] and e-mail can make even asking questions of the instructor possible.[97] One may properly be concerned about a legal education received wholly from packaged or online materials,[98] but as a supplement to live teaching in the upper-class curriculum, a way for persons working on advanced degrees to build upon groundwork laid in more traditional classes, and a way to make legal education more affordable, it seems inevitable that law schools and their students will turn to such technology.[99]

---

95. Such a vision is offered in DAVID I.C. THOMSON, LAW SCHOOL 2.0: LEGAL EDUCATION FOR A DIGITAL AGE 4–9 (2009).

96. *See* John Mayer, *Alternate Futures: The Future of Legal Education*; Ronald Staudt, *In Search of the Origins of the Electronic Casebook*; and James Hoover, *A Vision of Law Schools in the Future, all in* THE HISTORY OF LEGAL EDUCATION IN THE UNITED STATES, vol. 2 (Steve Sheppard ed., 1999). The Center for Computer-Assisted Legal Instruction, or CALI ®, has been working on such materials for at least thirty years.

97. Professors can now incorporate distance learning into classroom courses with the use of technology that allows class discussions to continue between classes. *See, e.g.,* Joan MacLeod Heminway, *Caught in (or on) the Web: A Review of Course Management Systems for legal Education*, 16 ALBANY L.J. OF SCI. & TECH. 265 (2006).

98. Currently, A.B.A. accreditation standard 306(b) treats both synchronous and asynchronous distance learning the same way and provides that a law student may earn credit for such courses only after the first year and may apply no more than 4 credits in any term, or a total of 12 credits overall, in such courses toward a degree in law. Surveys taken in 2002–2003 and 2003–2004 found that about 20 percent of law schools offer asynchronous courses, while 10 percent offer synchronous instruction. William R. Rakes, *From the Chairperson*, 38 SYLLABUS 2 (Winter 2007).

99. Concord Law School, www.concordlawschool.edu, the nation's only entirely online program, remains unaccredited by the A.B.A. Concord graduates may not take the bar exam in most states, but they may take the California

An even more basic way to cut the cost of legal education would be to reduce the time period required to complete the program needed to take a bar examination. Tuition and living costs, high as they are, are only part of the cost of going to law school. Often the greater cost is income not earned during the years of schooling. The ability to complete the "three-year" law school in two calendar years or less could substitute the relatively high salary of a first-year lawyer for the relatively insignificant salary of most students. Northwestern is the first "elite" American law school to initiate such a compressed program, although four other schools had taken the action earlier.[100]

Such an accelerated approach will not be attractive to everyone. Unless the student starts the summer before most law students begin—a practice Northwestern allows—it would deny both the student and potential employers the summer of employment many use to size each other up before offering or accepting a first position. What offering the opportunity recognizes, however, is that time is money, and cutting costs may be an important competitive advantage in the pursuit of good students.

G. NEW WAYS TO THINK ABOUT LEGAL EDUCATION

It is ironic that law schools are being pressed to teach law practice skills just as the need for expanded thinking about lawyer skills and their use in other than traditional practice settings has become more

---

bar, and several have become lawyers. NYU Law School has now announced plans to offer an LL.M. degree online. It can do that because a graduate law degree is not subject to the same A.B.A. accreditation standards. For a view of technology in education generally, see John L. Lahey & Janice C. Griffith, *Recent Trends in Higher Education: Accountability, Efficiency, Technology, and Governance*, 52 J. LEGAL EDUC. 528 (2002).

100. Leigh Jones, *Two-Year JD at Northwestern*, NAT'L L.J., June 23, 2008, at 4. Earlier, Southwestern University in Los Angeles had adopted a six-semester program. The University of Dayton Law School announced a five-semester program in 2006, and Syracuse University and the University of Kansas also had accelerated programs. Leigh Jones, *Law School in Two Years Flat*, NAT'L L.J., May 29, 2006, at 4. In all these cases, A.B.A. Standard 304(c) prohibits actually awarding the student a degree less than twenty-four months after the student began law study.

important. A call for better practice training begs the questions raised in this book about what the practice environment will look like in which legally trained individuals will work. It further ignores whether law firms themselves might provide better training than law schools in the transition to the kind of practice they do.

An education that might have prepared students adequately for work in the twentieth century,[101] in short, is not likely to ready students to enter the world in which we have suggested they will actually work. If this book is correct that yesterday's practice and ways firms operate will be changing rapidly, increasing a student's exposure to the old regime is likely to be a profound waste of time and money.

Contrary to the recent Carnegie Commission's assumption, for example, lawyers are not really much like doctors. They are not trained how to treat a single—albeit complex—organism, and they do not deliver their services by making regular rounds in a hospital, the setting for most clinical education in medicine. Rather, legal education might better be seen as consisting of four parts, comparable to the four kinds of understanding we suggested earlier, that lawyers need to develop.

1. Learning to Think Like a Twenty-First Century Lawyer

First, students should learn to think like a lawyer. More generally, students should develop a grounded understanding of sources of law and methods of legal analysis. The discipline to read carefully, become sensitive to ambiguity, and focus on facts most relevant to the matter at issue can be learned by doing, followed by prompt evaluation and correction both in classroom discussions and written papers.[102]

---

101. Even this was a contested proposition. *See, e.g.,* Duncan Kennedy, *How the Law School Fails: A Polemic,* 1 YALE REV. L. & SOC. ACTION 73 (1970) (written while now-Professor Kennedy was a law student); Robert Stevens, *Law Schools and Law Students,* 59 VA. L. REV. 551 (1973) (partial response to the Kennedy article); *Note, Making Docile Lawyers: An Essay on the Pacification of Law Students,* 111 HARV. L. REV. 2027 (1998).

102. Understanding of actual facts may be contested in any situation, and in a quest for the critical facts, lawyers sometimes tend to filter out the human realities that may be important in a situation, Thoughtful critics recognize that the professional distance lawyers learn to develop can cut the lawyer off from some of the emotional realities facing clients and the social implications or consequences that may be inherent in what superficially appears to be a

Substantive subjects addressed in the courses should be substantially broadened beyond traditional areas such as contracts, torts, and property. Statutes and regulations should be examined, not case law alone. A course in income tax might be used to teach close reading of statutes, for example. Vanderbilt has introduced a class in Regulatory Law into its first-year program.[103] Harvard has added classes in international and comparative law.[104] Elsewhere, a school might introduce

---

simple legal question. The consequence may be what some call a lawyer's assumption of a "moral void." Professor Roger Cramton was among the first to identify these issues. Roger C. Cramton, *The Ordinary Religion of the Law School Classroom*, 29 J. LEGAL EDUC. 247 (1978) (students are taught to be skeptical, to see law instrumentally, and to believe that process is more important than substance). *See also* G. Andrew H. Benjamin, Alfred Kaszniak, Bruce Sales & Stephen B. Shanfield, *The Role of Legal Education in Producing Psychological Distress Among Law Students and Lawyers*, 1986 A.B.F. RES. J. 225; Thomas D. Eisele, *Bitter Knowledge: Socrates and Teaching by Disillusionment*, 45 MERCER L. REV. 587 (1994). But at their best, lawyers can clear away less important facts to direct the parties'—and potentially a court's—attention to the facts on which a case is likely to turn.

The value of those instincts and skills will be as great in the future as it has ever been, although some writers express concern about the different effect of law school teaching on minority and female students. *See, e.g.*, Susan Sturm & Lani Guinier, *The Law School Matrix: Reforming Legal Education in a Culture of Competition and Conformity*, 60 VAND. L. REV. 515 (2007); Judith Resnik, *Gender Matters, Race Matters*, 14 N.Y.L. SCH. J. HUM. RTS. 219 (1998); Cruz Reynoso & Cory Amron, *Diversity in Legal Education: A Broader View, a Deeper Commitment*, 52 J. LEGAL EDUC. 491, 496–97 (2002).

Yet others have stressed the role of law professor behavior in forming long-term lawyer attitudes about their conduct. *E.g.*, Deborah L. Rhode, *The Professional Responsibilities of Professors*, 51 J. LEGAL EDUC. 158 (2001); Paul D. Carrington, *Butterfly Effects: The Possibilities of Law Teaching in a Democracy*, 41 DUKE L.J. 741 (1992); Carrie J. Menkel-Meadow, *Can a Law Teacher Avoid Teaching Legal Ethics*, 41 J. LEGAL EDUC. 3 (1991); Jack L. Sammons, Jr., *Professing: Some Thoughts on Professionalism and Classroom Teaching*, 3 GEO. J. LEGAL ETHICS 609 (1990); Norman Redlich, *Law Schools as Institutional Teachers of Professional Responsibility*, 34 J. LEGAL EDUC. 215 (1984).

103. *See* http://law.vanderbilt.edu/academics/curriculum/index.aspx. *See also* Edward Rubin, *What's Wrong with Langdell's Method, and What to Do About It*, 60 VAND. L. REV. 609 (2007) (Dean Rubin came to Vanderbilt with a commitment to revamping its curriculum).

104. *See* http://law.harvard.edu/academics/degrees/jd/index.html.

a class in business associations to analyze fiduciary duties that lawyers owe to clients. Evidence might consider the fact-finding process more broadly. Family law might stress evolving standards and the effect of the law on individuals. The point is that if we were to think afresh today about what twenty-first century lawyers will be doing, we would not begin by teaching all of today's first-year courses. Students would learn to "think like a lawyer," but the model would be a twenty-first century lawyer.[105]

2. An Appropriate Vision for Skills Training

A second part of a law student's experience should be exposure to the broad category of skills a lawyer uses to get things done. No one can seriously doubt that lawyers use more skills than they learn from reading cases, but likewise, the reality is that most practice skills will be most fully developed and enhanced by repeated efforts after the lawyer enters practice.

Some lawyer skills are far from glamorous. A lawyer's most basic skill, for example, is clear and careful writing. A second involves thinking in terms of alternative ways to get to a desired outcome. Yet a third set of modern skills will involve the use of technology. A fourth will involve developing the "people skills" to work in teams to solve problems. Each of these skills—along with the advocacy and negotiation skills discussed earlier—is important and can be developed by instruction, feedback, and experience.

Not all of these skills are best learned, however, in clinical settings that focus on cases involving real clients. Live-client clinical teaching is about the most expensive way to deliver law school training, primarily because of the extremely low student-teacher ratios involved in such settings.[106] As noted in the next chapter, law school clinics provide an important service to poor people in need of legal services, and there will probably always be a role for clinical education in law schools. The sense of the MacCrate Task Force and the Carnegie

---

105. For an only partly tongue-in-cheek account of the current first year in law school, *see* Michael C. Dorf, *The Five-Minute Law School: Everything You Learn in Your First Year, More or Less*, in FindLaw's Legal Commentary, Aug. 3, 2005, at http://writ.findlaw.com/dorf/20050803.html.

106. *See, e.g.*, John J. Costonis, *The MacCrate Report: Of Loaves, Fishes and the Future of American Legal Education*, 43 J. LEGAL EDUC. 157 (1993).

Commission that clinical training should be a centerpiece of legal education, however, largely ignores the diverse kinds of future roles many law graduates will fill.

Certainly, some advanced courses can be built around problems, i.e., complex fact patterns that require students to make choices from among several roads to resolution.[107] Other courses can provide training and simulated experience in negotiation and trial practice. There is no harm in organizing students into "law firms" to receive such training, and indeed it may be useful for getting students to work in groups. But we should not confuse course packaging with content, and we should not assume that law school will be the end of a student's education.

3. Training in Non-Legal Matter Needed for a Practice Concentration

The third kind of subject matter a student should study is that which will allow her to concentrate in a particular field of law. In addition to taking courses that go into more detail than an introductory course can, students should focus on the international, not just the domestic, aspects of their fields.[108]

Equally important, law schools should recognize that education about non-legal substantive issues will be at least as important as more law courses for the work of many legal advisors.[109] Courses in

---

107. Among the early books to take that course was THOMAS D. MORGAN & RONALD D. ROTUNDA, PROFESSIONAL RESPONSIBILITY: PROBLEMS AND MATERIALS (10th ed. 2008).

108. See, e.g., John Sexton, Thinking About the Training of Lawyers in the Next Millennium, NYU ALUMNI MAGAZINE, Autumn 2000, at 35; Panel Discussion, Legal Education in the 21st Century (DC Cir. Jud. Conf. 2000); Jill Schachner Chanin, Re-engineering the JD, A.B.A. J., July 2007, at 42; Tresa Baldas, Several Schools Adjust Their Curriculums, NAT'L L.J., Sept. 10, 2007, at S1.

109. This is by no means a new insight. See, e.g., Oliver Wendell Holmes, Jr., The Path of the Law, 10 HARV. L. REV. 457, 469 (1897) ("For the rational study of the law, the black letter man may be the man of the present, but the man of the future is the man of statistics and the master of economics"). From the more recent era, see, e.g., Carrie Menkel-Meadow, Taking Law and _____ Really Seriously: Before, During and After "The Law," 60 VAND. L. REV. 555 (2007).

economics, psychology, and communications—courses in accounting, computer science, and public administration—each now often seen as "interdisciplinary" and therefore collateral to a legal education— may over the next twenty years be understood as central to a lawyer's ability to function in the world he or she will face.[110] Indeed, law schools that have become used to having a certain independence within the academic community may again see themselves as dependent upon other departments to help them do their job.

Learning corporate finance in the business school, for example, may be equally or more important to an advanced law student as another course in corporate taxation. A year in China learning Chinese language may set a future lawyer more apart from her contemporaries than taking more courses in comparative law. The point is not to disparage legal study. It is to reiterate that a lawyer's task will be to give clients and other lawyers a reason to seek out that legal service provider rather than another one. As communications technology, as well as multijurisdictional practice rules, make it increasingly possible for clients to work with consultants located anywhere in the world, the need to develop unique qualities and skills with which to serve clients will be essential, and non-legal skills may be one of the best ways to differentiate oneself from the crowd.

4. Education for Breadth and Context of Legal Understanding

Finally, there should be a place for training in substantive law beyond the particular areas in which a student expects to practice. This might involve a corporate lawyer getting exposure to evidence, if only to know better the need for preserving certain kinds of evidence of the parties' intent. It might include a trial lawyer's exposure to litigation in a civil law system, or taxation, to know the consequences of settling cases in one way rather than another. The point, however, is that not every graduate is going to use his education in the same way, and breadth of legal understanding may be more critical for some graduates than exposure to skills training.

It is in these elective courses that technology may play a particularly important role. A student who wants to work in Europe, for

---

110. *See, e.g.,* John Palfrey, *The Law School Curriculum: What is Technology's Role,* Nat'l L.J., Nov. 13, 2006, at 30 (calling for law school instruction in uses and significance of technology).

example, might take courses taught from a European law school by a European professor on a satellite link. Or, she might move to Europe and take courses from her home school on her computer.[111] It is in these kinds of courses that schools should be encouraged to be as creative as possible in developing ways to deliver legal education to law students and even practicing lawyers, wherever they may be.

H. MULTIPLE POSSIBLE CREDENTIALS FOR LEGAL TRAINING

As a practical matter today, there is only one degree for Americans interested in legal training. It is the three-year program leading to a juris doctor (J.D.) degree. Earned only after a four-year college degree, it is costly both in money and time. Yet, as we have suggested, some familiarity with how lawyers approach questions is important to many people other than lawyers. Programs requiring less training than that for the J.D. are likely to be—and should be—an important part of law school programs as opportunities for three-year-trained law graduates decline.

A one-year program involving thinking like a lawyer, legal research and writing, and perhaps negotiation, for example, might be worked into an undergraduate college program, possibly leading to a major in legal studies.[112] Indeed, an even shorter introduction to law and legal skills could be offered to high school students and in programs of adult education. For other students, such a program might represent a first year of post-graduate study leading to a masters of arts degree. Graduates of such a program would be unlikely to hold themselves out as legal advisors, but such an education might be highly useful, for example, to business people trying to understand the way law impacts their activities. Even people who start law school and decide they do not like it would find such a degree a tangible reward for their efforts and a face-saving way to turn elsewhere.

---

111. Professor Thomson calls this Law School 2.0. *See* David I.C. Thomson, Law School 2.0: Legal Education for a Digital Age (2009).

112. The principal resistance to such a development would be likely to come from other liberal arts departments who may fear that people who would otherwise take their courses will be seduced into law instead.

A two-year law school program, in turn, would be the limit of a lawyer's basic and initial education if the Carnegie Commission's 1971 recommendation could be revived and given effect.[113] That recommendation deserves another look, given the clear decline in student attention to law school courses in the current third-year program at most schools.[114] My own view is that after the second year of law school, a student should be able to take the bar examination and be eligible to practice at least in one or more fields of law. Even without formal recognition of a two-year degree, however, such an education might be recognized as a basis for certification to give legal advice and appear before particular agencies and specialized courts.[115]

The three-year program might remain the legal education gold standard, at least until two-year graduates prove their success in the marketplace. Indeed, students might even choose to take a fourth year of legal training, as some do today,[116] while others might return to law school mid-career to take training in a new field and receive a

---

113. It is not clear what to name this degree. It might be an LL.B., which was long the basic law degree.

114. Mitu Gulati, Richard Sander, & Robert Sockloskie, *The Happy Charade: An Empirical Examination of the Third Year of Law School*, 51 J. LEGAL EDUC. 235 (2001) (showing class attendance and class preparation declines sharply in the third year of law school). The national Law School Survey of Student Engagement, produced annually, tends to be somewhat more optimistic about the level of student preparation for class and involvement in law school activities. The LSSSE annual reports may be found at www.lssse. iub.edu.

115. Thoughtful readers will see that such a two-year law degree would be analogous to the two-year education leading to an MBA degree. Further education—indeed, possibly further degree programs—taught on a basis analogous to executive MBA programs, would become a regular part of lawyers' lives as they keep up with new developments in their old field or transition to new areas of practice altogether as client demands change.

116. A world somewhat like this was foreseen in Russell G. Pearce, *Law Day 2050: Post-Professionalism, Moral Leadership and the Law-as-Business Paradigm*, 27 FLA. ST. L. REV. 9, 13 (1999). Professor Pierce foresees three tiers of practitioners. The top tier, or "members of the bar," will be eligible to appear in all courts. A middle tier of "advocates," who have completed one year of undergraduate work in law and a one-year training program after graduation, will be eligible to appear in trial courts but not appellate bodies. The third tier, called "aides," will have completed only a two-month training

certificate rather than a new degree for their work. In training beyond the second year, then, students would broaden their exposure to a variety of fields, concentrate their study in a single field, or even study non-legal subjects such as languages, finance, and science so as to enhance their ability to survive in a competitive world of client advisors.[117]

Accreditation of this range of educational programs should almost certainly not be the province of the American Bar Association. If courses in legal method are taught in an undergraduate setting at a university without a law school, for example, the regional accrediting agencies that review colleges would appropriately do the review. These agencies would also likely better review non-law course offerings and joint degree programs than the current law-dominated A.B.A. process is equipped to do today. Accreditation should be understood to be a process of protecting the public from deception about the quality of the education offered, and while the A.B.A. has largely done a conscientious job in the accreditation process,[118] the time has come to pass the responsibility to others.

If programmatic changes in legal education like these suggested here occur, the world many law professors now know is likely to change in ways most will find unattractive. At many schools, for example, teaching will ascend in importance, and scholarship will decline.[119] Experiential education, whether in the form of live-client

---

program and will only appear before administrative bodies or specialized courts, much as practitioners before some federal agencies do today.

117. LL.M. programs are already offered by many schools. They are particularly useful for lawyers who want to specialize in taxation, intellectual property, government contracts, or similar subject areas, and they are widely used by foreign law graduates to add an American degree to their resumes.

118. There is an opposing view. *See, e.g.,* George B. Shepherd, *No African-American Lawyers Allowed: The Inefficient Racism of the ABA's Accreditation of Law Schools,* 53 J. LEGAL EDUC. 103–56 (2003).

119. Judge (and former professor) Harry Edwards triggered an important discussion of whether legal scholarship must be useful to judges and practicing lawyers. *See* Harry T. Edwards, *The Growing Disjunction Between Legal Education and the Legal Profession,* 91 MICH. L. REV. 34 (1992); Harry T. Edwards, *The Growing Disjunction Between Legal Education and the Legal Profession: A Postscript,* 91 MICH. L. REV. 2191 (1993). *See also, e.g.,* Deborah L. Rhode, *Legal Scholarship,* 115 HARV. L. REV. 1327 (2002); Francis A. Allen,

clinics or simulation of practice, might remain part of a law school's program, but it will not be the center of focus. Most of any student's real experience will be obtained in the first years of practice in the specialized fields he enters—experience no law school could expect to duplicate or exceed.

In short, law school curricula will look more to the world students will experience rather than the world their professors faced. Today's random smorgasbord of courses will prove neither nourishing nor sufficient for a twenty-first century practitioner. In the years to come, today's relative homogeneity of law schools is likely to end as schools try to differentiate themselves in the education marketplace.

Almost inevitably, the nation will need far fewer law schools than it now has, or at least most will need to transform themselves and their offerings if they want to survive. Law schools rendered redundant in a world that requires fewer traditional lawyers will have to reinvent themselves and play a role in undergraduate education, continuing education, or some combination of these. Change will not be easy. Schools will not want to be first to concede defeat or to begin what might seem to be a revolutionary program. After the moves begin at a few "first-tier" schools, however, the rush will be on, and schools that have thought about the issues and are ready to respond to the challenges will have an enviable advantage.

The Causes of Popular Dissatisfaction With Legal Education, 62 A.B.A. J. 447 (1976). *Cf.* Margaret A. Schilt, *The Future of Legal Scholarship*, LEGAL TIMES, July 9, 2007, at 26 (discussing the increase in blogging and short articles that tend to be less theoretical than earlier scholarship).

6. COMMITMENT TO JUSTICE IN A COMPETITIVE FUTURE

Even after all that has come before, the idea of a "vanishing American lawyer" may seem anachronistic. In a complex and competitive world where legal regulation will be ubiquitous and varied, the need for people who understand legal issues seems likely only to increase. Indeed, some of the evidence offered here has been consistent with the view that more people, not fewer, may find it advantageous to know how legal analysis works. Further, many of the changes in how legal services are used and delivered will be affected by events in clients' circumstances over which lawyers have little control, so one might argue that American lawyers should do what they think is right and let the consequences play out as they may.

However, the changes predicted in this book are already under-way, and a major transformation of the American legal profession can be expected within the next decade or so. Almost certainly, there will continue to be a breakdown in the number of issues seen as distinctively legal in character. Knowledge and skills as to which lawyers were tested when they were licensed to practice law will relate even less than they do today to the work lawyers are asked to do for tomorrow's clients. Even traditional legal matters can now affect interests in other states or nations and can be beyond most lawyers' expertise. Clients, especially business clients, are likely to demand a varied mix of services for which traditional law firms will not always be the obvious supplier.[1]

---

1. *See, e.g.,* James W. Jones, *The Challenge of Change: The Practice of Law in the Year 2000*, 41 VAND. L. REV. 683 (1988); Bruce A. Green, *The Disciplinary Restrictions on Multidisciplinary Practice: Their Derivation, Their Development, and Some Implications for the Core Values Debate*, 84 MINN. L. REV. 1115 (2000).

A. MEETING JUSTICE NEEDS FORMERLY MET BY LAWYERS

But the changes predicted in this book will also take place in a world that has expectations that lawyers will continue to serve important functions for people other than paying clients. In many cases, the reality has long differed from the expectations, but it is important in closing this account to think about how those institutional functions might be performed even as lawyers' place in the world changes.

1. Guaranteeing a Right to Counsel in Criminal Cases

Since the Supreme Court's 1963 decision in *Gideon v. Wainwright*,[2] the Constitution has required that every criminal defendant have the right to a lawyer to provide "effective assistance" of counsel in the accused's defense.[3] For many years, that assistance was provided by private lawyers who were assigned by a trial court to conduct the defense without pay.[4] Now, much of that assistance is provided by public defenders who are paid by the state to engage full-time in criminal defense.

It is surely less than fair to criminal defendants to appoint random lawyers to defend them against charges that may affect their liberty for many years. We have already seen that legal work is becoming increasingly specialized. That is also true of criminal defense representation. Defendants' constitutional and statutory rights have been both expanded and contracted by court decisions, the need for use of psychological and scientific evidence in criminal cases is increasing, and a failure to raise issues at the trial stage may preclude a better-prepared lawyer from even raising the issues on appeal.

Because criminal defense specialists must be able to see themselves earning a living if they enter that field of practice, it seems inevitable that providing criminal defense to indigent persons should continue to be—in largest part—a government responsibility. The need for such

---

2. 372 U.S. 335 (1963).

3. For a good discussion of what *Gideon* did not say and has not been held to require, *see* Kim Taylor-Thompson, *Tuning Up Gideon's Trumpet*, 71 FORDHAM L. REV. 1461 (2003).

4. Today, when private lawyers are appointed to serve as counsel, they are usually paid something, albeit less than they would have earned doing their regular work.

services will not go away, and although skilled private litigators might be expected to volunteer to handle challenging, high profile cases, for the majority of criminal defendants, government will necessarily be the supplier of last resort for defense services.

Such services have been publicly supplied in most jurisdictions for many years, but the constitutional right to criminal defense counsel has in many places been more promise than reality.[5] Lawyers provided have sometimes been only marginally competent; it was not until recently, in fact, that the Fifth Circuit held that the fact that a defense lawyer slept through parts of the trial was constitutionally deficient representation.[6] But up to now, "counsel" at least has had to be a licensed lawyer with three years of training. In a world in which the pool of traditionally trained lawyers may become smaller and more specialized, what constitutes the "counsel" to which defendants have a constitutional right may become a matter for legitimate debate. Consistent with the analysis in Chapter 5, it is not clear that defense counsel in all criminal cases should be required to have the three-year training regimen they do today. What they might better have is the basic year of training common to all legally trained persons, plus a year's training in criminal procedure, evidence, trial practice, and negotiation, and then get experience working under supervision in actual criminal cases. Certification of the skills of such advocates could be done by lawyers with whom the candidate has worked and judges before whom the candidate has appeared.

What such a two-year-trained practitioner would lack is exposure to some collateral subjects—taxation, corporate law, labor law, and the like. There is obviously no harm in taking those courses, but they would be unlikely to help most indigent defendants who find themselves charged with criminal wrongdoing. It seems unlikely that the expense of an extra year in law school would justify requiring that all criminal lawyers have that broader training.

---

5. See, e.g., State v. Peart, 621 So. 2d 780 (La.1993) (funding of public defenders found to be so poor that it raised a rebuttable presumption of ineffective assistance of counsel).

6. Burdine v. Johnson, 262 F.3d 336 (5th Cir. 2001). See also Wiggins v. Smith, 539 U.S. 510 (2003) (trial counsel did inadequate job of determining whether a mitigation defense was appropriate).

The point of this suggestion is not to deny criminal defendants quality assistance. Felony cases involving the risk of substantial loss of liberty might require the help of a more trained or more experienced lawyer, for example. Many criminal cases today, however, fall short of that risk. Persons with a college degree and two years' specialized training to work in the criminal justice system might properly be held to provide constitutionally sufficient counsel, even though today they would not be eligible to take a bar examination. What such a system of defenders might do is produce defense counsel in sufficient numbers that each can give time to defend their clients effectively. Given the acknowledged failure of the present system to deliver high-quality lawyers to many defendants,[7] it just might be that the new system would provide a higher level of due process than many defendants receive today.

2. Providing Civil Legal Services to the Poor and Middle Class

Lawyers often say that without their willingness to make their services broadly available—regardless of a client's ability to pay—in noncriminal cases, the American legal system would be less able to make equal justice a reality. Making legal services broadly available is, indeed, a critical social objective, and if we lose sight of it, we will be diminished as a people.

The sad fact, however, is that most American lawyers do not make contributing legal services a significant part of their practice. No American jurisdiction requires its lawyers to provide free or reduced-rate legal services, and when an A.B.A. Commission considering changes in lawyer standards recently took up a proposal to require such service, the proposal was again rejected.[8] The current economic

---

7. The notorious underfunding of public defender services is likely to make reliance on public agencies insufficient standing alone. Private lawyers are today often paid to represent poor defendants when a conflict of interest makes public defender services unavailable, e.g., State v. Lynch, 796 P.2d 1150 (Okla.1990), and they might be asked to serve more often if judges believe they would be helpful to overcome an overworked public office. See, e.g., Zarabia v. Bradshaw, 912 P.2d 5 (Ariz. 1996) (county system for appointing lawyers held unconstitutional because it included appointing lawyers with no experience in either criminal law or trial work).

8. Report of the Commission on Evaluation of Professional Standards, Rule 6.1 (2000). Model Rules of Prof'l Conduct, R. 6.1

downturn has had a further negative effect on funds available to support legal aid programs.[9]

Voluntary legal aid societies around the country deserve praise for delivering legal services to the poor since at least the founding of the New York legal aid society in 1876.[10] Likewise, the view that lawyers have a moral obligation to serve the needs of individual indigent

---

asserts that "a lawyer *should aspire* to render . . . pro bono publico legal services. . . ." (emphasis added). In fairness, the A.B.A. Model Code of Professional Responsibility did not deal directly with pro bono work, so we should perhaps be grateful that the Model Rules say anything at all. When the Rule was first floated in the Kutak Commission's 1980 Discussion Draft, however, it was more demanding: "A lawyer *shall render* unpaid public interest legal service," the Rule said. The possible recipients of this service were broadly defined. "A lawyer may discharge this responsibility by service in activities for improving the law, the legal system, or the legal profession, or by providing professional services to persons of limited means or to public service groups or organizations." But each lawyer was to "make an annual report concerning such service to appropriate regulatory authority." *See* Thomas D. Morgan & Ronald D. Rotunda, 1980 Selected National Standards Supplement 67. The reaction to the proposal for mandatory service was extraordinary. The Kutak Commission was almost disbanded over the suggestion that a lawyer should be required to give something back to his or her community. The fact that no minimum-hour requirement was set did not make the rule palatable. The Commission was sent back to the drawing boards. By the next year, the requirement that a lawyer "*shall* render unpaid public interest legal services" had been changed to the current statement that a lawyer "*should* render public interest legal services. . . ." In 1993, the Rule was amended to assert an *aspiration* for a "50-hour" contribution of services, but that remains only a hope.

9. *See, e.g.,* NLJ Roundtable, *Economic Crisis Brings Pro Bono to Crossroads,* Nat'l L.J., May 18, 2009, at 10; Robert Weber, *Nonprofits Need Help Now,* Nat'l L.J., Apr. 27, 2009, at 18; Michael Moline, *There's Life Among the Ruins,* Nat'l L.J., Jan. 5, 2009, at 1.

10. *See, e.g.,* Emery A. Brownell, Legal Aid in the United States (1951) (part of the Survey of the Legal Profession); John MacArthur Maguire, The Lance of Justice: A Semi-Centennial History of the Legal Aid Society 1876–1926 (1928); Reginald Heber Smith, Justice and the Poor (1919). Others might date recognition of a right to free legal services to programs of the Freedmen's Bureau, established shortly after the Civil War but ended in 1868. *See* Maxwell Bloomfield, American Lawyers in a Changing Society, 1776–1876, at 345–46 (1976).

clients was at the heart of the legal aid movement advocated in 1919 by Reginald Heber Smith and later encouraged, at least in spirit, by the American Bar Association. A half-century later, the rationale for providing free services had become that—in a society based on a principle of equal rights under law—the inability of clients to afford a lawyer meant that rights could not be equal.[11] Because only lawyers may practice law in our society, the reasoning went, it falls to lawyers to overcome the inability of the poor to afford their services.[12]

In the future, legal services in civil cases are likely to be best provided by a mix of publicly supported neighborhood offices, law school and other charitable clinics, private lawyers paid by public

---

11. "Our legal system today faces crisis conditions. Innovative legislation and landmark court decisions from the 1950's to the 1970's have accorded to individuals, especially poor individuals, a new panoply of rights and remedies in addition to those traditionally available. . . . But the promise held out by newly-won rights has been illusory, because there simply are not enough lawyers available through existing legal-assistance organizations to serve all of those who need a lawyer and cannot afford to pay legal fees at prevailing rates." ASSOCIATION OF THE BAR OF THE CITY OF NEW YORK, TOWARD A MANDATORY CONTRIBUTION OF PUBLIC SERVICE PRACTICE BY EVERY LAWYER 7 (1979). The Special Committee that prepared this report had been formed in response to an American Bar Association in 1975 that declared it to be "a basic professional responsibility of each lawyer engaged in the practice of law to provide public interest legal services." See A.B.A. SPECIAL COMM. ON PUBLIC INTEREST PRACTICE, IMPLEMENTING THE LAWYER'S PUBLIC INTEREST PRACTICE OBLIGATION (1977); F. RAYMOND MARKS, ET AL., THE LAWYER, THE PUBLIC AND PROFESSIONAL RESPONSIBILITY 288–92 (1972).

12. These themes are developed very well in DEBORAH L. RHODE, ACCESS TO JUSTICE (2004). For an earlier statement of similar themes, see Roger C. Cramton, Delivery of Legal Services to Ordinary Americans, 44 CASE W. RES. L. REV. 531 (1994); Lester Brickman, Of Arterial Passageways Through the Legal Process: The Right of Universal Access to Courts and Lawyering Services, 48 N.Y.U. L. REV. 595 (1973). Creation of the Legal Services Corporation was in part a government response to a need that lawyers individually had refused to assume. The belief that individuals have a right to legal services was also at the heart of the A.B.A.'s extensive efforts in the 1970s to survey potential public demand for legal services. See generally BARBARA A. CURRAN, THE LEGAL NEEDS OF THE PUBLIC: THE FINAL REPORT OF A NATIONAL SURVEY (1977).

authorities,[13] and lawyers working in a private-pay legal clinic or paid as part of a client's prepaid legal services plan.[14] Offices should be staffed by both lawyers and non-lawyers. Private legal clinics employed paralegals before that practice reached traditional firms, and the model generally works well. Indeed, the advertising revolution among lawyers was in part designed to help legal clinics attract enough middle-class clients to create economies of scale that would make the work profitable. Further, some of what we once called "clinics" have transformed themselves into group legal service providers. It is hard to confirm how many people effectively have legal services paid for through their union labor agreements, but the point is that at least some middle-income people have more access to legal services than we may think.

Technology also may help provide part of the answer to providing such services. Law schools and other voluntary organizations could produce checklists, packaged forms, and other guidance that will allow at least some clients to do their own work and that will help others assist clients in areas unfamiliar to the practitioner. Translation of the documents into languages spoken by the clients will also facilitate these developments.[15]

If history is any judge, important interests will seek to resist such developments, but their objections will not necessarily succeed. Insurance company provision of legal services is well established in

---

13. The distinction between Judicare, which involves employment of private lawyers to serve the poor, and creation of separate legal services offices to serve the poor is developed in Samuel Jan Brakel, *Styles of Delivery of Legal Services to the Poor: A Review Essay*, 1977 AM. B. FOUND. RES. J. 219. *See also* Werner Pfennigstorf & Spencer Kimball, *Legal Services Plans: A Typology*, 1976 AM. B. FOUND. RES. J. 411.

14. MACKLIN FLEMING, LAWYERS, MONEY, AND SUCCESS: THE CONSEQUENCES OF DOLLAR OBSESSION, ch. 3 (1997). Personal service lawyers see themselves as delivering lots of pro bono service in the sense that much of their work does not get fully compensated. They resist mandatory pro bono, however, because they think most of the work would fall on them. CARROLL SERON, THE BUSINESS OF PRACTICING LAW: THE WORK LIVES OF SOLO AND SMALL FIRM ATTORNEYS, ch. 8 (1996).

15. *See, e.g.*, Julee C. Fischer, *Policing the Self-Help Legal Market: Consumer Protection or Protection of the Legal Cartel*, 34 IND. L. REV. 121 (2000).

the context of automobile and homeowner liability litigation.[16] Further, group legal service plans similarly pay the cost of an insured's house closing, adoption, divorce, and the like. In all these cases, clients receive services from lawyers they often hardly know, but one rarely hears an objection to the quality of the services.

As discussed in Chapters 3 and 4, the next step may be for banks, investment advisors, and financial planners to provide estate planning services or assist lay executors in the administration of estates.[17] In the early years, such services may be provided by lawyers working for commercial organizations, but the services may soon be standardized and delivered by non-lawyers either in person or via telephone or Internet. These developments will be a blow to lawyers who find that the individualized services they deliver have been turned into relative commodities, but from the point of view of the middle-class clients, these developments may spell the difference between adequate services and no services at all. In that sense, such developments will genuinely expand the sense of justice experienced by those clients.

Indeed, it increasingly seems likely that requiring pro bono service by all lawyers would not be practical even if lawyers were willing to assume the burden. Part of the problem is that lawyers will be so specialized that it will be harder to become familiar with legal issues facing the poor and middle class. More telling, issues of language proficiency will increasingly define who can and cannot deliver services to the poorest in the population. Individualized service for persons from all over the world will not be provided on a large scale by part-time providers. The future for poor and middle-class clients is

---

16. This kind of service has traditionally been justified as an exception to the usual rules permitted because the insurance company seems largely to be representing its own interest in minimizing the liability of its insured. *See, e.g.*, RESTATEMENT (THIRD) OF THE LAW GOVERNING LAWYERS § 134, com. f. *See also* Charles Silver, *Flat Fees and Staff Attorneys: Unnecessary Casualties in the Continuing Battle over the Law Governing Insurance Defense Lawyers*, 4 CONN. INS. L.J. 205 (1997).

17. It will be said to be not only unauthorized practice of law by a corporation, but a conflict of interest as well, because the corporate sponsor might engage in other business transactions with the clients that are prohibited by ABA MODEL RULES OF PROFESSIONAL CONDUCT, Rules 1.7(b) & 1.8(a).

likely to be offices with access to Internet information and computer forms in which volunteers help people fill in the blanks.[18]

Imagine that you were opening a new law firm to serve a population of individual clients who could pay for your services. How would you organize your practice? Presumably, you would try to have offices that your clients could easily reach, you would staff the offices with whatever mix of lawyers and non-lawyers would most efficiently serve them, and you would have central resources to provide help too specialized to have in each office. The Legal Services Corporation should work in much the same way.[19] Ideally, clients should be required to pay at least part of the cost of their services. Fees should not be so high as to deny service, but litigation should not become a recreational activity.[20] It is fine for researchers to estimate the demand for legal services by interviewing; real demand, however, will only be revealed when potential clients recognize that legal resources have a

---

18. In tax preparation, real estate services, and countless other areas, there have been few cases where a lack of competence has been shown. Indeed, "it is not self-evident that professional certification or supervision insures special competence." Deborah Rhode, *Policing the Professional Monopoly: A Constitutional and Empirical Analysis of Unauthorized Practice Prohibitions*, 34 STAN. L. REV. 1, 87 (1981).

19. Law school clinics and services of private charities should be included within the mix for planning and grant allocation purposes, and experienced retired lawyers should not be overlooked as candidates to staff such offices. *See, e.g.*, Marc Galanter, *"Old and in the Way": The Coming Demographic Transformation of the Legal Profession and its Implications for the Provision of Legal Services*, 1999 WIS. L. REV. 1081 (1999). It is important to remember that the poor also need legal services to help them become less poor. Small business clinics should be part of any services mix, and experienced private lawyers might do an excellent job in such clinics. *See, e.g.*, Ann Southworth, *Business Planning for the Destitute? Lawyers as Facilitators in Civil Rights and Poverty Practice*, 1996 WIS. L. REV. 1121 (1997).

20. *See, e.g.*, Stephen Yelenosky & Charles Silver, *A Model Retainer Agreement for Legal Services Programs: Mandatory Attorney Fee Provisions*, CLEARINGHOUSE REVIEW, June 1994, at 114. By no means would everyone agree. There is a strain of thought that receipt of any fee diminishes the selflessness of the lawyer's pro bono work. *Cf.* Lisa G. Lerman, *Fee-For-Service Clinical Teaching: Slipping Toward Commercialism*, 1 CLINICAL L. REV. 685 (1995).

cost and make genuine choices about when it will be in their interest to procure them.[21]

3. The Future of Cause Lawyering and the Defense of Civil Liberties

Lawyers have long been involved in representing public causes as well as private clients. There is no obvious reason that that will not continue in the future described here. At one end of the pro bono continuum are the individual cases just discussed that are important to the parties but have little or no significance for other litigants. At the other end is legal work on behalf of causes intended to establish fundamental legal changes applicable to many people.

To a generation of lawyers, the defining example was the effort to achieve equal opportunity that culminated in *Brown v. Board of Education*.[22] The case and its result were no accident. They were the product of a twenty-five-year-long effort originally conceived by Charles Hamilton Houston and Thurgood Marshall that began with efforts to desegregate law schools and universities and only later confronted public elementary and secondary schools.[23] Similar efforts later were employed to defend the civil rights legislation that sought to confirm the gains the litigation had begun.[24]

---

21. A related issue not often considered in discussions of pro bono service is the possibility of limited service agreements between clients and lawyers. Self-help systems using books, forms, and the like might be selected by clients with the advice of a lawyer, for example, followed by only a quick review, or perhaps answering some questions, but without the usual effort devoted to a "full-service" client. *See, e.g.,* Fred C. Zacharias, *Limited Performance Agreements: Should Clients Get What They Pay For?*, 11 Geo. J. Legal Ethics 915 (1988); David A. Hyman & Charles Silver, *And Such Small Portions: Limited Performance Agreements and the Cost/Quality/Access Trade Off*, 11 Geo. J. Legal Ethics 959 (1988).

22. 347 U.S. 483 (1954).

23. The story is told in Jack Greenberg, Crusaders in the Courts: How a Dedicated Band of Lawyers Fought for the Civil Rights Revolution (1994). While the most visible public interest litigation has been on behalf of the poor and excluded, conservative causes have had their representatives as well. *See* Lee Epstein, Conservatives in Court (1985). Concern about the whole process of policy-making through litigation is expressed in Robert A. Kagan, Adversarial Legalism: The American Way of Law 230–52 (2001).

24. The use of law and lawyers to achieve social change has spread beyond this country. *See* Austin Sarat & Stuart Scheingold, eds., Cause

These categories are described as the ends of a spectrum, but many examples combine elements of each. First, cases involving fundamental change are necessarily filed in the names of particular parties. There really was an Ernesto Miranda, for example, and it was the failure to advise Mr. Miranda of his right to appointed counsel that led to a right to such a warning for a generation of criminal defendants who have followed. There really was a Clarence Earl Gideon whose case established a right to counsel for criminal defendants around the country. Indeed, legal aid lawyers have long looked for ways to generalize the issues raised in a current case and establish principles beneficial to other clients similarly situated.

Likewise, some individual legal services are delivered to clients but only if the clients are within categories that a lawyer wants to support. The first legal aid society in the country, for example, was established in New York by a German immigrant to protect later immigrants from exploitation. The second agency sought to protect young women victimized after having been lured to Chicago by false promises of work. Today's counterparts of these agencies might be clinics that protect women against domestic violence and the International Justice Mission that uses lawyers to free children from sexual exploitation and contract slavery.

One could correctly say, of course, that there is plenty of room for pro bono work all along this spectrum. Drawing these distinctions is helpful, however, because the battles to define one kind of work as more important than the rest have long been the elephant in the room during discussions of how pro bono services should be delivered and to whom. Using public funds to support courtroom efforts to achieve legal change that legislatures fail to accomplish, for example, has been at the heart of debates over the proper work of publicly funded legal services agencies. In the early days of the Office of Economic Opportunity legal services program, which was part of President Johnson's War on Poverty, law reform activities designed to improve the position of the poor as a class were seen as central to

LAWYERING AND THE STATE IN A GLOBAL ERA (2001); Stephen Ellman, *Cause Lawyering in the Third World, in* AUSTIN SARAT & STUART SCHEINGOLD, EDS., CAUSE LAWYERING: POLITICAL COMMITMENTS AND PROFESSIONAL RESPONSIBILITIES (1998).

the OEO mission.[25] Those efforts continued in programs supported by the Legal Services Corporation, but from time to time, Congress has tried to impose limits on activities that the LSC may support.[26]

It seems inevitable that cause-oriented litigation will be pursued primarily by private groups established to achieve ends they favor, or by private law firms who undertake such cases out of interest in training their lawyers or commitment to a given cause.[27] Cause-oriented litigation can be challenging and a powerful tool for recruiting and training young lawyers.[28] Further, fee-shifting statutes may be another

---

25. Those early days are described by the first director of the program in EARL JOHNSON, JR., JUSTICE AND REFORM: THE FORMATIVE YEARS OF THE OEO LEGAL SERVICES PROGRAM (1974). *See also* Robert L. Rabin, *Lawyers for Social Change: Perspectives on Public Interest Law*, 28 STAN. L. REV. 207 (1976).

26. The debate is described in JACK KATZ, POOR PEOPLE'S LAWYERS IN TRANSITION (1982). For a debate on specific ways to make the Legal Services Corporation work more effectively, *see* DOUGLAS J. BESHAROV, ED., LEGAL SERVICES FOR THE POOR: TIME FOR REFORM (1990). *See, e.g.*, Legal Services Corp. v. Velazquez, 531 U.S. 533 (2001) (striking down Congressional limit on the Legal Services Corporation's use of appropriated funds to seek to amend or otherwise challenge existing welfare laws).

27. For a careful analysis of when and where such litigation might be useful, *see* BURTON A. WEISBROD, JOEL F. HANDLER & NEIL K. KOMESAR, PUBLIC INTEREST LAW: AN ECONOMIC AND INSTITUTIONAL ANALYSIS (1978). Ideas about the role of private law firms in public interest practice are found in ROBERT A. KATZMANN, ED., THE LAW FIRM AND THE PUBLIC GOOD (1995). For a more recent discussion of the state of pro bono practice, *see* ROBERT GRANFIELD & LYNN MATHER, EDS., PRIVATE LAWYERS IN THE PUBLIC INTEREST: THE EVOLVING ROLE OF PRO BONO IN THE LEGAL PROFESSION (2009).

28. Professor Marc Galanter's proposal for making more use of senior lawyers in a transition to retirement is yet another imaginative possibility. Marc Galanter, *"Old and In the Way": The Coming Demographic Transformation of the Legal Profession and Its Implications for the Provision of Legal Services*, 1999 WIS. L. REV. 1081 (1999). Ethical issues lurk within such cases. *See* Stephen Ellmann, *Client-Centeredness Multiplied: Individual Autonomy and Collective Mobilization in Public Interest Lawyers' Representation of Groups*, 78 VA. L. REV. 1103 (1992); Ann Southworth, *Lawyer-Client Decisionmaking in Civil Rights and Poverty Practice: An Empirical Study of Lawyers' Norms*, 9 GEO. J. LEGAL ETHICS 1101 (1996).

way to get private firms to vindicate public rights.[29] There are many statutes that reward litigants that bring successful public interest cases by requiring that defendants pay the plaintiffs' lawyers.[30] Many cases brought out of a desire to vindicate a principle have turned out to be profitable as firms get an award of legal fees when their clients prevail. If lawyers and their firms do see it in their interest to file cause litigation, the chances that it will happen will rise sharply.

4. Who Will Be the Future Judges?

Judges have traditionally come from a practicing bar that this book posits would be smaller and more specialized. There may thus be reason for concern that it will be harder to find judges who are qualified to manage the work of a court of general jurisdiction—one that potentially hears many different kinds of questions. Upon reflection, however, the problem does not seem nearly as great as it first might.

Even today, judicial roles differ widely. Many courts are actually very specialized. Some hear only divorce and custody cases, for example, or only juvenile cases, or only cases involving trusts and estates. Even persons with a very specialized practice should be qualified to act as a judge in a court in which the lawyer has spent several years practicing.

Further, while the training and experience required to hear most misdemeanor or small claims matters are not trivial, both kinds of courts often require more human empathy and common sense than comprehensive legal understanding. Judges of those courts often act more like mediators than legal oracles, and again, even two years' legal training and some years in practice should be sufficient for the work.

---

29. William A. Bradford, Jr., *"Private Enforcement of Public Rights: The Role of Fee-Shifting Statutes in Pro Bono Lawyering,"* in ROBERT A. KATZMANN, ED., THE LAW FIRM AND THE PUBLIC GOOD (1995).

30. No single law review article can capture all of the issues, but many of the possibilities and risks are seen in, e.g., Susan P. Koniak & George M. Cohan, *Under Cloak of Settlement,* 82 VA. L. REV. 1051 (1996).

Judges in federal courts or state courts of general jurisdiction, on the other hand, need broader training to bring them up-to-date on the law in fields other than those in which they practiced. Appellate courts that issue authoritative opinions that are broadly applicable similarly require judges with as much, or even more, legal training and experience than lawyers have today. As we have already seen, however, law schools would likely be more than happy to have lawyers come back for refresher courses at the time they are appointed or elected to the bench.

Thus, the challenge of finding judges in a world of multiple kinds of advisors and a variety of kinds of experience is not likely to be a forbidding one. Almost certainly, more than enough people will be willing to take additional training that is required if becoming a judge is the reward at the end of the process.

B. PROFESSIONALISM—A LAST LOOK

Everyone benefits from having lawyers—and others acting alongside and in competition with lawyers—act with high character and in ways one would proudly call "professional." The message of this book has simply been that to act professionally, one need not be part of a "profession."[31] The American Bar Association does and should continue to provide opportunities for education and networking. It should continue to offer informed opinions about law, legislation, and legal institutions. Ultimately, however, we should not let the label "profession" weaken the response to the realities that the future likely holds for legally trained persons.[32]

---

31. Use of the term "professional" to describe morally praiseworthy conduct was discussed in Chapter 2.

32. Membership in the American Bar Association used to be consistently fifty percent of all lawyers; now it is down to about 35 percent. Information about the A.B.A. can be found at http://www.abanet.org. The A.B.A. had over 400,000 lawyer members in 2008, out of almost 1,200,000 persons with a law license. Even within the A.B.A., the largest sections tend to be those that represent specialists rather than general concerns. The largest sections are Litigation and Business Law, each with over 50,000 members, while small "public interest" sections such as Individual Rights and Responsibilities have

All legal service providers exercise implicit moral judgment when they decide which practice organizations to join, which matters to undertake, which matters to decline, and how to act in the matters they handle.[33] A lawyer's and law firm's reputation increasingly will be the guarantors of professional quality assistance clients hope to receive,[34] and private actions against lawyers who fail to meet the promised standard are likely to replace formal discipline as the principal regulator of lawyer activity.[35]

The intense competition that this book has discussed might even have its own silver lining. Lawyers are likely to have increasing options for use of their services in areas other than law. Many lawyers have worked too hard, been appreciated too little, and spent insufficient time at home or working on matters that make a difference in public life.[36]

---

many fewer members. A majority of lawyers seem to be joining more specialized bar associations or no associations at all.

33. *See, e.g.*, David B. Wilkins, *Beyond "Bleached Out" Professionalism: Defining Professional Responsibility for Real Professionals, in* ETHICS IN PRACTICE: LAWYERS' ROLES, RESPONSIBILITIES, AND REGULATION 207 (Deborah L Rhode ed., 2000); Andrew M. Perlman, *A Career Choice Critique of Legal Ethics Theory*, 31 SETON HALL L. REV. 829 (2001); John J. Flynn, *Professional Ethics and the Lawyer's Duty to Self*, 1976 WASH. U. L. Q. 429.

34. Russell Pearce, *How Law Firms Can Do Good While Doing Well (and the Answer is Not Pro Bono)*, 33 FORDHAM URBAN L.J. 211 (2005) (rejecting the business/professional distinction and saying that honorable corporate practice can serve the public interest as well as private interests). *See also* Russell Pearce, *Model Rule 1.0: Lawyers Are Morally Accountable*, 70 FORDHAM L. REV. 1805 (2002). *But see* Elizabeth Chambliss, *The Nirvana Fallacy in Law Firm Regulation Debates*, 33 FORDHAM URBAN L.J. 119, 150 (2005) (increased mobility of lawyers decreases the likelihood they will internalize positive values of a law firm).

35. *See, e.g.*, David B. Wilkins, *Who Should Regulate Lawyers?*, 105 HARV. L. REV. 801 (1992); Ronald J. Gilson, *The Devolution of the Legal Profession: A Demand Side Perspective*, 49 MD. L. REV. 869 (1990). Even today, malpractice insurance companies have an incentive to audit lawyer compliance with professional standards more rigorously than lawyer disciplinary commissions will ever do.

36. *See, e.g.*, W. Bradley Wendel, *Morality, Motivation and the Professionalism Movement*, 52 S.C. L. REV. 557 (2001); Russell G. Pearce, *The Professionalism Paradigm Shift: Why Discarding Professional Ideology Will Improve the Conduct and Reputation of the Bar*, 70 N.Y.U. L. REV. 1229 (1995). There may be a concern that civic leadership and a concern for justice is missing from the

There is reason to believe such concerns may pass. The competitive forces that have made lawyers miserable may now provide them hope, albeit perhaps at lower incomes. Government offices, corporate legal departments, and law schools have attracted lawyers seeking better ways to balance time demands of work, family, and community, but lawyers may not have to choose between law firms and these other ways to use their training. Law firms competing for people who have such alternatives will have to offer comparable opportunities or lose the people upon whom they rely for the source of their competitive strength.

One should not be naive about the ease or speed of lawyer adaptation to the new reality. The rate of the changes outlined here is likely to depend in part on how quickly the world returns to vigorous economic activity. But almost no matter how quickly that occurs, consumers of legal services are likely to reward providers who deliver services more efficiently and at lower costs.

A lawyer's primary concerns should be integrity, loyalty, competence, and confidentiality. Those values have not and will not go out of date.[37] Ignoring the changes lawyers face does not constitute a mark of professional courage, and calling lawyering a profession cannot guarantee moral leadership. The lives of practitioners using legal training, whatever their number or the nature of their individual training and practice, will be the best instruments of justice.[38]

---

roles discussed for legally trained persons in this book. Former General Electric general counsel Ben Heineman, Jr., has proposed that lawyers be expressly trained as leaders, and that role could clearly be an important part of a lawyer's activity. But the effort is, I believe, a distraction. Some lawyers perform that role already, but so do people such as Howard Dean (a doctor), Newt Gingrich (a professor), and Mitt Romney (a businessman). There is nothing very special about lawyer/leaders.

37. Traditionally, the professional was understood to have a "calling," an obligation created by God to assume a role in serving the common good. The common theological understanding central to that understanding is much weaker today, but the idea still has resonance with many. See, e.g., WILLIAM F. MAY, BELEAGUERED RULERS: THE PUBLIC OBLIGATION OF THE PROFESSIONAL 14–19 (2001) (decrying the professional's shift from a calling to a career).

38. See Roger C. Cramton, Delivery of Legal Services to Ordinary Americans, 44 CASE W. RES. L. REV. 531, 611 (1994) ("I believe the major elements of a renewed vision [of professionalism] will be: [1] A lawyer who cares about

Failing to adjust the regulation of lawyers to the kinds of economic pressures this book identifies will only delay responsible efforts to do justice in the challenging world that lies ahead.[39]

clients, who is accountable to them, who engages in moral dialogue with them, and who wants the legal profession to see that client interests are protected, [2] a lawyer who cares about justice and who strives for efficiency in the provision of legal services, and [3] a lawyer who brings his or her conscience to bear on everything done as a lawyer.").

39. In August 2009, the A.B.A. announced the appointment of a new commission, Ethics 20/20, that was directed to address how "technological advances and globalization" will affect lawyers and how lawyer ethical standards should be amended to reflect those developments. The commission's agenda has not yet been announced, but its work will provide one setting in which the recommendations of this book might be considered.

INDEX

Demographics, U.S., 153–55,
153*n*64
Discrimination, within profession,
12–13, 12*nn*39–40, 155*nn*71–72.
See also Diversity
Dispute resolution, 133–34
Distance learning, 205–6,
206*nn*97–99
Diversity
as American value, 153*n*64
discrimination and, 12–13,
12*nn*39–40, 155*nn*71–72
within law firms, 153–55
in law schools, 80, 154, 198–99,
199*n*73
DLA Piper, 101, 147
Drinker Biddle & Reath, 164*n*94
Drucker, Peter, 127–28
Dwight, Theodore, 190, 190*n*34

E

E-commerce, 89
Economic crisis. *See* Global
economic crisis
Economic Opportunity Office,
227–28
Educated citizens *(patronus
causarum)*, 27
Education. *See* Law schools
Eliot, Charles William, 191–92,
192*n*43
England
history of legal education, 185–87,
185*n*15
history of legal tradition, 29–33,
29*n*31, 30*nn*33–34, 31*nn*36–37,
32*nn*42–43, 33*nn*44–45
multidisciplinary partnerships, 150
number of lawyers, 83
regulation of lawyers, 90
solo practitioners, 99
Enron scandal, 151–52
Equity (Story), 186
Equity Pleading (Story), 186

Era of Decadence, 39–40
Era of the Barnburners, 39–40
Ethics
client confidentiality and, 57–58,
57*n*137
in law school curriculum,
19–20, 75
self-regulation and, 73–79
social contract, 23–25, 40–49
Ethics 20/20 Commission (A.B.A.),
233*n*39
Ethics 2000 Commission
(A.B.A.), 63, 220
European Union (EU)
attorney-client privilege, 116*n*143
regulation of lawyers, 90
Evidence (Greenleaf), 186

F

Federal regulation, 152*n*62. *See also*
specific agencies
Fees. *See also* Salaries
antitrust laws and, 55, 55*n*134,
75–77, 76*n*18
billing models, 170–73
contingent fees, 105–6, 133
early American tradition
and, 34
fixed fees, 102–3
fixed retainers, 103
hourly rate billing, 53–54,
103–4, 171
percentage fees, 104–5
performance, 172
for persons of moderate means,
225, 225*n*20
Fiduciary duty, 59–60, 60*n*143
Financing, of law firms, 166–70
leveraged financing, 167
mergers, 167
stock sales to non-lawyers,
167–70, 167*n*104, 168*n*105,
170*n*111
Firm culture, 68, 68*n*174

Information technology
  commodified services and, 94–95
  data capacity, 93
  expert systems, 98
  globalization and, 91–98
  infomediary, 97–98, 97n90
  law school curriculum, 205–6
  legal information on Internet,
    95–98
  legal research, 93
  standardization of forms, 94–95,
    130n2
  work pace, 93–94
In-house counsel. *See also* Law
    practice (1970s–present)
  for insurance companies, 131–32,
    224, 224n17
  rising power of, 112–23, 114n136,
    115n138, 123n169
Inns of Court, 32–33, 32n43, 185–87,
  185n15, 186n16
Insurance companies
  in-house lawyers, 131–32, 224,
    224n17
  malpractice, 79, 231n36
International Justice Mission, 227
Internet
  e-commerce, 89
  free legal information, 95–98
  global marketing, 92, 145
  legal services delivery, 224
  networking Web sites, 136
  Web-based instruction, 206

J
Japan, 82–83
Jefferson, Thomas, 188
Job offers, 3
Johnson, Lyndon, 227–28
Journalists, 183, 183n11
Judges, 229–30
Juries, 37–38
Justice, commitment to, 217–33
  civil liberties defense, 226–29

criminal defendants, 218–20,
    220n7
  institutional changes and,
    218–30
  judges, 229–30
  legal aid, 220–26, 222nn11–12,
    223n14, 225nn19–20, 226n21

K
Kritzer, Herbert M., 125n175
Kronman, Anthony T., 62

L
Landon, Donald, 111n132, 132n10
Langdell, Christopher Columbus,
  191–93, 191n42
Laumann, Edward, 111, 111n131
Law practice (1970s–present),
  71–128
  bar hemispheres, 110–12,
    111nn126–27, 111n132
  firms as premier practice
    organizations, 99–110
  billing models, 170–73
  contingent fees, 105–6
  financing of growth, 166–70,
    167n10, 168n105, 170n111
  fixed fees, 102–3
  fixed retainers, 103
  hourly rate billing, 53–54,
    103–4
  lateral hiring, 109–10
  lawyer loyalty and, 161–66,
    163nn92–93, 164nn94–95
  leverage and, 106–7,
    107n118, 162
  mergers, 167
  percentage fees, 104–5
  size, determinants of, 99–101
  tournament theory, 108–10,
    110n122
  globalization, 83–91, 87n48
    T. Friedman on, 83, 83n40,
      86n46, 88n51, 90–91